Your growing child

Your growing child

Mark Lovell

Routledge & Kegan Paul

London, Henley and Boston

First published in 1976
by Routledge & Kegan Paul Ltd
39 Store Street,
London WC1E 7DD,
Broadway House,
Newtown Road,
Henley-on-Thames,
Oxon RG9 1EN and
9 Park Street,
Boston, Mass. 02108, USA
Set in Imprint
and printed in Great Britain by
Ebenezer Baylis & Son Ltd
The Trinity Press, Worcester, and London

ISBN 0 7100 8431 5

Contents

Illustrations

Figures

Tables

My intention, when writing *Your Growing Child*, was to bring to parents' notice a lot of what we now know about the way children develop. The book is specially meant for those parents who want to know more than just what lies on the surface. There is so much that we tend to take for granted—yet at the same time there is so much interesting work that has been done in recent years to increase our understanding of *how it is* that children do certain things at certain stages. I wanted to point out what is actually going on when a stage is reached, and why children come to vary so much in their skills, interests, personality and ambition.

The first volume I wrote, under the overall title of *How Children Grow*, covered the period *From Conception to Two*. *Your Growing Child* picks up the story at the age of three, and continues right on into adolescence.

I hope that this will give parents some help in understanding their children better, so that there can be better contact with the growing generation.

Once again, I am indebted to a large number of doctors, psychologists, teachers, and—significantly—to children of all sizes, for their patience and their good nature in trying to help me pick my way through very complex territory.

Mark Lovell

1*

Becoming a real child

Of course a baby, or a toddler, is perfectly real. He has begun to be a child, and an individual at that. But three years old is a milestone that heralds real childhood.

Many parents welcome it with a sense of relief. The physical dangers of infancy have been survived. Whatever happens to him now, a three-year-old will be stronger, and will meet it with more resistance.

But there is also, at about this time, a big change taking place in the amount of communication that a child can have with his parents. He can be asked to do a number of things (and very often *not* to do things) with a bigger chance of his understanding, and complying. He asks more interesting questions, too, and has interesting suggestions to make about the world around him. He is becoming an individual character in his features, in his mannerisms, and in his words.

It is to this time of life that many, if not most, people's earliest memories date back. It is notoriously difficult to establish how far somebody can remember (mainly because children might be told of something happening to them a year or so earlier, and they claim it forever afterwards as part of their memory), but many have at least one very vivid recollection from their fourth year that stands out so clearly that they are convinced that this *must* have impressed itself directly on them, and that it was the first event to do so. This suggests that, apart from being impressionable, a child of this age is starting to 'run over' in his mind some of the happenings of the day. We do not understand a great deal about how the brain stores memory traces, or what processes allow some stored material to be 'accessible' (i.e. recalled consciously) and some not. But a need to run over what happened, again and again, and a feeling that whatever it was, it was in some way important, are usually regarded as pre-conditions for the brain to store an accessible memory trace. Before this, some children might already be doing this, but after three, very many will.

It is possible to link this with the development of a sense of time. This is nothing to do with telling the time or with knowing the difference between a day ago and a week ago. It is a change from living from moment to moment, recognizing and accepting a pattern to the day as it unfolds, and paying attention to certain things that happened and are in the *past*. This goes together with expectation of future things and having a picture of what happens *generally*, at particular times. Somebody with no sense of time does not need a memory. So it is logical that these two developments should occur at about the same age.

Another way of looking at memory is to consider the growth of the brain and the rest of the central nervous system. Memory functions have been localized in a part of the upper brain, or cortex. This is the part of the system that is still growing at a particularly fast rate, right through childhood. The implication is that the maturation process does not equip a young child for complex memory work until about the age of three. Figure 1 shows how much a child's brain has had to grow *since* birth and how much growth there lies ahead of it, until at the age of ten it reaches nearly all (95 per cent) of its adult weight.

Most, although not all, three-year-olds stand upright, walk and run around. Their reactions are still not as fast as those of older children, so they cannot always keep their balance in, say, a moving bus or train. Nor are their muscles used to the idea of conserving energy. This means that on a long walk they will start with great fire and purpose, bounding ahead. They get impatient with adults accompanying them and cannot, anyway, see the point of continuing always in the same direction. So they change course every now and then and run back to collide into a hug with their mother or father. After half a mile or so, they are likely to be very tired. Parents who sigh, and think, 'Oh no! Now I shall have to carry him the rest of the way', often do not consider that by this time their three-year-old will probably have covered about half as much again as they themselves have done, or that a lot of this was at a run or at a pace that was exaggerated for them. If you try to keep up with someone who is cycling slowly—perhaps at eight miles per hour—you get something of the feeling that a three-year-old gets when he is told, '*Do* get a move on, David!'

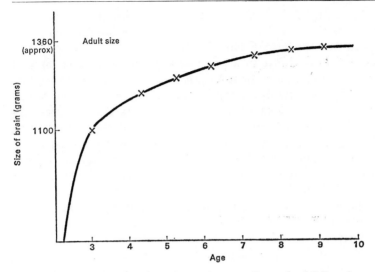

Figure 1 How the brain continues to grow through childhood

Notes
1 At the age of three, a child's brain is a little over three-quarters of its final adult weight.
2 The growth rate decreases very gradually, until by the age of ten most children have a brain that is over nineteen-twentieths of its final weight.
3 The maturation of the brain and the whole central nervous system is not limited to physical *expansion*, but includes the development of *connections* which service an increasing range of brain activities and allow for increasing precision.

Walks are much easier for parents in one way: not being entirely dependent on a push-chair, they can go further, using public transport more freely or crossing stiles. This means greater manœuvrability and more freedom. But a three-year-old is never unmitigated delight as a walking companion. Most of the time, either he goes too slowly for you or you go too fast for him.

Sometimes he will be too much of a prey to his curiosity and slow reflexes have to be allowed for as well as his limited ability to comprehend orders. For instance, 'Come away from the edge, John, there's a train coming' should never need to be said. Even if he grasps the implications of the train coming, they take time to sink in, and John needs time to turn a wish for escape into action. Besides this kind of problem, which boils down to a need to hold hands unless the situation is completely safe, there is the child's fatigue threshold, which varies from day to day. It is often a difficult question deciding whether to take a push-chair just in case it is needed over the last part of the journey. *Taking* a push-chair at all is sometimes bad psychology—provided you are not going too far. It is then a constant reminder that an easier form of progress is near at hand, which can prompt some children to ask for it. Another form of constant reminder is a younger brother or sister who is always in a pram or a push-chair. Sheer envy of attention to a brother or sister can make a three-year-old cry that he is tired and needs a carry or a push. But, as well as exercising judgment on push-chairs, parents *can* make walks with three-year-olds more enjoyable by calculating the distance they are expecting to cover and deciding whether stops might be needed; by calculating the time needed, so that there is no urgency or rushing, which can of itself help make a child more tired; and by *encouragement*. This means complimenting the child on how well he is doing and paying at least as much attention to him as to adult conversation or to the occupant of a push-chair.

Visits to shops can be more harassing for a mother and at the same time more interesting if she has a three-year-old in tow. Even if he is in a push-chair, he will scarcely be satisfied with remaining outside a shop. If he is mobile, even strapping him in is a dangerous practice (although one sees it done), and it is anyway most unlikely to increase his pleasure in going out with his mother. But inside a shop he needs careful watching. In supermarkets, it is as well to remember that he does not fully appreciate the principles of shopping: he sees you taking packets and tins down from the shelves and putting them into a wire basket, and he sees no reason why he should not join in. This has led to many embarrassments at the check-out desk. A lot of his time is spent in copying his parents, and since he is making great progress at this age at distinguishing and reaching for things at odd angles and on tiptoe, the supermarket seems an obvious invitation to try out his skill at adult games. Paying for what you buy is a ritual, in his eyes, not an obligation. There is no harm in starting to explain the obligation, provided that you do not expect him to understand it fully until some time later.

Parents make it easier for themselves when they *involve* a three-year-old in what is going on. Obviously, this must depend on the time you have, the amount to be done and the child's temper and energy that morning. But as a principle, it is far preferable to tugging a tearful creature around the shop, saying 'No—this way!' There are certain jobs in the shopping expedition that a toddler can be safely given to do. Be firm about handling the glass jars yourself, but he can take pleasure in reaching for packets of sugar, say, or cereals. Some supermarkets provide miniature wire baskets for him to use, but he will enjoy putting his particular purchases into his mother's basket too. If he feels that he is an active part of the scene, co-operating in something adult, he will be far less inclined to become tired, bored or frustrated by what he is not being allowed to do.

This principle can be extended to all kinds of outings. If watched and helped, he can be the one to show the family's railway tickets to the inspector. He can hand over money in a newspaper shop and receive the change—provided there is no queue behind. But he should not be given too much responsibility, since he does not understand the principles underlying, for example, the inspection of train tickets; therefore it is unfair to be hard on him if he makes a mistake. Early happy experiences in shopping are probably more important than most psychologists have made out—not just to make shopping less of an embarrassing experience later on, when children are older and more anxious to do things correctly and unobtrusively, but because it is one of the first kinds of formal encounter between a child and society, or the world outside the sheltered circle of the family. If his first impressions are of an unfriendly and impatient world, which is either disregarding him totally or making too many demands on him too quickly, he may start to regard having transactions with other people as difficult, unpleasant or liable to expose him to feeling shamed. A few early, easy and satisfying encounters make for confidence in relations with people that go far beyond the simple matter of buying a few groceries.

If this seems to be laying too much stress on this area, it is worth asking friends about embarrassing experiences they can remember vividly when they were very young. Or ask them about things they can remember being afraid to do. Events in shops often loom surprisingly large in the answers people give.

Reaching for something in a shop is easier, at three, because of better eye-and-hand co-ordination. A very simple experiment involves using a collection of different objects, such as pencils, pens, egg cups, spoons, rubber bands, etc. A two-year-old who knows what a spoon is can be asked to reach for the spoon in the collection, and he will get it for you. But it takes time and effort. He may well use both hands, especially in those many cases where he may only just have developed a preference for being 'right-handed' or 'left-handed'. He will touch objects on either side of the spoon and perhaps he will not clasp the spoon properly the first time. The three-year-old, given a similar instruction, will go for the spoon more directly and more neatly. In nearly all cases he will use his preferred hand. If you watch his hand, you will note that he is better at grasping the object between his thumb and fingers and at holding it there.

Colours are intriguing to a three-year-old. Even if he was an early talker, he may not have built up a sufficient vocabulary at two to recognize differences between hues and name them. Many children use some colour names for a while without knowing what the words *mean*. Usually these are children who are in their first year or two of learning to speak: one of their toys may be called 'the blue train', which is taken by them as a phrase that names the toy, rather than a description of the toy's colour. They do not apply 'blue' to other objects because that is not part of their name. If they meet a green train and note the words used to distinguish the two toys, something clicks and colour generalization starts; *or*, they notice a similarity in the hue between different objects that are called 'blue'. A set of building blocks of different colours helps speed up this process when the child hears his father say, for example, 'Now let's put the blue bricks along the top of our castle.' But a three-year-old is *expecting* to meet more colours and their names, because he knows some of the principles. He looks on a new object as something which is likely to have a particular colour, and his eyes are more capable of differentiating between colours that may be close to each other because they are both bright or both dark. It is amusing to listen to three-year-olds arguing about colours, each convinced that he is right. This often happens with check material or a carpet with a striking pattern. But whether the same shirt is called 'mauve', 'purple', 'violet' or even 'plum' will vary from house to house, and this provides more grist for argument.

Getting colours correctly named is important to children because it is part of getting control, symbolically, of what is surrounding them. Knowing another child's name and sometimes keeping his own name dark is even more important, for the same reason.

Some children will find difficulty with colours—particularly in distinguishing red and green. In most cases these will tend to be boys. It has been calculated that approximately one boy in twenty has some form of colour blindness. Often this is restricted to a difficulty in telling some shades of green from some shades of red. These are complementary colours and are more likely to be confused by a child whose colour vision equipment (particularly the 'cone' receptors in the retina of the eye and the nerve pathways that carry information from the eye to the back of the brain) is peculiar in some way. Other children may have difficulty with yellow and blue, the other complementary colours, but this is rarer. Complete colour blindness is extremely rare.

Parents whose children seem to be having difficulty with colours in their fourth year may find that this proves to be a matter of linguistics, or becoming able to use the right words. But it is worth noticing whether particular colours—especially red and green—cause more problems. Sophisticated colour blindness tests (such as the Ishi-hara cards) are dependent on number recognition and cannot usually be applied at this age, but a doctor or an eye specialist will be able to see whether colour blindness can be ruled out as a diagnosis. Further checks can then be made when the child is older. It is worth being forewarned about this. Colour blindness cannot be corrected, but compensations can be taught: for example, a child can be told that when the top light of a set of two traffic lights (facing him) is shining brightly, this means you must stay on the kerb. It is worth adding that this is what people mean when they say 'The lights are red.' Explain, of course, that during this time the traffic will be moving across his path.

The earlier that traffic lights are taught, the better, for all children of this age. This does not mean that they should be allowed to cross the road by themselves, under any circumstances, but simply in order that they pick up the habit of looking for the lights. Very rarely does a three-year-old object to pressing the button that operates lights at some pedestrian crossings. Seeing the lights on the other side of the road obeying your instructions is usually a great mystery and a great delight.

This is the age when some first impressions can be very important. A typical three-year-old knows very well by sight about twelve to fifteen adults, and there are about twice that number who are familiar faces. He probably knows many more adults than children, because unless they are in the family, daily visitors or older children, he is only just starting to take real notice of them. Some first impressions are weak. A visiting relative or friend may come several times and play with the child, but remain unrecognized. 'Oh, *surely* you remember Uncle James', a mother will cry, possibly in some embarrassment, when her three-year-old asks bluntly 'Who are you?' But Uncle James may remain a cypher. Meanwhile, Patrick, Daddy's friend from the office, may arrive *once*—but in a red sports car, say, or whistling as he walks. Two years later, when Patrick is seen again, the child may cry 'Where's your red car?' or 'You're the man who whistles!' Memory is starting to be very selective about people. The first striking or notable thing that they do or say, or the first feeling that this person is fun, or dangerous, or kind, or sarcastic, may colour the child's view for a very long time.

Boys and girls look and act very much the same at this point in their lives. They get dressed differently, but for a large part of most days they may be in interchangeable jersey and overalls. Gradually they are being encouraged to do different things, which will give them a consciousness of sex role, long before they have any clear idea of how and why boys are different from girls. Even parents who consciously support a unisex ethic in fact promote role differentiation unconsciously. They encourage boys to be brave, determined and energetic, while they cannot restrain their smile of approval if their daughters are being winsome or winning, or dancing rather than climbing trees. But at three years old, much of this has not begun. It is often only at parties that the boys look like boys and the girls like girls, unless the girls have very fast-growing hair or natural curls.

Both the sexes are just over three feet tall. Their weight is nearly the same, with the boys having a slight edge. Both are likely to be walking and running with similar proficiency. They are equally matched in terms of what they can do with their hands and in the energy they possess. Children coming up to three do not fight very much, as a rule. But if they were trying to snatch something from each other or push each other out of the way, a girl is just as likely to win as a boy.

It is somewhat early, if not premature, therefore, to suggest to a boy that he should be gentle with girls. To a three-year-old, there are stronger children, weaker children, faster ones and slower ones. If you stopped and wondered whether you are confronting a girl—you might lose valuable seconds!

Three-year-olds usually talk a lot, although many of their comments are in a kind of personal jargon which is difficult to understand. The fourth year is a time during which they need to be given a lot of encouragement to talk more and more, and to talk at *all* levels: they should not be addressed in baby language because it sounds cute, but neither should they always be put off nonsense words or jingles in favour of neo-Victorian adult conversation. The greatest width of talking experience is going to be an enormous help to them, not just in communicating with others but in learning to enjoy language and in gaining a feeling over the years that they can make language do what they want it to do. For an academic, this is an invaluable groundwork. For anyone else, making of language is always useful and is usually a source of pleasure.

Width of talking experience is encouraged by parents doing both these things: taking an interest in a new phrase (English or jargon) that their child is using and playing it back, perhaps elaborating it, but letting the child make the running, and using grammatically correct language but not insisting that he corrects his language; and making conversation with him in simple, but grown-up language, using a normal tone, when you feel like it. This can best be explained by contrasting two mothers' ways of putting the same thing to a three-year-old:

Mrs A.: (rather arch voice, more highly-pitched than when speaking with her husband) 'Mister sun's come out, Tommy! Want to go walkies? Hold handy-pandy and go walkies in the reckie (recreation ground)?'

Mrs B.: (normal voice—neither off-hand nor sugar-coated) 'Tommy—look! The sun's shining. Shall we go for a walk together? Let's hold hands, then. Shall we go to the recreation ground?'

Well . . . with which of them would *you* rather go for a walk?

If Tommy has picked up 'reckie', there is no reason why he shouldn't use it, until he tires of it. Nor is there any reason why you should not use it yourself, occasionally, if you like it. But using it simply to talk down to Tommy is absurd, and limiting. The important thing is to make it clear that you enjoy talking with him and by implication that he can have access to grown-up conversation any time he wants it.

Trying to find a middle path is also important when it comes to interruptions. If his parents are succeeding in encouraging conversation with him, he may want to burst in on their discussions. This is not only normal, but is a thoroughly desirable trait in three-year-olds. But yielding each time to interruption is wrong. Most parents work out a compromise—continuing their talk and

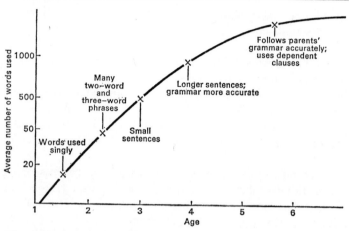

Figure 2 Vocabulary gain and use of language

then allowing their child in to make his point. There are few things a child likes better at this age than to be part of a conspiratorial threesome, of father, mother and child sharing their thoughts, or a joke, or whatever. This depends on the subject being intelligible, but looking out for the right moment can mean a lot of happiness for a child.

The opposite extreme to yielding too often is to react in a way one sees all too often in buses or trains, when a mother is near the end of her tether, and the following non-conversations take place:

'Mummy, why doesn't the bus go faster?'
'I can't be bothered with that now, dear.' Or (depending on social background) 'Shut your cake-hole!'

It is impossible not to reflect, when you hear this kind of thing, that years hence the young generation will be blamed yet again for creating a communication gap and having too little concern for their parents.

A more immediate consideration, however, is the help that language development gives for starting to read. Parents sometimes worry a great deal about getting reading started quickly, but pay scant attention to conversation in the home. Yet reading must mean using words confidently, which is what conversation is all about.

In the fourth year, a lot more new words are developed. These include many more verbs and adjectives, by comparison with the noun-dominated language that children tend to pick up until the age of about three. The graph in Figure 2 shows the average development of vocabulary at this time: it is an amazing increase, which will stand comparison against any other intellectual achievement that the child may go on to gain in his lifetime.

Not all children are talking so easily. Figure 2 shows the *average*: there is a wide range overlapping either side, within which most children will fall. A minority will have a speech problem or a learning problem of some kind. Late talking is by no means such a rare thing, but if speech does not start expanding rapidly by the middle of the fourth year, especially if communication in general seems difficult, then the advice of a doctor must be sought and taken. This will probably lead to consultation with a speech therapist, although other specialist help may be needed. Nowadays, a great deal can be done to help children to talk, whatever their problems.

Chapter two

What is a four-year-old thinking about?

Very young children can be understood without too much difficulty. A baby cries and his mother can think of several reasons why he should do so. He is fed, made comfortable and cuddled. He smiles and is obviously, for the most part, understood. At some point in early childhood most parents suddenly realize that their child cannot be read like a book. This occurs earlier to some and later with others. If he is their first child, the realization may come as a shock.

When they reach four years of age, many children are proving a mystery to their parents in one way or another. Their personality is very likely becoming more individual and less like mother's or father's. They have their own ideas, their own tastes, preferences and crazes. They change not only in mood—which is to be expected—but in direction of interest, too. Sometimes, at this age, they make it clear that they are not content merely to have the world interpreted for them by their parents. They claim the right to question what their parents are doing, too. Here are some comments from parents who have been puzzled about their four-year-olds.

'Looking at her now, it's obvious that Clare is an out-and-out tomboy. She's always climbing things, or leading the boys next door into mischief. Just recently she's started throwing stones. She seemed such a good-natured girl before. I mean —she always laughed a lot and showed she had a lot of energy. But she's always on the rampage now. The other day my husband watched her through the french windows having a rough-and-tumble and asked me, "Did *you* ever behave like that when you were a girl?" I said, "I certainly don't think so", and this made me realize how different she is from both of us. . . . I expect she'll cool down as she gets older. But she's quite a handful at the moment.'

'Dennis looks at me very severely sometimes. I've only really noticed it this year. It's unnerving when he watches you getting everything ready for the wash, and then tells you you've forgotten something. . . . It makes me short-tempered sometimes. Once I told him that if he's so clever he ought to do it himself. I kicked myself afterwards, but you don't expect that sort of thing from a little boy.'

'When Linda was younger and she was upset, it was easy to bring her round again, by starting doing something she liked. She loved being read to, or sung to, or simply being picked up. She still likes all those things, but sometimes I just don't seem to interpret what's wrong, and she refuses to be consoled. . . . There are some things about her moods that I just don't understand.'

There is nothing to be ashamed of in making an admission of this kind. Very many mothers admit as much, at one time or another, and are the more honest for doing so. What *is* there to be ashamed of in stopping to care whether there is understanding between you and your child or not?

The basis of a four-year-old's thinking is that, at the very centre of his life, he has a family bond to rely on. This is usually with his mother, or he may have a mother-substitute. He is in the last year of the period during which it is extremely important that a close bond of this kind should form and be protected. There is no magic date on which this need will change, but investigations of childhood disturbance tend to focus attention, in the end, on whether this bond existed during the age period up to five, and whether it was broken or threatened. However advanced or individualistic a four-year-old may seem, he is still within a danger zone. He may rebel and appear to resist all proposals of authority or of winning back his affection; but such rebellion is only skin-deep. When he is at his most dismissive, he has great need of his mother's reassuring presence and concern.

One pointer to this conclusion is work done among children in hospital. It has been shown by Robertson, in particular, that when children under five are admitted to hospital and left there by their parents, they undergo a kind of trauma. This is not necessarily a scar for life, and it is clear that individual children's personality and illness play some part in this, but it often has results that last far beyond convalescence from whatever the child's condition happened to be. Above five, the danger is there, but less great. Where mother stays in hospital with her child, there is far less danger of real disturbance. Many hospitals, over the past decade, have shifted their policy towards allowing mothers to 'live in'. This has also been the official policy recommended by successive Department of Health and Social Security (DHSS) circulars, since the publication of the Platt Report. Mothers who encounter opposition to a request that they accompany a young child into hospital and that they have unrestricted visiting, have a duty to others, as well as to themselves, to complain and, if necessary, enlist the support of NAWCH (National Association for the Welfare of Children in Hospital).

It is worth mentioning this not simply because it could help some children, but because it makes an important point about the four-year-old's mentality. His verbal skills, which have been growing very fast, as described in the last chapter, have grown faster than his ability to understand all the arguments that can be made with the words he has learned. His mother explains, in simple terms, that he will have to go into hospital for a few days, where he will be helped to get better and where everyone will look after him nicely, that his mother will visit him and that after a few days, when the doctor gives the all-clear, she will gather him up and take him home again. He may show, by asking intelligent questions, that he gets the superficial meaning of what she says is going to happen. He may be curious about doctors and nurses and about how meals are prepared in hospital. But this is very different from appreciating that he is actually going to be *left* in the hospital, that his mother will actually *go away*, that he is going to spend a long time—night-time, even—without having her within calling distance, that someone else is going to remove his clothes and give him a bath; and that he (possibly) will be given a pre-med before an operation by a team wearing gauze masks. Naturally mothers who are not going to live in may tend to gloss over the fact that they will not be at hand all the time. But even if their warning is clear, the importance of the mother–child bond is such that a child cannot really get the full meaning until it happens. In other respects his understanding may be in advance of speech, but not where hypothetical conditions are concerned.

However, some mothers whose attendance at hospital is restricted by other family commitments have had considerable success with booklets and games based on those booklets, which give a child a chance to learn by means of *play* about the experience this going into hospital will bring. (Some titles are suggested at the end of this chapter.)

The strength of feeling for his mother (or mother-substitute) comes out in other ways. One is the rather bizarre interpretations that children sometimes put on separation. They are not sure about whether their mother is punishing them, and if this may have been deserved, or if their mother is really the naughty one, who deserves punishment herself. The basis of good behaviour and punishment is only very sketchily understood at four, so it is not surprising that there should be this confusion. Occasionally, a four-year-old will blame himself for a parent's illness; he does not understand *how* he has done it, but it may seem all the worse to him for that reason.

Adele was a very bright, lively and rather coquettish three-year-old. She had boundless energy and a distinct sense of fun. She used to get into scrapes because her curiosity led her to explore everything she could get hold of—father's attaché case, mother's cosmetics, everything. She was stopped from doing these things, and sometimes told she was a naughty girl—but usually this was with good humour all round. When she was just four, her mother was found to have tuberculosis and had to leave home. Because of the danger of infection, contact with Adele was broken for several months. In order not to alarm her about the seriousness of the illness, not much was explained to Adele about what exactly was wrong, or why life had to change in the way that it did.

Her father moved Adele and himself to live in with his sister and her family. They all knew each other well, which helped. But Adele's father noted, over the weeks, that Adele became less cheerful, less energetic, less mischievous. She seemed to have fewer ideas about how to amuse herself and less motivation to put them into practice. She clung to him more, and she clung more to his sister. On some days her emotions became entirely unpredictable: a more lively hour, playing with her cousins, would suddenly give way to a temper tantrum, to be followed by whining and being negative about everything. Her sleep was often interrupted and she spoke of events that were clearly derived from nightmares. She ate poorly. She also had sessions by herself, in which she would sit down with some of her toys and break them up, while refusing to have anything to do with anyone who approached her.

Her father wisely took a week off work and devoted most of his time, except for hospital visits, to being with Adele, playing with her, distracting her and trying to talk as much as possible with her. She responded quite well to this. At first he noticed that she would only talk about her mother in very superficial tones (e.g. 'Mummy liked the flowers? Good. Can we have an ice cream, now, Daddy?'). Later in the week, by coincidence, he was able to give her some good news. 'Another few weeks and Mummy will be able to come back. Won't that be wonderful?' Adele agreed. She did not display much emotion, but she was obviously pleased and thoughtful. By now she was talking more easily with her father. They talked for a while about how they could make the house look nice for when her mother returned. Tacked on to the end of a comment about clearing her toys away was this significant comment from Adele, '. . . and I won't be naughty again, I promise.' Both her father and their doctor probed this promise carefully; it seemed that Adele was convinced that in some way or other she could not fathom, she had been responsible, by her naughtiness, for her mother's serious illness. This burden of guilt could not vanish overnight. But once it was all in the open, her father and her mother could gradually help her to understand that she was not to blame.

A mystery surrounding a separation is a spur to a four-year-old's imagination, and some very unfortunate interpretations can be thought up for it. Death is a common source of this kind of problem. Thinking to spare the child's feelings, nothing is told. A funeral happens, from which the child is kept at a safe distance, and later the person's name is only mentioned with a tear or a reverent hush. It is far better for a child to be told a simple fact—not necessarily elaborated—so that his natural curiosity is satisfied and so that he does not work out a macabre explanation involving himself as a guilty party or a return of the loved one on which great emotional store is set, but which never happens.

The four-year-old believes that his mother knows best about some things and (usually) that his father knows best about others. He notices arguments and he notices where, and how, one parent defers to the other. This is part of his observation of adult sexual roles. Later, when he models his behaviour on either parent, he will expect to be an authority in certain areas himself. He will also be prepared to listen to advice and to adapt or change his views, if he has seen evidence of this in his parents.

Children copy their parents more often than their parents usually suppose. It is natural that they should try to please and to be like these people who have such kindness and authority. They need little encouragement to be like them in questions of independence—dressing themselves, and so forth. But if they feel hurried at this kind of task, deflation and resentment can set in.

Four-year-olds are not particularly logical when their parents admit that they do not know the answers to a question. They expect their parents to know most things. They do not expect to understand all answers. Sometimes they will repeat questions, irrespective of whether they have been given an answer or told 'I don't know'. It is almost as if they are trying to come to terms with this kind of answer, along with the other information they are given.

Repetition of questions, particularly repetition of the dreaded 'Why?', is often a compound of two wishes. The first is to be engaging parents in conversation, which means both getting attention and participating in something with them. The second is to dig for a little more understanding, as if sheer repetition of an answer might make it more comprehensible or help it to fit into the child's frame of reference. The degree to which a child pursues questions for either reason depends on the personality of the child, and particularly on how far he feels he needs extra attention or on how strong his curiosity about the world has become. Young children, who are generally very curious, can sometimes be heard repeating their parent's answer to a question, almost as if it had some special magic about it that the child wanted to claim for himself. The 'magic', in fact, is knowledge (and therefore *control*) over the subject. Here is an example overheard on a bus:

Four-year-old: 'Why is the driver getting out of the bus, Daddy?'
Daddy: 'I think somebody's going to change places with him.'
Four-year-old: (whispers to himself) 'Somebody's going to change places with him.'
Several minutes later, a second driver clambers up into the driving seat.
Four-year-old: 'Is it his turn now, Daddy?'

The child in this example knew nothing about bus drivers'

working schedules, and probably saw no reason why anyone should give up his place. But he knew about taking *turns*—we may suppose this was something he was always being encouraged to do with other children. Consideration of his father's remark led him to make his interpretation. It may sound comic, but at his age it was a very intelligent deduction to make.

At four, the world is seen very much in personal terms. This affects a great deal of children's thinking. In the first place, it means that they tend to make judgments on the goodness or badness of people or events, according to how these affect their own security and personal pleasure. They are hard on visitors who take up too much of their mother's time; they are jealous of other children in whom their parents show an interest. On the other hand, they like people who amuse them or give them apples or ice cream. But they give short shrift to anyone who asks questions on first meeting, which seem to have the purpose of getting a laugh, or of causing them to be confused or embarrassed, or of simply testing them. Paradoxically, more intelligent children often go through a period of 'clamming up' when introduced to strangers who may have heard how bright they are supposed to be. Presumably one aspect of their intelligence is to be sensitive to situations where they risk being put to shame.

Another function of their personal outlook on the world is to encourage them to ascribe reality only to things which *they* can see or imagine. Another child's house, described in *that child's* terms (e.g. big, warm, with lots of toys and a cat or two), is meaningless, by comparison with his own observation from outside that the house is a red house. Piaget's work on the development of children's intelligence shows that they are not ready, at four, to allow things to keep their nature when they are not under scrutiny. Three eggs put into a bowl and whisked up, look like *more* eggs. A four-year-old who has observed the whole process is quite likely to say there are more eggs now. What is called the Constancy Principle does not yet apply in his mind.

When he explains something that has happened, he tells his story as if the hearer had been there too. This is because he cannot take into account the hearer's point of view. There is only one point of view, and that is his own.

Child: 'I was on the beach and we went up on the rocks. We were looking for crabs. He said, "No crabs down here", but—'

Parent: '*Who* said?'

Child: 'Martin of course! He pulled up this stone and he said, "No crabs." But I said, "Look, there's a crab!" And he fished around with mine, because he dropped his, and he can't catch it—'
Parent: 'Your *what*?'
Child: 'He took my shrimping net. . . .'

And so it goes on. The child's account is very similar to what he would say if they were both watching the sequence being played through on a cinema screen and both had exactly the same visual information.

A simple and interesting test of the degree to which a four-year-old is learning to consider other viewpoints can be tried out if he has a sibling—say, a sister. 'Have you got a sister?' will get the answer 'Yes'. 'Has she got any brothers or sisters?' may very likely get the answer 'No'. He can't see her viewpoint of himself. Typically, a four-year-old will start seeing himself as his mother's son (or daughter), before starting to consider any others' views, probably because this is the easiest possessive relationship to grasp outside his own possessions but also because it is the most important relationship to him.

Not seeing others' attitudes makes it very difficult to interpret what others are thinking, with a few important exceptions. He has always, even as a baby, been very sensitive to fear and anxiety on the part of his parents. He can also sense their love and—if it applies—their disapproval. Laughing and crying are easy for him, because they have always been part of the communication form he has picked up. But smiling and frowning mean much, much less. It is worth while looking up some pictures in a new picture book, showing them to him and saying, 'I wonder how that man is feeling. What's he saying do you suppose?' In most cases, the four-year-old will take his cue from whatever *situation* is in the picture. A facial expression in a static scene may mean very little indeed. Gradually this changes, until at six he may retort, 'Well he doesn't look exactly happy, does he?'

This inability to distinguish mood means that four-year-olds are often felt to be very insensitive, or even callous. Other parents may interpret his indifference to facial expression or others' feelings when they are expressed in a low key as evidence of naughtiness or egocentricity. A psychologist called Vygotsky has stoutly defended four-year-olds from this kind of judgment by pointing out that since they do not understand that there *is* another point of view of the world other than their own, they cannot logically be called selfish: they are not, in fact, making a choice, which is what selfishness implies.

But four-year-olds can be charmingly sympathetic and kind, when they understand that somebody they love is unhappy. It does not last long, because it is not in their nature to concentrate on unhappiness longer than they have to. In this, they often have a healthier attitude than adults. But their first expressions of sympathy may come through at this age—possibly at a moment when you need it badly.

Rules have a big attraction and a kind of sacred authority for children from about their fifth year until they are at least eight. This may seem odd, given that they view the world so much from their own angle. But rules have a kind of simplicity about them that implies order and stability, and they enable somebody to control what he does not fully understand. In some houses, there may be a rule that Wellington boots must be removed on the threshold, or in the kitchen. It is much easier obeying a simple rule like this, than a general one about being tidy or not getting the house dirty. A mistake made by a number of so-called 'permissive' parents is to have no rules, but to insist on a general code of the tidiness kind, such as 'We must all try to be helpful to each other'. At four, this means nothing, unless it is very carefully illustrated.

Rules also help children when they meet each other and play. Four-year-olds are still very much at the experimental stage of finding out what it is like to have transactions with other children. They are like two early navigators meeting in mid-channel, each with their own, very idiosyncratic maps. Rules provide a basic framework in which they can start to discuss and explore that channel. Children who are used to different rules (e.g. one may come from a house where everyone knows about and respects personal belongings, the other where most toys are held in common) tend not to mix as well as those who recognize similar rights and taboos. This does not mean that these children will not bend the rules to their own advantage. They certainly do. But they do not question the rules themselves, or the way they have been constructed.

Other elements of common language are important to four-year-olds learning to play together. It is worth noticing the satisfaction and delight among members of a play-group of this age when they recognize words, phrases, bits of childhood lore, songs and 'cult objects' that they have in common. This is more than finding a language: it is discovering points of contact where the other child is regarding something from *your* viewpoint.

Inevitably, while some of these things (e.g. one sings part of a Womble song, which the other recognizes and plays back; or one says, 'Witchie-poo is in that box' and the other picks up this play-theme by saying, 'What's she doing? Can she see us?') are the kind that adults are amused to hear, there are others which are more painful to a fond parent. 'Where have these "Bang-bangs!" and this gun-toting come from?' a parent may ask himself. '*I* don't encourage it. Billy isn't allowed to watch it on television. And his little friends seem to come from decent homes. . . .' If he listens a bit closer, he will hear more unsavoury themes, which may disquiet him further. 'Why are they so *obsessed* with what they do in the lavatory?' he then wonders. 'What's all this talk about pees and poos?' Perhaps, he feels, he ought to intervene and put a stop to it. In fact, although parents can distract children from an interest of this kind, and can make it less intensive, they have no hope whatever of quenching lavatorial interest completely.

Where does it come from? Well—where do flies emerge from in spring-time? It is pointless and unfair to pick on one child among several playmates and forbid him to come to the house because he is thought to be the purveyor of crudity.

The Freudian view—and one which is accepted by many psychologists who do not go the whole way with Freud—is that in their fifth year, children are coming to the end of their pre-occupation with anal functions. This has been the dominant form of interest for them since their 'Oral Phase' ended at about eighteen months. It has been a source of pleasure, concern and achievement. Now, at four, children have language, and can talk about it. They meet others, who have been similarly pre-occupied. Talk they do, although in many cases there is a kind of code, or symbolism, because they know that parents do not like attention focused on the lavatory. They discovered this when (usually at about three) they experimented at painting a lavatory wall with their faeces. (*No* parents should be ashamed of this in their child: it is the rule, rather than the exception.)

It is interesting to work out just how much symbolic value children's games and cult objects have at this age. At the end of a paragraph above, mention was made of overt lavatory references. Earlier in the paragraph there were guns and explosions: the

former are usually expressions of power and have phallic symbolism for a child, the latter are often more anal. Then there is the
legend of 'Witchie-poo', who crops up from one generation to
another, with varying but appropriate names. She is a dangerous
authority figure, from whom children usually have an exciting
time escaping in their games. The children, typically, make
believe they are playing tricks on Witchie-poo, but are frightened
of her at the same time. This is an analogy with life, where you
derive what fun you can from defecation, but must not get
caught or make a mistake in where or how you do it. And what
about those delightful Wombles from Wimbledon Common?
Freud would have no hesitation in noting how neat and tidy—in
short, how anally obsessive—they are, and he would point to
their shape, their movement and their homes to show that these
are faecal symbols, and for that reason of great attraction to
children at this age.

Certain things are clear, whether Freud's work is believed or
not. This is that lavatorial interest is normal; that it usually
reaches a height, during which children are likely to encourage
each other, and then it declines thereafter; and that this decline
is all the faster if the interest is not driven underground by well-
meaning parents trying to root it out, but succeeding only in
making it more guilty and stimulating.

They have another focus of interest which is of growing concern.
For a boy this is the penis and for a girl the vaginal area. Children
naturally become aware of pleasure when these are touched. Most
children, nowadays, either at home or on the beach, notice that a
boy is different from a girl. Very likely, they will at some stage
ask why—either at four or at five. It is important to bear in mind
that children can easily be made to feel peculiar and that this is a
source of great anxiety—if they are not told clearly that their
equipment, whether male or female, is perfectly in order. They
are fast approaching the 'Phallic Stage' of Freud, which (again
whether you accept Freud or not) is going to explain a great deal
of children's thinking and conversation.

It is worth reviewing those things which are more difficult, if
not impossible, for most four-year-olds, for what light they can
throw on the kind of help they need educationally.

First—time. In the last chapter it was suggested that time is
beginning to have a meaning for a three-year-old, in terms of
what is past, what is happening now and what is coming up in the

future. The five-year-old can usually differentiate between morning and afternoon, with lunch in the middle. This is the first concrete and practical way of dividing up time, in which he is
involved. There are other 'times' that he knows, which have less
practical value—e.g. 'day-time' and 'night-time'. (He cannot *do*
so much with these concepts as with morning and afternoon,
when he is equally active.) Meal-times, bath-time and bed-time
are also recognized by him as staging-posts, and he knows which
is the next one that is coming up. But 'yesterday' and 'tomorrow'
are problematical. Either term could mean a very long time away
on either side of the present. He does not organize his memory
or expectations on a scale that is at all precise, as yet.

Second—the span of apprehension. A four-year-old has difficulties in organizing (virtually or manually) a large amount of
anything. This can apply to objects or information. Faced with
the task of comparing two sticks, they have no difficulty in saying
which is larger and which smaller. To put these sticks in order of
size may seem to us to be an easy stage forward from this beginning, but it demands concentration and possibly trial-and-error
from a four-year-old. Sorting a large number of sticks into big
ones and small ones is, again, more difficult than we might expect.
This seems to be because the child is confused by the numbers,
and has a tendency to compare two things at a time. It can also be
that the instructions for a task become more difficult to understand when they are applied to a large number of objects, rather
than a small number. But certainly a child finds it hard at this age
to think of 'classes', or categories, in which to sort objects. 'Get
me all the daisies you can from the lawn' is understood and acted
on. 'Get me all the dandelions' is also understood. But 'You see
that pile of flowers? Put the daisies on one side and the dandelions
on the other' is not so easy.

Third—negative and passive forms. The active voice in language comes first. People *do* things. It is often that passive forms
are more subtle, and may be too subtle for a young child. It takes
time for 'good to eat' to mean the same as 'I like to eat it' or 'tastes
nice'. 'Pigs are good to eat' can suggest to a four-year-old that
pigs are *good at eating*: he may visualize them with big jaws.
Similarly, 'less weak' is much more difficult to grasp than
'stronger'. The words 'less' and 'few' are often omitted from perception by four-year-olds as being difficult, and so 'less weak' to
them may sound like 'weak'.

2

Fourth—internalization. This means that four-year-olds find it hard to commit a complex command to memory, and produce the right action at the right moment. To do so demands that the sequence be 'internalized', so that they are poised, ready to complete the sequence when they perceive the right stimulus. An experiment by the Russian psychologist Luria gives a good demonstration of this difficulty.

Luria compared children of three age groups, testing each child separately. He showed each one a button which operated a buzzer, and told them to 'Press it when the red light comes on, but *don't press* it when the blue light comes on'. The three-year-olds found this task impossible to perform consistently, and many could not perform it at all. Yet Luria had made certain that all the children taking part knew what 'blue' and 'red' meant, and what the button was. A signal that meant *withholding*, as opposed to making a response, was a foreign and a very difficult concept. At about four and a half, children were able to comply, after a struggle, but they needed to repeat aloud their instructions each time a light flashed. By the age of six, children could fulfil the task correctly and silently.

This was a significant experiment, because it hints at so much that is important in the development of children's thought. The need to repeat instructions might be called 'incomplete internalization'; or it might be linked to the fact that children are throughout this age period developing their ability to store data in their memories, and to retrieve it efficiently. It could also be linked to the fact that positive instructions are easier for a child than negative ones, in all areas of his life: part of this may be a problem of obvious, as opposed to less obvious, reward. Putting on a shirt when you get up makes sense—it keeps you warm and prepares you for the outdoors. But being told *not* to put on yesterday's shirt when you waken is hard to follow. The advantage here is to the mother, who presumably wants to wash the shirt in the morning. The eventual reward is the avoidance of displeasure, which is at some remove from getting up and shirts.

This problem that they have, together with the others referred to before, suggests ways of helping four-year-olds:

(a) Avoid giving them instructions they cannot understand *and* explain negative instructions in a positive way (e.g. 'When you get up, bring down the blue shirt and we'll put it in the washing machine').

(b) Help them to learn, gradually, what happens in different segments of the days and different days of the week.

(c) Show, with examples, what negative words, phrases and concepts actually mean. Let them play with the material so that they can work it through for themselves. The material can be more or less sophisticated—from cuisenaire rods to pebbles.

(d) Give them easy sorting tasks, which help them learn to organize groups of objects and to start to categorize.

Books for introducing children to hospital

Ages two to seven:
M. and H. A. Ray, *Zozo Goes to Hospital,* Chatto & Windus, 1967.
Children's Hospital Painting Book, National Association for the Welfare of Children in Hospital (NAWCH), 1972.

For older children:
A. Weber, *Lisa Goes to Hospital,* Blackie, 1970.

Chapter three

Social life at four

Some pointers towards the development of the four-year-old's social life are given in Chapter two. Chief among these are his dependence on the bond with his mother and his high regard for both parents in terms of their love and authority. Also important are the development of communication through language and a greater preparedness to be social—to go up to another boy in a playground, to do something with him or to talk to him, instead of keeping an eye on him and playing in parallel.

All children are likely to appeal to their mothers in times of distress in the playground. Many fathers wrongly believe that their young sons must be the worst cissies in the neighbourhood, for crying and shouting 'I'll tell my Mummy' when thwarted in a game. They forget that, once, they did exactly the same, and they do not notice the other children doing it. In any event, the fourth year is not the time to discourage this with a curt 'Fight your own battles!' They cannot be *made* self-reliant or tough. These qualities are more likely to grow if there is a basic belief in home security, that behind one there is a mother and a father who will help if all else fails.

First approaches to other children in strange surroundings are often alarming, probably to most children. This is very different from the behaviour they show to the same children in their home territory, where they feel much more confident. It is true that some children of four seem remarkably tolerant of being taken to a strange house and left to play with another family for the after-noon. But these are more the exception, not the rule. Generally, they have had experience of 'mini-separations', in which they gradually got used to being left for short periods of time with relatives or well-known friends, at first at home, and later with nearby neighbours, in well-known houses. They have also, usually, had a very close, warm relationship with their parents which has given them a confident frame of mind.

Contrary to popular belief, children who have had a looser relationship with their mothers—perhaps their mothers have been going out to work every day or have travelled a lot, leaving their children with relatives and friends for varying periods—are *not* more self-sufficient in strange surroundings. Generally, they are more nervous and less socially advanced. There are exceptions to this. The first kind of exception is where a child has developed a strong bond with a mother-substitute. The second is where he has developed a glib, rather precocious sociability, which is his particular answer to a situation where normal mother–child bonding has been denied him or has been broken. This superficial flair and charm brings the child short-term rewards, by contrast with the long-term rewards of a deep, stable relationship that are founded on the pattern of the mother–child bond. Children in institutions where there are few personal links between them and the staff sometimes become like this—making friends quickly, but in a shallow way.

It is sometimes noticeable that as children get more used to making contact with each other, they become less eager to meet adults. When this switch-over occurs, it is often during the fifth year. There is probably no causal relationship between the two, because some children continue to be extrovert before all-comers. Increasing shyness with adults can sometimes be traced to experience of situations where the child has suddenly felt that his dignity is threatened. Increased language ability can lead to a child being pushed (consciously or subconsciously) by their parents into the foreground. When he is on show, so to speak, a child is very sensitive to reactions that are not so much admiration but amusement. When adults laugh at children's early efforts to get a complicated phrase right, they are contributing to a feeling of acute danger from which those children will suffer when they meet adults later on.

Interestingly enough, it often seems to be children who are conscious of having something extra to defend who are shy in this way. They may be intelligent and aware that they are highly thought of by their parents. Shyness at this age may be more akin to a feeling of superiority, despite our tendency to think of a shy adult as probably feeling rather inferior. When children who are shy with adults are observed in a play area with other children, they often seem eager to organize the others, to tell them off, to play a leading part in games.

Four-year-olds cannot be made less shy. Forcing them to shake hands and talk with people they instinctively distrust is self-defeating. Experience of success in meeting people is the only instruction that will help. This is best begun from within the broader family and a circle of close friends, where there is a chance to get used to others gradually. Pushing shy children forward merely makes them retreat further into their shell, apart from causing no little discomfort and prejudicing their feelings for their parents. At the same time, it must be said that cocooning a child from contact with strangers or checking up assiduously to make sure they are getting on all right can also increase and extend a shyness phase. Silent encouragement works far better than radiating sympathy in these circumstances.

Grace was a very bright three-year-old whose self-composure with outsiders contrasted nicely with her suspicious and competitive attitude towards her younger brother. Just before she was four, however, she took to disappearing from view whenever an adult male hove in sight. This went on for about nine months, in all. At its height, she would rush through the house to greet a four-year-old friend when told he was at the door, only to stop with a scream and rush behind a sofa when she realized that his father, not his mother, had brought him. This disconcerted visitors, who had to have it all explained.

The only adult male excepted from this treatment was Grace's father. He tried, as his wife tried, to talk to Grace about why she should be afraid of men. 'I don't like men' was all he got in reply. When he protested, 'But *I'm* a man, Gracie,' she told him, 'No, you're not. You're Daddy.'

There was no occasion, let alone evidence, that either parent could find of a story that had frightened her off men; or of a man exposing himself, or otherwise alarming her; or of any tale being transmitted to her about men from another child. None of these things could be *entirely* discounted, but they seemed very unlikely. The only situation that might have influenced her, that they could work out, was a visit they had made to a friend's house, when Grace was coming up for four. She had only recently come out of nappies by day—the delay in progress being probably connected with a desire to be 'like' her baby brother—and was using a nappy again for the visit because of a stomach upset that rendered her unreliable. Someone had made a joke about her being 'well-padded', and when she did, in fact, fill her nappy, she was very tearful.

A doctor and a psychologist were asked their advice. When they asked to see her, it created an obvious difficulty, because they were male. Both advised Grace's parents to try not to pay too much attention to it, while avoiding leaving her in situations where she was likely to take fright. They had watched her at play and decided there was nothing else abnormal about her.

Grace was taken to a birthday party, where the father appeared half-way through to organize some simple games. Predictably, Grace cowered in a corner. Grace's mother, in the kitchen with other parents, peered through the doorway in case her daughter showed need of a rescue act. The other child's father knew of Grace's shyness and ignored her. The other children joined in a singing game and then matched up cards which had been cut in two. Grace edged out from behind the dolls' house to have a look at some cards. She helped another child to fit two together. When offered some cards to match up, however, she scampered back. Then there was a farmyard noises game, in which Grace associated herself with several groups of animals, mooing, barking and bleating just as loud as the rest. By the end of the session, when there was a simple quiz, in the form of a story which the children had to interrupt with answers, Grace had infiltrated into the centre of the front rank and contributed more than anyone else. Then her mother came into the room and she beetled back into the corner of the room, behind the dolls' house.

Grace had a very strong need to shine and to compete, and any situation which threatened her star status was shunned. Male adults threatened it, for some reason, quite possibly because some had laughed at her embarrassment over nappies. The birthday party provided her with an opportunity not just to copy other children, but to excel. This, I believe, is partly why shy children rarely respond to the suggestion that they 'be like the others and join in'. It is at least in part because they feel they should do better than the others, that they are shy. As soon as the adult male at the party was seen to be organizing a platform on which she could in fact excel, Grace had no fear of him whatever. *But*, at her mother's appearance, she picked up her role again of being shy in front of men. Her mother began to sense from that moment, that they concentrated rather too much on the 'problem' for the problem to be allowed to disappear gradually as Grace grew up. In fact, Grace showed very few shyness symptoms from about two months after that.

The party referred to above included both four- and five-year-olds. They mix reasonably well, provided mothers are in a nearby room, or *known* to be coming back. The sight of familiar faces among the other children is reassuring. If the home is too large or there are too many children (twelve should be the maximum), this can be disturbing. The children understand enough to be led into singing games, and at this age they perform them with a delightful blend of delight and a solemn sense of ritual. Now they *enthuse* about being allowed into 'In and Out the Dusty Bluebells', etc., particularly if an adult or an older child is participating (not just giving orders). For many, it is an introduction to movement in rhythm with music. This is excellent both as an exercise increasing muscle control and as a stepping-stone to musical appreciation. In a couple of years they will do the same game with more obvious fun, but sometimes with a faint suspicion that they are doing what the grown-ups seem to want. Then, some will enjoy adapting the game or even sabotaging it. But now, the roles are almost sacrosanct. They can be very hard on each other for getting them wrong, which is often why some will back out.

But they do not want to be organized the whole time. They benefit a great deal from being given access to a wide variety of materials—preferably in sequence but not all at once—and simply being allowed to explore them. For parties, this can be difficult because they tend to appear in special clothes for the occasion. But any play-time in a sand-pit, or with finger paints, or with an inflated pool with water (supervised, of course), or with 'Plasticine' or wet clay on newspapers in the kitchen, is enjoyed enormously by four-year-olds at the same time as it is extending their experience of handling and dealing with various basic elements. These also allow children, from a social point of view, to make contact in a co-operative way. They grouse at each other and complain when one transgresses the other's territory, but this is *part of* learning how to make co-operative contact and what oversteps the mark with different partners. Children deprived of social experience at this level are often nonplussed when embarking on a joint activity later on; according to personality, they may then be either too retiring or too bossy.

Some children will be much more competitive than others at

this age. Some will set great store by winning at, say, Passing the Parcel, when they are at a party. Some will insist on going first, or on being the one who hands round the ice cream, or on helping light the candles. They may also intend to seize some trophy from a strange house and carry it away. This can naturally be interpreted in various ways, and there is often a link between taking others' things and a feeling of losing out on affection or attention at home. But when it occurs in children who are otherwise very secure and who look for comparisons with others at which they may shine, it does suggest that they are more piratical than defensive.

When a child is four, his parents will already have a good idea if he is very competitive, and they will also have noted if he does not seem to be competitive at all. There may be doubt about the whole range in between. Psychologists still maintain sometimes that children 'learn to be competitive at school'. When they believe this, they usually add 'unfortunately'. But there is really not much evidence for this. Many, if not most, children who are unquestionably competitive give evidence of this long before they reach school. The function of the school may be to offer, suddenly, a range of new ways in which they can express their nature. Admittedly, schools sometimes go too far in stimulating it.

Competitiveness is nowadays something on which many parents and many educationalists preserve a double standard. Because there is now much more accent on encouraging co-operation, on stigmatizing the rat-race ethos and on the benefits of an egalitarian society, competition is played down, by teachers and by parents too. It tends to be regarded as a source more of problems than of advantages. A sense of competition, it is felt, causes harm to the many who fail, and though it may have been a spur to those few who are successful, it gives them false horizons. And so methods are deployed to divert or dampen down the competitive spirit. But the double standard comes in when plans are being made for the future. Parents, certainly, and many teachers too, tend to believe in the principle that 'if you don't push, you don't get anywhere'. They make comparisons between their children and others, even if they discourage the idea. When their children are four, they are already looking for signs of future academic success. Parents are pleased, in their heart of hearts, if they are told by nursery school teachers—who may run a strictly non-competitive nursery themselves—that their child will probably benefit from, and come to no harm in, the cut-throat every-boy-for-himself atmosphere of the local preparatory school. It is wonderful, in fact, to create an egalitarian society, provided your own children do not have to depend on brotherly love for higher education and a good career.

There are scores of ways in which parents encourage competitiveness. Some are open, such as delight in watching sporting events on a Saturday afternoon. Whether it is horses or football teams, somebody has to win, and the concentration is on the winning. Other ways are more subversive, such as watching another child turn a somersault, and asking yours in a disingenuous way 'Can *you* do that too, Sandra?' Even complimenting a brother or sister on an achievement stirs competitiveness.

I believe that we should be more honest with ourselves about this trait. It is really a question of degree. *Preventing* competitiveness is an absurd concept. *Blaming* children for being competitive certainly does not help them. But learning from social science that *feeding* competitive spirit into a child can give him an intolerable burden if he does not match his own expectations, and can make him intolerable to others even if he does match them, is only reasonable. Providing a mixture of activities on which there are sometimes rewards for individual, sometimes for joint, achievement is a process that could usefully begin about this age.

Girls and boys are equally likely to be competitive now, and they pursue the same goals. Gradually, girls are encouraged at home and at school that losing and winning is not the whole of existence, while boys are led to set a higher store by coming first. This is more or less inevitable, although obviously this too should be seen as a question of degree. For instance, there is no reason why a girl should be treated any differently from her brother if they are both fighting over toys. Equal treatment for both means much more, in all its implications, than telling her she should 'behave more like a girl' and either condoning his actions or telling him he should 'be gentle with girls'. Forcing sex role on to children at this age suggests unfairness and can lead to resentment of the sex role.

Four years old is a fascinating age at which to study concentration. Children vary enormously in this—not merely among themselves, but from day to day as well. When they are together for periods of time, it is possible to tell those children who get stuck into a game or a problem very easily, which holds their concentration, from those who tend to pick at things, moving restlessly from one to another. This affects social development, because those with poor concentration lose out on the number of contacts of any length or complexity that they make with other children. They tend to become less popular, too, either because they give things up listlessly or rush from one diversion to the next, bursting in on what someone is doing and leaving the very next moment.

What causes 'good' or 'bad' concentration is a mixture of things. The capacity to concentrate well is closely correlated with intelligence: since there is a large genetic factor in the latter, there may well be one in the former also. But however intelligent he is, a child who is disturbed will find it hard to concentrate, because what he attends to fails to make him forget his problem or his anxiety. Similarly, a bored child, or one who is tired or ill, will concentrate poorly. These are all transient states, provided they are properly dealt with. Children who are hospitalized in certain institutions have been on a diet of boredom for a long time, and those who teach in hospitals bear witness to the fact that many of these seem to have lost the ability to concentrate and need to be trained back to it. A child who seems to have trouble with concentrating, that seems to go on and on, should certainly be brought to a Child Guidance Clinic for an objective view. The sooner this is done, the sooner help can be given; this is more important from a social development point of view than an academic one, because academic tricks can be picked up more easily later.

Opinion in the last fifteen years has swung round dramatically where nursery schools are concerned. This has come with the realization that those who could get their children into a nursery school gave them a flying start when it came to primary school. This applies to education, but it also applies to social maturity and the avoidance of personality and behavioural problems when primary school begins. From being a low priority, it has relatively quickly become a leading candidate for more educational spending—when that can be afforded.

This does not mean that children without nursery school experience are necessarily going to do badly at school. It is just that it helps get certain ideas clearly established in a child's mind very early on:

(a) There are schools to which you go, where there are a lot of interesting things to do.

(b) There are lots of other children who go to schools, too, of all kinds—sometimes nice, sometimes not so nice to deal with.

(c) There is a rhythm to the school day, which starts and ends with seeing mother.

(d) You do more school as you get older.

(e) Teachers are there to help and are accessible to questions, rather than being jailers.

In short, the nursery school provides an easy start, in which the curriculum is fun and based on co-operative rather than competitive effort. Having a positive attitude towards what happens at school makes more serious study much more palatable later.

Most children will start going to nursery school when they are just four, but some will have started a bit younger. There is no optimum time for starting, except that it is better for both the nursery and the child that he is happy to be left for an hour or so when he starts. Some nurseries allow mothers to be in attendance (although usually out of the way) for the first week or so, so that they can come to the rescue if needed. There is obvious merit in this. The argument that children go on expecting their mothers to be at school if they see them there at all does not really hold water. Normally they start by attending for three mornings a week, and this is extended as they get used to it. Often they extend it unofficially anyway: children of four who are completely engrossed in a project are not always easy to bring home.

There are many difficulties about starting nursery school. Fortunately, most parents realize that it is natural and normal if their child flinches at the idea of staying in the big room with all the other children, when they first take him there. It is a credit, in a way, to the excellent relationship that they have, that their children prefer their company and are cautious about other people's. Here are several points which can help, however:

(a) Arrange for children to get used to playing happily in other homes, with other children, before going to nursery school.

(b) Get them to know the nursery school teacher beforehand.

(c) Arrange for several children, who know each other, to start at the same time.

(d) Attend for all or part of the time on the first few days.

This last point is a specific example of a general aim, which is to help the child to feel that the nursery school is a natural extension —if not of home, of what the child has been used to meeting and experiencing with his mother. Some advocate going further and equipping him (as if on a visit to hospital or on holiday) with a favourite toy. But nursery school teachers are not always receptive to this idea, since one of their aims is to help children to treat what is in the nursery as communal property that they can all use. Adjudicating in arguments and separating personal property can be a big job.

But the majority of children will not, at least over the next five years or so, be able to go to a nursery school. In the United Kingdom, there are simply not enough places. (The same applies to play-groups.) Many local groups of mothers organize events in their homes, now, for mini play-groups; these are restricted to a few families who know each other, using those playrooms and gardens which are the largest and pooling equipment. Others are based on church groups. These do a great deal to make up for the lack of nursery schools. But they do not, as a rule, extend the children's experience of social backgrounds. The best nursery would prepare them to meet children of all kinds of families and of all shades of colours, as well as establishing a broad platform on which their education can be built.

It must be obvious that there are two main categories of experience that a four-year-old may have before facing the outside world. The first is to have a brother or sister of about the same age or younger; the second is to be an only child or to have a brother or sister who is considerably older. Nursery school teachers usually grant that the first type often fits in best, at nursery school, because of their awareness that they cannot always be dealt with first and that they have to compete for attention. They may also be more used to a high noise level. But then the teachers think of the exceptions, and by the time they have finished, much of the logical advantage that those with brothers and sisters seemed to have evaporates.

Part of this is due to one of the side-effects of 'sibling rivalry'. *All* four-year-olds are jealous, at some level or other, of brothers and sisters—particularly if the latter are younger than they are. If such a brother has only just arrived, the barely contained emotion at having been ousted from pride of place can be released by being thrust into nursery school. It *can* come, if not tactfully handled, as a final straw in loss of attention, which can be given a misinterpretation similar to those worked out by children when they find they have been left in hospital. This is one reason why it is worth choosing the time to start nursery school that is not just convenient to you, or to the school, but right for the child as well, in terms of his being happy and secure. It is also a reason for not 'tossing him in at the deep end', as being the quickest and least fussy way of getting him established there; that is even more liable to misinterpretation.

It would be absurd to under-play the value of having a brother or sister with whom to act out or rehearse experiences with other children. It helps a great deal. But the tensions that are present with a brother are very different from the vibrations when little strangers meet for the first time at nursery school. It is sometimes a welcome release for a child to play with those of whom he is *not* jealous, just as it is pleasant, sometimes, for him to return home to his brother, who has a more instinctive understanding of him than the other children seem to have. The two forms of social contact are complementary, but different.

It is rare for four-year-olds to make lasting friendships that are at all deep. They are much too exploratory, finding out what other children have to offer, to invest a great deal of feeling in one outside relationship. But of course they may resume a relationship and deepen it, later.

Father, naturally, has a big influence on the way a child approaches others. Girls usually learn that they have a set of subtle psychological controls that can get their fathers—when he is in a receptive mood—to do things for them that their mothers either refuse, or judge on a more practical basis. They do not see it in these sophisticated terms, but they soon learn that fathers respond to a soft voice and a happy smile. These first victories increase the chances that femininity, and probably social sensitivity will be among the arts that they learn to deploy in a wider sphere as they grow older.

Boys, too, appreciate that their fathers can be persuaded by more subtle means than howling. They are impressed by his authority. It is often instructive to watch four-year-old boys playing in a garden, and see how they vary between imitating each other and making approaches in ways that suggest a larger figure they are trying to be like. If you try to guess what their fathers are like and have an opportunity to meet them later, it is remarkable how close you find you can get. They are usually competitive with their father, envying his closeness with their mother: but this adds fuel to their desire to emulate him.

To sum up, four is an age at which children's social development grows very fast. It can be helped by having, at root, very close relationships with mother and father, *and* a great deal of contact with them at play, conversation, outings, and so forth. They also need, at this age particularly, a lot of opportunity to meet other children from all backgrounds; they need to meet other four-year-olds, but can gain from meeting older and slightly younger children, too. Further, they can be helped by being given a realistic middle-of-the-road view about jealousy: they should not be allowed to create havoc on a brother or on his possessions, but neither should they be made to feel ashamed of having feelings of rivalry that they cannot ever completely suppress. This will help them to feel they do not have to carry their jealousy difficulties with them into the playground and inflict them on others. Being thrown in with too many other children, too soon, should be avoided. Nursery schooling undoubtedly helps from many points of view: my personal belief is that if one has to buy private schooling of any kind, every pound spent at this stage is worth considerably more than what may be spent on older children's education. It is worth exploring play-groups and small-scale private groups, when all the local nursery schools are full—as is often the case. There are plenty of ex-teacher mothers who can, and do, help.

Finally, all this social contact means very little if a child is not actually *enjoying* himself. A happy half-hour in a sand-pit with one friend is probably worth more than a day or two of feeling nervous and timid among a gang. Do not think of the latter as 'toughening him up': it is putting him off. If your observations suggest he is always unhappy with others or is lagging behind them, go back to the nursery school teacher, your doctor or your Child Guidance Clinic, and keep talking until you are satisfied that you know how he can best be helped.

Chapter four

What do children learn at four, five and six?

Speech is the key to so much other learning that it is important to start there. Chapter one described the enormous strides that a three-year-old makes in communicating with others. The progress made during the ages of four, five and six may seem less dramatic in terms of the number of new words mastered per month, but it is, or can be, very important.

When he is four, a child's talking is becoming more conformist, both in terms of the sounds he makes and in the words he uses. The speed of this change depends on several factors, not least among them being the way his parents talk, in general and to him. If they descend into baby talk, they will put off the day by which he abandons it. But this is only a small example of their influence.

Here are two extremes: at one end, parents ignore the child and his requests until he actually shouts what he wants and forces their attention; at the other, parents are habitually consulting the child, interpreting his expression to see what he wants, hanging on every sound he makes and anticipating his needs. Neither of these kinds of parents is doing much to improve their child's speech. In the first family, he will scream or rely on abrasive sounds and phrases to be attended to and to get what he wants. In the second, he will lack any spur to express himself more clearly or more maturely. Most parents are at some point between the two extremes. They enjoy their children's company, but do not smother them with attention. If they also talk to them a bit, in simple but in natural language, and if they avoid laughing at their mistakes or correcting them compulsively, they are giving them the best help they can.

As far as grammar and syntax are concerned, these appear gradually, in the measure to which a child's parents have good grammar and syntax. The influence of other children on grammar and syntax increases very considerably at primary school. The six-year-old, therefore (depending partly on his teacher's influence), may start bringing home some odd grammar and syntax, to his parents' surprise. Other children's accents are liable to creep into his voice, as well. This is because the importance of being part of his peer group is then beginning to weigh heavily with him, so that anything that makes him more recognizably an acceptable member of his contemporary crowd is picked up into his repertoire.

But that lies ahead. At four and at five, parental speech remains the strongest influence, even if the child is going to a nursery school. During this period it is interesting to keep a periodic measure of:

(a) the length of complete sentences that they make;
(b) the proportion of complete, as opposed to part, sentences that they make;
(c) the number of times they use 'you' and 'he' (including 'him', 'me', etc.) as opposed to 'I';
(d) the number of statements and questions they make that do *not* include 'emotional' words (e.g. 'lovely', 'nice', 'nasty', etc.).

As he gets older, a child's speech increases on all these counts. All are measures of general maturity, as well as the ability to use language, which is why the process has to be gradual.

It may seem a paradox that during this period, while they are becoming less tied to 'emotional' phraseology, children are learning to use language to each other in a way that is not always friendly. It is one mark of a bright five-year-old that he can assert or defend himself verbally, as well as physically. One will call another 'silly' and get called 'silly' back; both may then feel aggrieved, because they perceive the strength of abuse turned on themselves as much as they appreciate its effect on others. It is natural for a child to try out these new weapons. It does *not* mean —unless he uses them to excess—that he is over-aggressive.

One aspect of speech development that can be puzzling is the way children often find difficulty in deciding which form of a word is right. 'Mouses' and 'mice' may be used by the same child within the same day. He sees no reason why only one form of the plural of 'mouse' should exist. If he likes the sound of both, he uses both. It is only adults who see a need for precision. In the end it is they who impose the rules, suppressing the 'mouses' either by looking amused when they appear or by simply stating 'mice', and implying correction. Children themselves contribute towards this later, at five and even more at six, when they can be more censorious to each other than most adults. Whether their own preference is right or wrong, correcting each other's language is a way of asserting superiority. Parents are often taken aback when they have themselves only issued a mild suggestion that 'I gave it' is better than 'I gived it', to hear their child telling another, 'You silly nit! You've got to say "gave" not "gived". Everybody knows that!' Many six-year-olds being told this will stubbornly hold out against 'gave' for the rest of the afternoon, but adopt it the next day.

Children do apply logic in the way they build up language, despite entertaining different versions of the same word. This is more easily observed in the case of children who are brought up listening to two languages. They can be seen to apply a principle they have noticed in one language to the other. The implication of this is that a similar process, though one more difficult to follow, is used by all children with a single mother-tongue. Here is an example of the speech of a five-year-old with English parents, living abroad and spending a lot of time with a German house-keeper: 'Mummy, come and see what Beate has gecooked!' Beate's English extended only to 'please' and 'thank you', so she could not have supplied the specific word 'gecooked'; but the boy picked up the principle of past tenses beginning with 'ge' from his conversation with her, and put it logically into practice.

It is sometimes said that children brought up bilingually have a tremendous advantage because it prepares them *both* to speak a second language well *and* to learn the idea of slipping into another tongue in a natural way, which will help them master other languages too. Against this, others claim either that when children learn languages in this way they have difficulty with the grammar of both or that it is confusing and an unfair imposition on them to struggle with two forms of communication at once. There is no research evidence of any weight that demonstrates that bilingual children are less secure or more liable to confusion, which convincingly rules out other factors. Two points tell against this argument anyway. First, a large number of Swiss families would be very insecure if this were the case, and this seems highly unlikely. Second, there are *other levels* of communication than spoken language, which are crucial in establishing the basis of love and understanding between parents and child; if these are working efficiently, a second language should present no special problem. On the question of grammar, there is no doubt that a bilingual upbringing can result in children having a feeling of superiority in the language they can speak fluently and confidently, which leaves their contemporaries (and sometimes their teachers) gasping —with the result that they feel supercilious about learning grammatical nuts and bolts. But this is an educational problem that cannot be insurmountable, otherwise there would be few Swiss language scholars. It is possible that some children who get on well in two languages during these years are subjected to too much pressure to be correct in both; this could certainly make them insecure, but it is nothing to do with being bilingual *as such*.

Most investigators studying speech development in schools have noted that good progress made during the ages of four, five and six is closely correlated with socio-economic status and the terminal education age of the parents. Bernstein offers an interesting concept for understanding why this should be. He suggests that at one end of a spectrum are parents who use only a 'restricted code' of language; at the other, parents use a highly 'elaborated code'. 'Restricted' means, in this sense, language that is stripped down to its bare essentials, in which descriptions are adequate but not imaginative, and in which positive and negative feelings are expressed by blanket terms. 'Elaborated' means using words more carefully, to give particular shades of meaning and overtone. Education (which ties in with socio-economic status) increases the 'elaboration' which parents use. These parents encourage (mostly unconsciously) their children to perceive and use nuances of language when they are talking with each other as well as when they are talking to the children. They feel pride when their children show signs of acquiring an 'elaborated code', and they encourage this.

Piaget, the Swiss psychologist, made a comprehensive study of the *kinds* of language young children use, and how this develops with experience. The categories he uses include 'monologue', which means a child talking out loud to himself, and 'collective monologue', which is a comment made partly to himself, but also attempting to involve the person or the group near him as well. Imagine a child sitting and drawing at a table, with several other children. An example of 'monologue' statement would be 'There —that's his whiskers', as he puts the finishing touches on a cat.

The communication is essentially to himself, for his own satisfaction. Part of a 'collective monologue' might be 'I say, I'm drawing a super cat!' Again, nobody needs to act on or answer this comment, and he may not even look around. But he is keen to make himself and his work stand out in some way, and perhaps to cut across the others' consciousness. Across the years of four, five and six there is a gradual decline in 'monologue', matched by an increase in 'collective monologue'. This is a close parallel to the development away from playing separately from others, towards playing *with* others. It cannot happen more quickly than it does, because, as described in a previous chapter, a four-year-old has an entirely individual view of the world, which is only gradually adapted to the ways of others.

Other Piaget categories cover those comments which are made directly to someone else for a specific purpose—e.g. questions, comments, threats and the giving of information. It is these last aspects of children's speech that parents become aware of more easily, because they often have to attend to them. Sometimes a four-year-old seems to be perpetually asking questions. And yet *more* of a four-year-old's output is monologue than conventional speech. At five, a child is beginning to offer less monologue, and more of it is 'collective' at that. At six, he is still offering quite a lot of monologue: it varies between a third and two-fifths of his total speech output.

For most parents these are exciting years, in which they can listen to their child acquiring new words and phrases, putting them together more and more boldly, and correctly at that. But for others it can be a worrying time, because their child seems to be lagging behind. In these cases, it is possible that he is a slow developer; it is possible that he has some kind of speech impediment, which may or may not be linked to some other handicap; he may also, just possibly, be emotionally disturbed. Many children can be helped, nowadays, by speech therapists: if you are anxious about your child's progress it is well worth discussing with your doctor the various possibilities of what might be wrong.

There are many ways parents can help children with their speech. By far the best is to *talk*. Even if you don't get much by way of answers, it is encouraging the use of words by showing that you enjoy conversation with him. Avoid questions if they are obviously causing him problems. Even when a child is handicapped, talking helps. Many case histories tell of handicapped children's parents persevering in saying simple things to them, again and again, in spite of being told there was little hope of intellectual advance. They have often been rewarded by the realization that their children understood gradually more and more as time went on.

Singing and singing games are a great help for a child who will not enunciate clearly. Certain programmes for mothers and children on television are also very useful at giving clearly spoken examples of speech, in rhythms that make them fun to repeat.

Many children take to reading at four. There is a noticeable difference nowadays in attitudes of education authorities towards early reading, compared with the mid-1960s. Then, there were dire warnings against teaching children to read before they started primary school at five. There was even the implication in some of these warnings that children should be *distracted* from reading, if by some mischance they had been taught a word or two. The main argument against starting at home was that children would be confused, possibly bored, if they had to start a new method at primary school. There is much less of this now. Talking to primary school teachers in areas where there is a bigger middle-class intake of pupils, it is clear that they expect, now, to get quite a number of children who are at very different stages of learning to read. They assess their reading age, their interest and their problems, and plan to help them in groups accordingly. In prep schools or other private schools with a five-year-old 'junior' section, they tend to *expect* most of the children to have at least started reading.

Why has there been this change? Partly, it must be the parents' simple instinct to help their children to read—sometimes in response to the child, sometimes because they are ambitious for him. Partly, it may be put down to teachers gradually accepting that there is no guaranteed optimal method for every child. (The ITA, Initial Teaching Alphabet, is still used, but children are not automatically processed through it.) It is a dispiriting fact that the number of children who *cannot* read by the time they finish primary school has steadfastly refused to decline. With increasing class sizes and the shortage of teachers, it is not surprising that many welcome the advent of some children who have mastered the first steps. Another big influence has been Glenn Doman, and his advocacy of teaching in the home by 'Look and Say' methods.

The principles have spread further than the number who have ever heard of Doman.

Some children are also taught to read at their nursery school, if they are lucky enough to get a nursery school place. Most teachers at these schools seem to be very conscious of the fact that some of the children in their care are simply not ready for reading. Children mature at very different rates from this point of view. The skill of the teacher lies in sounding them out, sensitively, to see whether they are ready for this stage or not. They will notice that some are practically 'self-starters' and have started to enjoy some reading at home. Others soon find there are interesting games to play with words and parts of words, and take pleasure in recognizing them and being told they are right. But there are undeniably some who find it hard to understand the principles whereby differences in sounds correspond to differences in the shades of lines on paper. With these children, we may suppose that their central nervous system or part of their basic function is taking longer to mature (although they may be ahead in other respects); that their visual perception is not yet as acute or well-developed as in others; and that sometimes they are less motivated to learn to read. The latter may be natural to them, as individuals, or it may be the result of too much pressure to read from their parents.

This means that two kinds of under-motivation can exist. The first is typical of a child whose family read little and see little purpose or enjoyment in it. The second applies in cases where the child is all too aware of the concern that his parents feel about reading, and feeling the tension mount each time they renew the struggle to get him going properly, chooses escape rather than risking his self-esteem.

In many cases, a mother has tried to help her child to read, and got nowhere. Then he goes to school, takes to the teacher, and starts learning very quickly. It happens too often to be just a matter of timing. What does it mean? It is nothing to do with preferring the teacher. It can have a lot to do with the fact that different children seem to respond to different ways of teaching reading. But, more than that, teachers are trained to explain carefully and to judge the pace at which to progress. It is a professional job. Also, the atmosphere between a particular mother and her particular child may simply not be the best one for a formal learning process. The vibrations between them may be much better suited to informal, casual exploration of things—or simply to having fun together. Many adults recollect that, as children, they could not learn the piano from a parent—or maths, or typing. And yet they loved their parents very much. This is probably a reflection of the same difficulty that a perfectly intelligent child can experience when taught reading.

It is well worth while, if you would like to try to help a young child to read, to get hold of Glenn Doman's book *Teach Your Baby to Read*. This outlines a simple and successful method, and more importantly it stresses the need to go slowly, with plenty of encouragement. Praising means far more to a child who loves you, and loves your attention, than correction: it follows that successful teaching avoids the need for correction as much as possible. But above all, you *must* accept the fact that if it does not work, it is no discredit at all either to your child or to you. Give in gracefully and leave it to his teacher.

Four-year-olds may vary a lot in skill at drawing. It needs a very high degree of co-ordination indeed to pick up a pencil and transmit through it on to paper a picture you hold in your head. Some people find difficulty with drawing right through their lives, and nobody thinks the worse of them for it. But it is a skill that can give an enormous amount of pleasure, if it is there.

Most children start with a pencil or a crayon that is the wrong shape for their hands. The right implement for an adult is not necessarily right for a child to grapple with confidently. His first efforts might as well be with chalks or small stubby crayons with fat ends. Finger paints are always fun to use. Few representational results will come off, except by mistake, but the squiggles that he produces will please him. Because drawing something is one of the first self-expressive gifts that a child makes, he will be doubly pleased if he is congratulated. Watching him at work is instructive, too. For a while, what he actually puts on the paper or the bfackboard is very much a part of him, psychologically. Where does he go? Confidently, right into the middle? And then, does he cover the page as if to say, 'I've got so much to tell you about myself, I can't possibly give it all'? Or is he a bit timid, cautiously limiting himself to a section down in the bottom left corner? Children reflect a great deal of how they are feeling, at four, in how they *use* the surface they are drawing on. Later, their choice and treatment of subjects will be even more revealing, both of their character and of what is going on in their minds at the time.

At three, some children manage to copy or **draw a circle that** just about qualifies as being round. There is often a tail where the join is made. Now, at four, they can go on to do crosses, getting the second line well and truly over the first one. With encouragement, they can make a reasonable shot at a tree, at their mother, at a cat and at the house where they live. Children who are really taken with drawing show an early liking for odd shapes, such as a star, a worm, or an elephant's head: they can be seen trying again and again to perfect one, entirely lost in what they are doing. Such children also begin early to announce what they are going to draw, before they actually accomplish it.

Round edges are easier to do than sharp ones. The first houses are usually bulgey, with sloping corners. Then, as well as circles, a child develops the extra control needed to produce triangular and rectangular shapes too. This is usually at about five.

While they are learning more and more colours, children enjoy colouring as well as drawing. Colouring books give them a chance to feel they are making pictures as beautiful as ones they see in magazines or in their older brother's work. It takes time for them to have the concentrated effort needed to complete an entire picture with crayons, and they will get more satisfaction from *simpler* colouring books at first. It may seem less 'educational' for a child to be using these books, but what a child enjoys doing often proves to be of more value to him than trying something about which he is none too confident. Simpler efforts with brushes and chalks give him the confidence to be more ambitious later. At five he usually becomes much neater at colouring, keeping the colours separate and within their borders.

Some children at five and six are much happier drawing objects that they know well, and which they can represent more and more clearly. Others are more experimental and will try to draw the wind or machines that they feel should exist, even if they do not as yet. Those who are more original may in fact be more creative, over time, than those who are drawing neat little houses with flowers in front and chimneys on top, despite the fact that they have less to show off at this stage that excites admiration. This has little to do with intelligence—it is a reflection of differences in the extent to which children want to be different and surprise others.

Skill at drawing often seems to go hand-in-hand with acquiring early skill at making letters. Obviously, pleasure and assurance gained at one will make a child happier about applying himself to the other. Parents sometimes worry because the first letters a child writes are often the wrong way round, like Z for S. This is very common, and it may take a few years to grow out of it completely. The first letters to be learnt are usually those which look the same whichever way round they are—O, X, I, V and T. These are all easy to form. An H, M and W are rather more difficult, and require more skill. A few children confuse Ms and Ws, in the same way as bs and ds. It all comes out in the end. Exceptional problems with seeing the letters the right way round for writing them seems to go together with reading difficulties, as if these children tend to see words or parts of words backwards instead of forwards.

Those who, at six, look as if they are lagging behind at reading and writing may need particular help. There are special aids, nowadays, for children with a visual recognition problem. These are mostly based on getting him to use his other senses, in combination with vision, when learning about letters and words; textured letters allow a child to feel the shape of a letter while saying it out loud and looking at it. Sometimes distinctive colours are given to certain letters. Some children find early reading easier if all the words are in bright red, anyway, rather than black.

It is important to discuss the possible reasons for a child's difficulty with his teacher. This reduces the chances of the teacher being impatient—which in itself can be a cause of slowness—and it can certainly reduce a parent's anxiety, to be told more, from an objective source, about his child's progress. It is worth noting that many more parents worry unnecessarily about their child being slow to read and write, than those who in fact have a child with a serious perceptual or emotional problem to overcome.

Chapter five

Physical development through ages four, five and six

The last of that early chubbiness will gradually disappear from most children during their fifth year—but not from all. Some children are, by nature, more bulky than others. This can be because their metabolism does not break down the foods they eat as efficiently as that of their skinny friends, and part of this may be a hereditary characteristic. But there is also a possibility that a child is being fed too much of the wrong foods and is overweight. This is a problem that has grown considerably in the United Kingdom since the Second World War. There has been plenty of food available, except among very poor families, and malnutrition is exceptional. But some parents, often for psychological reasons, overfeed their children, with the result that they can be on the road towards having a serious problem in later years. Without going as far as dieting, corrective action now is both possible and desirable.

Table 1 Average weight of children across the ages of three to ten

Age	Average weight lbs	'Overweight' lbs
3	30	37
4	36	45
5	41	51
6	47	59
7	53	66
8	59	74
9	65	81
10	71	89

Note
Each of the average figures is calculated in terms of what is expected of most children in the *middle* of the year—i.e. at 3, etc.

Table 1 shows the average weight of children across the ages of three to ten. There is a wave band which allows for some variation either side. It is natural that weight should be greater among children with greater height and who are endowed with a heavy build.

But there is a limit beyond which a child has to be called over-weight. The second column indicates thresholds for this. Some doctors may draw attention to it, but the mother may have to take this up herself, finding out first of all if there are any physical reasons why her child should be developing in this way. The doctor is there to help, and he may recommend tests at a hospital, where there are specialists to determine what is wrong. This is important, because diet adaptation may be needed. It may prove, however, to be a situation in which the child is simply eating too much, especially carbohydrates. What is likely is that the doctor or the paediatrician will recommend a gradual decrease in con-fectionery, bread, cakes, pastries, crisps, potatoes, sweetened drinks and anything with a rich fat content. He will warn, very likely, against giving too much milk. As alternatives, he will suggest apples and most other fruit, salads, and less sugar with everything. The success of this will depend on three things:

(a) Tackling the problem gradually, and not trying to change a child's eating habits all at once.
(b) Making the alternatives seem a treat, rather than an imposition; e.g. giving a carrot as a reward, not as a poor second-best for a chocolate bar.
(c) How far eating has been taught as a compensation.

This last point may seem obscure. It refers to the degree to which a habit has been encouraged in the child to ask for or to expect something nice to eat as a substitute for attention from his parents. Where this has been continuous, changing expectations takes a long time; the child must not be made to feel he is being punished for being huge, and sudden withdrawal of compensation food without more love and playing time with his mother may point in that direction.

In this context, sweets are a threat to health. They will be criticized later in the chapter, too, on the subject of teeth. But they cannot be cut out altogether. The United Kingdom has the highest *per capita* consumption of sweets and chocolate in the world. When children go to nursery school and primary school, they talk about them, enjoy them and share them around. It is well nigh impossible for a child to be the odd one out. But alternatives to sweets can be successfully promoted by parents to decrease sweet-eating frequency. Some children find that a carrot is a very agreeable snack between meals—if they are offered it as something special and if they see their parents munching happily on a carrot too. But in a family where the parents are dipping into bags of humbugs every so often, children will note their example and follow it.

Sugar has been suspect for a long time as detrimental to teeth, but it has only more recently been discovered to be a long-term enemy of the blood circulation system as well. Keeping a child to small helpings of sugar and encouraging savoury rather than sweet tastes is good for him on three counts. First, it reduces unnecessary calorie intake; second, it is a start towards making him less prone to arteriosclerosis in later life; third, it will undoubtedly help his teeth.

The age of four is the time to take careful stock of a child's teeth and lay the foundations for a healthy mouth. The United Kingdom has an unenviable record in this: 27 per cent of those over the age of sixteen no longer have their own teeth. Think of it. It is a huge proportion of the adult population, even allowing for the elderly. It is worth care and practice to help your child to avoid joining their ranks prematurely.

From two until five, most children have their full complement of deciduous, or milk, teeth. The second teeth have yet to come through. But at five, and often at four, a dentist can tell how these second teeth are coming along and whether any corrective treatment needs to be planned for the future.

One of the reasons why British teeth are so bad is that dentistry is usually concerned with treating problems as they arrive, instead of preventing their occurrence. For preventive dentistry to become widespread, the whole basis of remuneration needs to be changed, since it *pays* dentists to do fillings rather than stop them becoming necessary. In China, doctors used to be paid so long as their patients were *well*: that is the principle to which we should possibly try to return ourselves. But there are steps that can be taken, and it helps if parents *ask* for them:

(a) *Fluoride* protects the enamel of the teeth. Most families now live in areas where the water contains fluoride. Where the water does *not* contain fluoride, regular fluoride tablets are worth while.

(b) *Fluoride treatment* can be provided by a dentist. This involves preparing a small saucer-like tray with a jelly-like substance containing fluoride. This is put into the child's mouth and the fluoride automatically transfers to the surface of the teeth. This is an excellent protection for young teeth and should be repeated every three to six months.

(c) *Regular tooth cleaning* must be supervised by a parent and handled by a parent. A child should be encouraged to brush his own teeth and be praised for it, but he is not ready to have the job left to him for a year or two yet. A soft to medium brush is best, because it is unlikely to scrape the surface of the teeth. A fluoride toothpaste is the best to use.

But this is not enough. It is well worth investing in a 'floss', which can clean out the spaces between the teeth by means of a white nylon string. A 'floss aid' makes it easier to manœuvre in the mouth. Both are obtainable at chemists. It is worth observing, now and then, just how efficient your tooth cleaning operation is. You can now get 'disclosing tablets' which contain a harmless vegetable dye. After taking the tablet, those parts of the teeth which are still not clean show up a vivid red: a very revealing and instructive exercise.

Even more important is for children to be used to the sight of their parents cleaning their teeth regularly—if they still have them. This means the difference between feeling that tooth care is important to grown-ups, too, and that it is a nuisance phase they want to grow out of.

(d) Visits to the dentist must be regular: on a six-monthly basis if there seems nothing wrong, more frequently if there has been trouble. Family visits are best, with mother (or father) going first and with the children watching, provided there is nothing more to be done than a filling or two. This gives confidence in the dentist, and makes for belief that he is on the family's side and that his advice is worth taking. To be avoided at all costs are suggestions that the dentist causes pain or that visits to him are to be feared.

(e) Teeth should be cleaned after meals. Why particularly? Because (especially if there is some form of sugar entering the mouth) there is a build-up of acid after the meal reaching its peak inside the mouth in about half an hour. Bacteria work best in acid conditions; therefore the most dangerous time for the tooth enamel and the gums is half an hour after the meal.

(f) The foods that a child eats have a direct bearing on how his teeth develop. Sugar has already been mentioned as pernicious. Any food which preserves sugar in the mouth for a length of time and any which leaves a patina of sugar behind, or particles in crevices, is going to be harmful. It follows that some sweets are worse than others—toffees in particular. Drinks containing sugar are less dangerous if taken through a straw, because less of a coating is left on the teeth. A sweet drink late in the evening is a threat which is often overlooked. Naturally, it is not so bad if teeth are cleaned thoroughly afterwards.

If all this seems to be going excessively far in the direction of a puritan revival, it is worth recalling the last time you, yourself, had an unpleasant experience in the dentist's chair and reflecting that your child could be spared all that. The ages of four and five are very important indeed for tooth protection. If a child's milk teeth and his gums are infected (it could be either or both), then this can automatically infect the second teeth as they come through. Chronic gum infection will mean that the second teeth never establish themselves firmly—a condition which would help them to be more resistant to decay.

The dentist can also tell what kind of orthodontic treatment may be necessary. This might take the form of removing certain teeth in order to improve the shape of the mouth and to stop teeth crowding each other out of position as they grow. Strategic extraction of this kind is not usually done until the child is about eight. But advance planning is always worth while, so that the development of the teeth can be watched. This has nothing to do with 'cosmetic dentistry', or just making the child's smile more entrancing. It is basically a question of protecting the mouth and limiting the chances of pain.

Table 2 shows the order in which the second teeth come through.

A five-year-old will probably have a 'wobbly' milk tooth or two. Most children brag to each other about the tooth they have lost, and this becomes a matter of pride. They are adept at infuriating adults by wobbling their teeth, which is sometimes compulsive. Since the only harm they do is to their mother's nerves, there is no real reason for stopping them: they cannot do any damage to themselves. Only when a tooth is *very* loose should a parent give it a tug or use the time-honoured method of tying it with thread attached to a door handle. It hurts—unless it really is very loose. Parents worry that if they do not do this, the tooth may come out while chewing and so get swallowed. They should remember that this is rare, and doctors are reluctant to recommend surgery when it happens unless it is obvious that it is stuck or is causing pain.

Table 2 Development of teeth

Age	Development
2	The average child acquires his last four molars to give him his full complement of twenty *milk teeth*.
4, sometimes 5	His first milk teeth come out. These are usually one or both of the lower central incisors, but may be one of the molars nearest the incisors. *Permanent teeth* replace these quickly.
$6\frac{1}{2}$	He has six permanent teeth: two lower central incisors and two lower and two upper molars.
$8\frac{1}{2}$	He has all eight incisors.
$9\frac{1}{2}$	He has both lower canines.
11, sometimes 12	He has all eight bicusps (two-pronged teeth) and both upper canines.
12, sometimes 13	He has four 'second molars' (leaving four 'third molars', or wisdom teeth, to come through between the ages of seventeen and twenty-one); i.e. thirty-two permanent teeth in all.

At five, or six, it is possible that a playground accident may result in a second tooth getting knocked out. *The big mistake is to throw this tooth away.* It may be very useful to a dentist or an oral surgeon at a hospital for rigging up a natural replacement which will cause minimal change to the shape of the child's mouth.

Teeth are more obvious than some of the other important changes happening in the body. Possibly the biggest differences between growth over the period of four, five and six and that of the preceding three years is the way in which the legs grow much longer, relative to the rest of the body. The legs are also developing very considerable skills. Parents spend so much time noticing (and often worrying about) the speed of their children's movements, that they may not remark on the increase of skill that goes with those movements.

Longer legs go with better balance: the brain becomes better at interpreting information from the inner ear about how the body is positioned in space and information from the feel of the foot and leg muscles and of the ground beneath the feet. The brain is also improving at organizing appropriate action, according to this information.

At four, then, this combination of better comprehension of how to position oneself in space, and sheer physical growth, enables a child to negotiate stairs in an adult way—one step at a time, upstairs or down. Obviously this does not happen perfectly overnight. A temporary illness may very well set him back on his hands and knees for a while. But paediatricians often keep a sharp lookout for the way in which a child, who is suspected of being backward, deals with a small flight of stairs. Although this seems a physical problem, some complex mental events are involved. When a child takes a very long time to master stairs, the possibility of brain damage, although it may be slight, cannot be ruled out. Of course, a spastic child has a handicap that specifically involves these mechanisms, but he is likely to have been diagnosed a long time before this, at the clinic. It is worth remembering that quite a few spastic children prove to have very considerable intelligence, despite their co-ordination problems: therefore a parent who observes that his child is very slow in this area must not assume that there is no skill which he will enjoy developing.

Other signs of physical-cum-mental skill at this age are learning to stand and to walk on tiptoe. Depending on whether there are suitable trees within range, many a four-year-old will try his hand at climbing them. Like cats, they sometimes go up a good deal further than they feel is wise when they start looking down and thinking about the descent. Just when they seem to have become really independent, they cry to be helped down.

The more adventurous children need careful watching at this time. They have the turn of speed to get down the garden path quickly and the dexterity to open simple garden gates, in order to be out on to the street before their parents can catch them. At the same time, they do not understand the danger that is on the street until it is right on top of them. It is a time to reassess regularly what they can reach, what they can open and what they can get into. Shallow garden ponds are notoriously dangerous at this age: even if he can stand upright in one, with his head and shoulders well above the water, a child may panic if he falls in the water and be unable to get up.

Less dangerous forms of panic are liable to overtake physical feats at any time. I personally remember going indoors from the garden to answer the telephone while looking after two children aged six and four. I put the receiver down on hearing a scream for help. In the intervening three minutes they had climbed on top of a dustbin, grasped hold of the top of the fence and swung themselves along for about five yards' distance. No doubt they had pushed at the fence with their toes, but the strain was almost entirely on their fingers. Their feet were three feet or so off the ground, and as soon as they despaired of reaching the dustbin again, they simply screamed. Two minutes later they were running around again, without a care. They had worried *me*, but their own physical courage was resumed immediately.

At four, a child also learns to handle a tricycle. His direction, his control of speed, his ability to turn at speed and his acceleration all improve markedly by the time he is six, when he should be a tricycle expert. Children vary a great deal, on the other hand, in their confidence where bicycles are concerned. Some five-year-olds pick it up very quickly, but this is certainly advanced. Others will not take to the idea of committing themselves to two wheels for a long time. This difference in attitude is often difficult to account for. Occasionally, a slow cyclist is a child who is less nimble and less well co-ordinated. But there are many more cases of children who are at least the equal of others in these respects, whose reluctance to learn goes with a conviction that balancing on two wheels must be difficult, and possibly with greater imagination of the dangers involved in falling off. Motivation enters into this as well: children in the same family usually *all* learn to cycle quickly or they are all late, suggesting that copying a brother and not letting him get all the glory of fast travelling is a significant spur.

An early mistake on a bicycle can prove a shock to a child and put him off for a long time. (He may come back, time and again, to the machine—but in a suspicious, almost defeatist, frame of mind, which is not conducive to learning.) 'Fairy' bicycles with two detachable small wheels on either side of the back wheel, and a lot of experience of just being propelled by father gripping the back of the saddle, are therefore good as general confidence builders. Most important is the *size* of the bicycle on which he is trying to learn. If a child is in difficulty manœuvring his feet down over the pedals to create motion, it is unrealistic to expect him to be able to pay attention to balance and direction as well. It is most unwise to let go of the saddle before you believe there is a real chance that your child can balance, and it can be dangerous to let go without telling him, because this undermines confidence in you as an instructor. A very good tip for nervous children is to tell them to watch the front wheel, *not* 'Look where you're going'. If they do watch the front wheel, balance is easier and direction comes naturally.

3

Girls are, if anything, more intrepid than boys at physical feats and new experiences like cycling. As with all generalizations, there are countless exceptions. But the principle is borne out very clearly in horse riding, for example. At four, children can, with caution, be helped in the saddle and given their first instruction on a good-natured pony. Whereas few girls cry out for help, many boys become nervous. Most riding teachers will vouch for this. This difference seems to increase with age, up to about twelve. An early start with riding, therefore, probably helps boys even more than girls.

While riding, skating, ski-ing and gymnastics can all be dangerous, they do not have to be so. And there is no question that starting during this age bracket gives a tremendous advantage, both for enjoying these sports and for learning to do them well. The only provisos are a good teacher who will not hector the child and avoidance of anything really frightening. At this age, a child's muscles can develop in many different ways, relative to each other. This means they can adapt to sports demanding subtle physical development more easily. There are also sports where mastering basic movements is needed before anything like technical brilliance is gained. If they start older, children are that bit more impatient to be brilliant immediately, which is self-defeating.

Swimming and diving come into this category, too. Some Olympic swimming trainers suggest that learning to swim by the age of six is absolutely crucial if a child is to reach the top class. For this, correct technique is important, too. But while ski-ing, and so forth, cannot be said to be vital to man's existence, there is a very strong case for *all* children learning to swim, as early as possible, irrespective of whether they go on to win competitions. It can be, literally, a matter of life or death.

There are big differences between children, however, in their readiness to take to water and their aptitude at coping with the element. Most children who fight against swimming have been frightened in some way or other; they reach a point beyond which they do not develop, because they dare not. This is commonest with children who have been taught by people who are impatient. Enjoying the water is a prerequisite to learning to swim. Enjoyment stops as soon as a child feels he is being criticized for not overcoming a sense of alarm that sweeps through him as soon as his feet are off the bottom, or a steadying hand is released. It is worth comparing different people's earliest memories of being taught to swim:

'I started in a class of about fifteen at the swimming baths
on Saturday mornings. I was six at the time. The first time
was fun, because we just held on to the side and kicked
backwards in the water. Then, in the second lesson, we had
to stand—in the shallow end—about two yards from the edge.
One by one, we were supposed to hurl ourselves, kicking
hard, towards the side. I watched the others, and got more
and more worried as my turn came nearer. "Come on,
Curly!" the teacher shouted at me when I hesitated. I threw
myself forward, and kicked, and struggled, but my head went
under before I could get there. I remember my hair being
pulled upwards, and the teacher demanding, "Well! What
happened to *you*?" Everybody laughed. I learned absolutely
nothing at those classes and I begged my father not to take
me there any more. Years later, at twelve, I was at a school
where all non-swimmers had to join a class. So there was no
escape. Along with a few others I was given up as hopeless.
We were allowed to fool about by ourselves. One day, right
at the end of term, I suddenly found I could float on my back,
if I took it calmly. Then, gradually, I moved my arms a bit,
and went in a circle; soon I could actually swim. But I didn't
tell anybody in case I suddenly found I couldn't.'

This is a clear example of a child being put off by both fright and
humiliation. Here is a contrasting account:

'I must have been just six when I started learning in a small
group in the local swimming pool. We splashed about in the
kiddies' pool, which was separate from the big one. The
teacher used to take each of us in turn over to one side, to
help us get going. We all had inflatable armbands, and a ring
round our middles. I remember her proving to us that we
were quite safe with this equipment, just by pretending to
push down on us in the water, and crying, "Oh, there! I
can't push this child down into the water!" We all laughed.
She was very easy-going and full of fun. She got us floating
on our fronts and our backs, and pretended to be so
impressed whenever we did something well that she had to
duck her head under the water and then leap out again
with a splutter. This always had us laughing, and we used to
copy her. That way none of us ever got really frightened if
we went under. Very gradually, lesson by lesson, she released

the air from our armbands, and she had a game that meant pretending to lose the ring round her body, so that she had to hold on to it in front of her, and kick to follow it. She soon had us copying that, too. When *exactly* I was swimming unaided I really can't say—there wasn't any clear dividing line. . . . It was only some time afterwards, when I was older and looked over to where she was teaching a new gang of young kids, that I realized she looked funny, on all fours in the paddling pool with a ring round her middle. Later still, I realized how clever she was to do this—to make us feel that she was really one of us.'

Here it is worth noting how any danger of fright was avoided at all costs; how something potentially frightening like ducking was made into a game; how the children were constantly motivated and rewarded for making progress; and how the teacher made her own achievements seem capable of being imitated *by getting down to the children's level* and becoming accepted as a friend. Obviously, this is easier in small groups. She was probably able, although this does not appear in the account, to give individual help, and adjust the armbands of each individual according to that child's progress and confidence.

Rhythm in movement is usually very pleasing to a child during this period. Whereas before he was four it was very difficult to move his whole body rhythmically, the four- or five-year-old generally gets great delight out of matching the beat of some music with his arms, legs, head and trunk, all in unison. Singing games were intriguing before. Now they are something to be mastered. Dancing and musical appreciation can take firm root, now, if children are given plenty of chances to enjoy it and if they see their parents enjoy it too. Moving the body to music is not exactly an instinct—because some children never get beyond foot-tapping—but surrender of the body to a rhythm must be very basic to our nature, given that very few races can be found which do not practise it in some form. This being so, it seems a shame that it is encouraged more in girls than in boys. Children will accept most music at these ages, although they show a clear preference for something that has melody and a beat that they can reproduce.

Some children will now be able to start a musical instrument. Others will be quite unprepared for it. Apart from some hereditary

disposition towards playing music, the main factors that are likely
to influence musicality are early experience of hearing it round the
house and being *drawn* into enjoying it, rather than being *urged* to
attend to it. Requiring a child to concentrate on it in an abstract
way is self-defeating. Singing with him, however, and dancing
with him, or playing with him and asking him which piece he likes
best, so that you can repeat it, encourages enjoyment. But another
factor is manual dexterity, in terms of getting the fingers or the
mouth and fingers to obey the sequence of instructions quickly
and accurately. This is a specialized kind of co-ordination. It
can be improved by appropriate training and practice, but there
has got to be a facility there in the first instance. If training is *not*
appropriate, habits of playing can be acquired now that will be
very hard to shed later on. If you believe your child to be musical,
therefore, and if he seems to enjoy a trial lesson or two, it always
pays to try to find him the best teacher that you can.

Lots of little skills reflect improved co-ordination by the time
a child is six, even if he shows no interest in the piano or recorder.
Girls can be taught the rudiments of sewing or knitting, while
boys are encouraged to take pieces of machinery apart and (occasionally) to piece it all together again. There is no reason whatever
why each sex should not do as the opposite one does, but both
parents and society tend to approve of what they feel is appropriate to each sex. Their developing skill is therefore channelled,
and takes expression in one kind of activity rather than another.

But both sexes play ball, and it is very interesting to compare
the sexes at, say, the age of five when you see a group playing with
a ball. Unlike their older sisters, the five-year-old girls show no
more awkwardness about throwing overarm than their brothers.
They are good catchers, too. Extremely complex physical and
mental problems are posed by a ball flying through the air: the
young child must judge the angle of approach, the speed, the
spread of his hands needed to stop and trap the ball, and the right
position for his own body. At five, most children develop a good
talent for catching. A child who is having undue trouble with
catching at this age should be given a sight test, in case a slight
visual defect is threatening his progress and needs timely help.
This kind of perceptual difficulty often shows itself in exaggerated
fear of what the ball will do to him. But most boys and girls are
equally likely to do well at this, and they tend to be equally
courageous.

Sex differences come out in *how* they play ball and the way in which they enjoy the game. Boys tend to be more aggressive, especially in throwing. They become fascinated, very often, by the concept of hurling the unstoppable ball—at a brother, a playmate or, significantly, at father. Many a girl and many a parent has protested that 'Bob is spoiling the game'. But this is because it is *his* idea of the game, and for a while it is not comparable with theirs. Boys are often more genuinely competitive with a ball, too. They play 'pig-in-the-middle' ruthlessly. Girls will play this too, but accept the idea more readily that the 'pig' should be relieved from his post, if he gets stuck in the middle for too long. Girls often prefer *ritual* ball games to *competitive* ones: 'broken bottles' is a good example. (Here each player has to pay a forfeit for missing a catch, being reduced to one hand first, then going on one knee, etc.) Watching them at it, one soon observes that most girls are enjoying the procedure, rather than the idea of beating somebody else.

Competitiveness and aggression are *not* exclusive to boys—as will be discussed in Chapter six. But they add a kind of flavour to the way that boys use their skills, which are essentially equal to those of girls.

Girls seem as fast as boys now, too. They can run as far as boys, if they want to. Sometimes they make it obvious that they can fight as well as boys, but conflict between the sexes is discouraged so that this may only become apparent by accident. Gradually, boys do more fighting and so their experience at this often makes them physically harder.

The child who is turning six is very close to half the height that he will have as an adult. His brain, which has been growing throughout childhood, is now about nine-tenths of its eventual adult size. From now on its functions will be developing more visibly than its physical capacity. But it is worth bearing in mind that the child's mental equipment is still not fully formed, and the maturation of the central nervous system still has some way to go as well.

Chapter six

Emotional and personality development at four, five and six

Across this age span, most children make an enormous amount of progress in coming to terms with their own feelings, and in finding new ways of expressing them. The four-year-old is easily moved to tears, or a tantrum, if he does not get his way. The six-year-old *may* cry, and he may have a tantrum, when faced with a similar block, but his repertoire for dealing with the situation is much wider. He may start an argument, pressing his case for being allowed what he wants; or he may try cajolery; or he may look pathetic and play on sympathy; or he may try his luck on another member of the family, to see if he can improve his chances; or he may pretend that he wants to do something else, anyway; or he may deny that he ever wanted it in the first place; or he may pick a fight, to distract himself and others from his failure; or he may even, in some cases, discuss rationally and objectively why he is not being allowed what he wants in this instance. It is often remarkable, in this event, how philosophical a young child can become: he may want to know, 'When can I do it, then? When I'm ten?' and comment, 'Oh, well, you can't have everything, I suppose'. This last example is unusual, and a rather precocious remark for the age. *The same* child who says it may still throw the occasional tantrum, when tired, ill or under pressure. The point is that a wide range of different attitudes and behaviour has been developed. Some of these tend to recur, in ways which indicate a pattern that is individual to the child. This pattern we call personality.

Much of a child's personality has been developing before his fourth birthday. But he is still very open to influences that will shape it significantly. The fifth year is the last in which the mother–child relationship is what one might call 'crucial'. At the age of five (this is, of course, a convenient average and not the same for all children) the relationship shifts to being 'important', rather than 'crucial', for a strong, positive, helpful and confident personality. But his mother (or his mother-substitute) remains his natural reference point. When things seem to go wrong, or he cannot decide how to contend with the demands being made of him by others, or when he finds his own emotions confused and difficult to control, at these times his instinct is to go back to his mother, to approach her as if he were a year or two younger, and cling and cuddle until the tide passes by.

It is usually a mistake to tell five-year-olds that they are now 'too old for that sort of thing'. So they are, in a sense, but it does no good to tell them so. It merely adds to their own sense of inadequacy at the time. A child who knows he can always go back to his mother in time of real need becomes, paradoxically, more self-reliant. The child who rushes back to be hugged every so often—when it is not out of sheer affection, of course—is often one who is worried that he is being persuaded to keep his distance when he feels troubled. Brothers or sisters who are close in age almost inevitably feel a desire to re-establish close contact when either sees the other doing precisely that. He may hang off for a while, particularly if he feels he might be told off for hurting his brother, but the fear of being supplanted in terms of attention or embraces proves stronger in the end.

Providing physical reassurance is important—at four, at five and at six. So is being consistent in offering interest and help, in talking and playing with your child, and, perhaps most of all, in simply being there—if not all the time, most of the time, and if not most of the time, regularly and often.

This is a very different matter from either giving in to your child whenever he asks for something or wants attention, or cushioning him completely against having to sort out his problems by himself. 'You must fight your own battles' is said, quite reasonably, by parents to their children in each generation. It is neither practical nor useful to be drawn into every playground argument about whose turn it is in the swing or who was responsible for a toy getting broken. A parent is there to be turned to for advice and comfort, but not to come forward as a referee every time the odds appear to favour the other side. Children can only learn about life through making social contacts themselves and developing a repertoire for different kinds of encounter. Occasionally one sees a mother rushing backwards and forwards into the fray, as if trying to orchestrate all these encounters. She is delaying social maturity.

When it looks as if a serious battle is imminent, then intervention may be necessary. It is also sometimes necessary to tell a young child, 'Well, I wouldn't play with those two for a while, if I were you.' In the short term, this advice can get a child out of danger. In the long term, curiously enough, it makes him more interested in trying his luck with the tougher kids, when he feels better equipped.

It is always worth bearing in mind that *yours* may be the tougher kid and that, somewhere, some mother is advising her daughter not to play with *him*. Most mothers are very surprised indeed when they are confronted with this sort of situation. This shows how selective one's perception of one's own children's behaviour usually is. If you notice that your child seems to get into scrapes rather often or is shunned by some of the others, it can be worth trying to observe him objectively, from another mother's point of view. Should you need to advise him not to snatch other children's toys, not to hog the rocking horse or not to push other children off the climbing frame, he will listen to you and you will help him to be more popular.

How he behaves in the playground often reflects the behaviour he is used to meeting in his own home. During this period, children copy their parents far, far more than they copy each other. Later, the balance shifts. Right now, their speech, their ways of regarding or offering help to each other, their comments, commands and jokes, or their reserve, are usually reproductions of the kind of encounters they are used to having at home. Sometimes they misinterpret what they hear or experience at home, with the result that they may seem far stricter or more aggressive to other children than their parents ever feel to them. But the tendency is still to recreate the standard and example they have been given by their parents.

Misinterpretation of the kind mentioned above is all too easy. Sometimes a child misinterprets a fact or a reason for something bad happening and feels guilty for no real cause, or imparts a feeling to his parents that they never had. Alternatively, the misinterpretation may be one of degree: taken aback by his father's outburst of anger when his tea cup is overturned by a tennis ball, a five-year-old may feel that he is not just angry for a moment, but hopelessly enraged for all the foreseeable future. In families where

3*

emotion is not openly expressed, exposure to sudden high feeling can be much more alarming than in a home where irritation or glee is brought to the surface immediately, as a matter of course, and then passes. A mild-mannered introverted parent who uncharacteristically registers rage is likely to be embarrassed about going to his child afterwards and re-establishing harmony. But it is very wise to do so, for the child's emotions—whatever the parental loss of face.

It is useful to remember that a young child's *fears* are worse for him if they are under the surface. Long-term, nagging fears sap his confidence and make him less capable of dealing with ordinary, everyday demands on his emotional control. Such fears usually concern a serious doubt of some kind about being together with his parents, being loved by them or being inadequate in their eyes, either in his own right or by comparison with a brother or sister. Sometimes, though, these fears can have their origin in a real or imagined threat to the safety of the family from outside, or a feeling that retribution may be in store for something bad that he has done. Not being able to talk about it makes it hard to live with a fear of this kind. A breakdown in communication between the child and his parents may be a compound of these features:

(a) Not having a sufficient range of phrases to start to express his feelings.

(b) Concern that his parents might confirm his fears or that the discussion might reveal a real gap between them.

(c) Anxiety not to appear stupid or bad.

(d) Anxiety not to be criticized by, or unfavourably compared with, a brother or sister.

(e) Experience of short temper or impatience at previous attempts to talk about the problem.

Occasionally it seems as if a child who is more intelligent in an imaginative way is more liable to a communication block and more subject to complex fears in the first instance. But *any* child can arrive at this situation.

One way of telling that a child of this age group may be hindered in his progress by nagging fears is to note that he has difficulty in concentrating for long on a game by himself or with another child, and that he cannot maintain his temper or his patience with other children for any length of time. His drawings probably reflect it, since it is often easier to release tension on paper than to voice it out loud. It will be reflected in work done at primary school, too. But here, as with interpretation of drawings, it is difficult for most parents to know what the evidence is indicating for *their* child.

More telling is the give-away tendency to 'hover'. 'Hovering' means approaching, asking a diffident question or two (often about nothing in particular), accepting and toying with the answer, retreating, and then repeating the whole process again. Sometimes, the same questions get repeated. This is a sure sign that something lies behind the hovering, which the child is unwilling or unable to broach. It also harks back to an earlier stage of childhood, at two or three, where repeating questions and phrases was part of a joyful explanation of the power of speech. The hovering child is *not* joyful. He wants more companionship and a more intimate conversation than he dare admit. Asking him bluntly 'What's wrong, then?' is likely to drive him back into his shell. If you give him the impression that your time and patience are limited, *that* is effectively part of his answer. He wants to have his worries teased to the surface and to feel that you genuinely want to help him, to hug him and to be with him.

Some other fears may be more evident and more dramatic in the form they take, but are much less serious. As an example, let us consider the behaviour of Gregory (aged six) and Samantha (five) on a Saturday afternoon. They are taken for a walk with another family and progress to a corner of a park devoted to slides, swings and a variety of other playground structures. The children rush on ahead. But half-way there, Gregory turns and faces the adults who are bringing up the rear. 'We won't miss *Dr Who*, will we?' he demands, with a worried look. He is told that there are at least two hours before the programme starts. Samantha has caught his mood and demands at regular intervals whether it is time for them to be getting home to see *Dr Who* on television. Meanwhile, both children enjoy themselves, going from one game to another. Gregory decides that a certain climbing frame, with a ladder at each of four corners and a spider-like object in the middle, is one of the dreaded monsters that make Dr Who's life so perilous. Samantha gets half-way up one of the ladders. 'Quick! It's seen you! Run away quick!' her brother shouts to her. She shrieks, jumps down and both scamper away.

Later, on the way home, they continue interrogating the others to make sure that they will not miss the start of the programme. As soon as they are home again, they rush to the television set and switch it on. It might be expected that they would sit still and watch—but no. They are too excited and frightened to watch consistently. During the quiet bits they are attentive, although Samantha is a bit restless, almost as if disappointed at the lack of action. Then, when a monster appears, both shout 'Oooh!' at the screen and while Gregory calls to his mother that the monster has come, his sister is already in the next room, burying her face in her mother's skirt. In fact, for a good third of the programme the two children are on their feet, as if checking their lines of retreat, and often they are not watching the screen at all. You might say that they are participating, rather than watching. It is a high spot of the week and missing it means tears, but they spend a lot of time running away from it.

This is the kind of fear which fascinates. Part of the fascination comes from knowing that other children of like age are alarmed by what happens to Dr Who as well. It is slightly hysterical, in fact. When parents intervene and say, 'Don't worry, darling, it's only a story you know', they are sometimes put out by the children's failure to register this. Some of the problem is that the children are only just learning to distinguish truth from reality, and they are not sure where television comes into this scheme. But they do not entirely *want* it to be just a story, either. Being alarmed is exciting, despite the fact that it can go too far.

When children watch a frightening film, or hear a frightening story and remain very still, saying very little about it, they need help, because they are not so much frightened as terrified. But Gregory and Samantha are different. They rush to their mother and talk about the programme, often magnifying their feelings. When the programme ends, they look around rather crossly for something to do, and then do it. They incorporate *Dr Who* adventures into their games. This is a sign that they are assuming or getting control over the emotions aroused by the series. They have no nightmares.

Even so—some parents, and probably some psychologists, would not allow a five- or six-year-old to watch *Dr Who* if it were so exciting for them. Does it do them harm? What about other programmes, films, comics and books where the entertainment is calculated in terms of fright? Every parent has to pick and choose. It may be helpful to reflect that parents have worried about this for quite a number of generations. They will continue to worry, because *they* have to pick and choose among programmes, according to what they feel is reasonable for *their* child. However, children will always continue to look for excitement rather than boredom, and will tell each other in playgrounds about the creepiness of the monsters in *Dr Who*. A most important consideration is that Gregory and Samantha turned instinctively to their mother for moral support whenever the going got rough for the intrepid doctor, and they could rely on her being there. Children vary greatly in what they are ready to confront, and having a solid base to which to retreat is a big factor in this. It is also worth noting that some children are more seriously alarmed by, for example, films like *Snow White*, which bring to life people and situations which were worrying enough when read from a picture-book in the nursery at bed-time. If *Dr Who and the Daleks* were forbidden, by what right would we preserve stories about wicked step-mothers, bad fairies who curse baby princesses at the christenings, witches in gingerbread houses with a penchant for baked children, or even bears creeping up on girls who are injudicious enough to sleep in their beds?

Material which is *too* frightening for children often has one or more of these characteristics:

(a) A realistic situation, in which the child can readily identify with the hero and the circumstances, and where the relationships between him and his family are threatened or disturbed.

(b) As (a) and where the hero is shown as giving way to strong emotions, over which he has no control.

(c) As (a) and where horrible but believable things are done to the hero, who seems to have no prospect of recovery or survival at the end.

Less lurid, but more real, are the many encounters that a young child has with others who do not seem to him to have his best interests at heart. His character has for a long time been geared to getting most of the things that he wanted, most of the time. This is not selfishness, but a natural determination which serves to protect the species. Gradually, at four, five and six, he meets people who regard him more as incidental and less as some-body to be loved, helped and fed. Other parents have their own children, he learns; they are polite and kind to him, but he is not their main concern. Other children have their own wishes and intentions, which do not often coincide with his. The main social skills that a child has to learn during this time are how to com-promise and negotiate, and how to overcome or compensate for the feelings of not always getting what he wants.

The more that children are held back from the company of others, especially from children of like age, the smaller are their chances of equipping themselves, through experience, with sufficient of these social skills to fend for themselves in a way that increases their acceptance outside the home. There are numerous ways in which children vary at this. A common assumption is that children in larger families must have an advantage over others in the playground, simply because they have had to get used to accommodating to the wishes and ways of others. There is very little research support for this, however. In fact, the follow-up study described in *From Birth To Seven* (which examined a large, representative sample of children at successive stages of their lives, from birth onwards) suggests that single children are not at any great disadvantage when their 'social maturity' is measured. A stable background and opportunities for meeting and playing with other children, especially when combined with nursery school help on learning to work and play co-operatively, are particularly important—much more than the shape of the family.

When they are encouraged to talk with their parents, children are disarmingly frank in their questions. Learning social tact is a slow business. This should be regarded as only to be expected of normal children at this stage; it is intellectually cramping and emotionally menacing to try to press children into guarding their tongues before they are ready to read situations accurately. More people appreciate the naturalness of a five-year-old's 'Mummy, why is that boy a brown colour?' than those who long to shut him up because of the embarrassment he may be causing. Children have a licence to ask this kind of question. They deserve more than 'Hush!' A smile, yes, and a simple answer like 'He was just born that way, and perhaps he's wondering why *you* are so much lighter'. In certain circumstances, such as when a child persists in commenting on personal features in a way that is unconsciously hurtful, it makes sense to distract him by switching the conversation. But it is worth noting that an obvious, abrupt switch often causes more offence than the child's comments themselves.

Sometimes embarrassment can be anticipated, in the home. This is the age when curiosity about his physical features and those of everyone around him will give rise to a lot of questions. Frank, patient answers are best, because evasion only increases curiosity, adding to it mystery and possibly guilt. But *having* answered frankly, it helps to explain to a child that this is a subject usually avoided outside the close family. For example, most children who are normal and alert will probe their mother's bosom, and ask 'What *are* these, Mummy?' and, perhaps, 'What are they *for?*' A girl who is beginning to identify her future role may add 'Will I get them, too?' Similarly, two young children will compare, in all probability, each other's genitals at bath-time. They will want the differences explained. All these questions can be answered directly, although at this age relatively few children ask for a comprehensive explanation of reproduction and it can be alarming (some psychologists feel it is 'overstimulating') to give more information than what is actually asked for. Having explained that these are called breasts and that all women have them, possibly adding their function if this is demanded, you could add 'We can talk about them here, but most people don't like talking about them out-of-doors' and, possibly, 'Ask me anything you like, or ask Daddy. But I would choose something else to talk about with Grandma.' Children *like* simple, social rules. They do not always follow them, but it makes life much easier for them if they have a few guidelines, instead of running into tensions which they do not understand.

Part of their social difficulties lie in the fact that a child under seven cannot discern subtle differences of expression on people's faces. Parents who believe they are giving their children a clear hint, by looking suddenly stern or 'meaningful', are deluding themselves. Children do not *expect* to have to read faces in this way and they are not much good at it either. Laughing and crying they notice. These involve *actions* and are easily interpretable. Frowns and smiles, curiously, mean much less to a four- or five-year-old than many suppose. They take their cues from actions and words—not looks. Sometimes, when somebody is bleeding or wearing a bandage, their look is accepted as a significant communication, but these are exceptional cases. It may seem, for example, after a bereavement, that a young child is being perverse about not noticing how sad everyone is; but typically they are not expressing their sorrow in a way that children readily grasp, although Latins are better at this than Anglo-Saxon families.

At about the age of six, one of the most useful accomplishments that children develop is to distinguish between looks, and to assign them to moods and meanings. But it should be remembered that this is a slow process.

Occupying a great deal of their attention are other children outside the family. From four onwards they play together much more than during their earlier years of wary encounters and mutual observation, where they tended to play in parallel. But the wariness has to remain, because so much of what other children do is, in their eyes, unpredictable. These others have different ways of behaving, different interests and often different words and different rules. A lot of getting accustomed to social behaviour can be considered in terms of unpredictability. This is partly done by noticing how John, or Jane, reacts and how best to treat them, but much depends on skill at generalizing from particular experience.

The degree to which children are successful at this is very much bound up with the degree to which they *want* to socialize. Psychologists who study personality have often remarked on the way in which one particular dimension (introversion–extraversion) seems to underlie many other character discriminants. This is not to say that any child's character can be described fully by knowing just how outgoing (extravert) he is socially or how much he retires from contact (introvert). But there are many traits which seem related to this dimension, either directly, such as 'friendly–unfriendly', or indirectly, such as 'confident–diffident'.

Some of the prompting to be an extravert with others comes from a natural curiosity towards a new stimulus. Those who feel more of this may well have a hereditary predisposition to being more outgoing. Others may be, from conception onwards, more self-sufficient. But this can be inhibited by fear of a contact being either threatening to oneself or liable to lead to a failure of some kind. The strongest basis for a child not having such fears, or for his dismissing them, is a confidence in his relations with his parents and a secure sense of his position within the family. Enjoying the company of brothers and sisters obviously has a part to play here; sometimes having a brother close in age is more a delight than a threat, sometimes the other way round, so that the influence on wanting to socialize further is not consistent.

Allied to introversion–extraversion, but a separate issue, is the degree of competitiveness that a child has. Children who are going to be *very* competitive have already shown clear signs of it—some mothers would say from birth. Others show their hand more clearly *now*, when they make more contact with other children. It is a key element in how young people treat each other. It is also an interesting link between emotions and social behaviour, and deserves a section to itself.

Watching any group of five-year-olds shows that some of them are consistently more curious about each other and are more confident in moving towards each other and taking opportunities for an encounter. In most cases, although not invariably, the more extravert children are also those who are more naturally competitive. Being competitive is sometimes obvious and sometimes concealed. A proportion of those children who are less eager for contact with others are (or become) envious of others, and reveal that they are competitive only when it seems safe for them to do so. When it comes to choosing the most appropriate kind of school, it is well worth getting an understanding of how competitive—and in what ways—your child is likely to be and finding out how well, or badly, different schools may be matched to his character. State primary schools, as well as fee-paying schools, can vary considerably in the amount of competitive interest they presuppose among their pupils. Too much competitive pressure in a school may be very dispiriting to a child, as well as intellectually irrelevant, if he is resentful of constantly being compared with others.

It is wrong to talk, as some do, of competitiveness as being one dimension on which children can be compared precisely, as if they were being measured for their height. Competitiveness can be open, and compatible with friendliness and with taking pleasure in co-operative games or activities. It can also be compulsive and a source of frustration and unpopularity. It can be covert and gnaw away at somebody. It can be harnessed within other values (i.e. kept within bounds) or it can overwhelm all scruples.

Christopher, Bill and Laura had not met each other before. They were in a waiting-room with other children, while their mothers were discussing arrangements for them to join a primary school. Their movements, words and actions were noted objectively by independent observers who compared notes afterwards. These three children were singled out because they represented the best contrasts in their relationships to each other.

Christopher went straight up to Bill, as he did to others, and looked at what he had in his hands. 'That's a car,' he said. 'I've got lots of cars. Give it to me. I'll show you how it works.' Bill didn't want to hand over his car. He turned round, trying to shield it with his body. Christopher, however, would not be diverted. 'Give me the car. I'll show you how it works.' He took it, rubbed the wheels against his chest and then put the friction toy on the floor, where it obediently covered several yards. 'I've got lots of cars at home,' added Christopher, watching it with a satisfied smile.

Bill looked at the car on the floor and seemed to make a conscious decision not to cry. He is, in fact, bigger than Christopher, despite being the same age, so that it was not a case of his being afraid. He edged away towards a corner.

Laura seized the car as soon as it stopped. 'I can make it go better than that!' she cried. Going to the place where Christopher had started its last trip, she rubbed the wheels vigorously with the flat of her hand. Christopher thought he could show that he, too, could do it better, and made a grab for the car, saying, 'Give me. I must do it.' But Laura hugged it to her and gave a little screech. She knew that this screech is good for defending or sometimes claiming property. It surprised and inhibited Christopher for long enough for Laura to prepare her turn. She did not do as well as Christopher, partly because she was hurried.

'Can Bill have his car back now, please?' This was a student teacher, anticipating trouble. Laura lost interest in the car at that point, but Christopher dived for it, determined to be the one to bring it back to Bill. His competitive sense extends to organizing or leading social situations. He wants to be the first to be helpful, but he likes to boss others as well.

'Anyway, we've got a Hot Wheels set at home,' Laura told him. 'I don't care,' said Christopher. (Christopher did not seem quite sure what a Hot Wheels set is.)

Bill *did not want* to have a go with his car on the floor, although both the student teacher and Christopher suggested it. He hugged the car, but turned away to a hutch in the corner, where he could look at a guinea pig. Only when both Christopher and Laura had left the room did he try, somewhat diffidently, to work his car across the floor. In some children, awareness of competition can retard social progress, because it makes them shy away from a meeting which might end up with their losing face.

Not all non-competitive children, by any means, are like Bill. Some will be mildly surprised at the rivalry expressed by others, and will adapt to it or bypass it. They may *become* competitive in particular activities, where it suits them to be so. They have an advantage in some ways in that they can choose their battlefield, rather than feeling a compulsion to fight in all circumstances.

Despite all that is said, quite rightly, against excessive competitiveness, there can be little doubt that a measure of it helps a child in any normal playground or classroom, or in relations with children down the street. Guardian angels do not hover around to guarantee fair shares. Most sport is competitive and children generally respect success at this. Bill seems likely to be at a disadvantage. He can best be helped by having a lot of contact with a few children who are friendly but not overbearing, or determined to compete and win. This will give him some confidence at dealing with others and—hopefully—encourage him to press for his rights and to show off a little.

Laura is a long-term competitor, while Christopher is soon ready to consider a chapter closed. At one point in the afternoon he pushed Laura out of the way when she was threatening to interfere with his plans for which of the children should do what in the Wendy-house. She picked herself up and led an attack, with another girl, on the other side. The student teacher intervened. Much later, Laura found Christopher at a disadvantage. *He* had forgotten everything, for he practically disregarded her, but *she* was waiting. Suddenly she plunged her teeth into his leg and he howled with surprise.

There is a streak of vindictiveness in Laura which is absent in Christopher. She *generalizes* rivalry with others, so that a determination to be superior to another child is carried over from one situation to the next. Christopher is entirely *particular* about his rivalry; he does not bear grudges and is taken aback when others obviously do.

Part of this has to do with their backgrounds. Laura has two twin sisters, who are both nearly two. They have held the centre of the stage for some time. She is continually trying to get the attention from her parents that she feels is her due. There is a taboo, at her home, about harming the twins in any way. Her resentment finds other forms of expression, and this is paid out to other children. (Some psychologists might well hypothesize that she is worried by the violent feelings she has against the twins and projects this animosity into the minds of other children, whom she therefore wants to get the better of and occasionally to hurt. Possible—but it exceeds the knowledge we have to hand.)

Laura can best be helped by being given, by her parents, a better *identity* within the family and a clearer sense of being loved for what she *is*, as opposed to whatever clever things she does. Right now, she is not quite a tiny tot, not quite a big sister, not quite a mite who needs help all the time and not quite an independent child. Giving her more responsibility in the household may help a good deal, if done gradually. Time will also help, anyway.

Christopher is an only child and has masses of self-confidence. He identifies strongly with a big, autocratic but benevolent father, who thinks the world of his son. He is often compared with other children, almost always to his advantage, in his hearing. If this were done less, he might be more amenable to the principle of give-and-take and will be less of a target for the Lauras he will meet at primary school, operating alone or in gangs. He stands to be admired—or disliked. School will help him to grasp both the idea and the desirability of co-operating with others, and accepting their ideas sometimes. He needs a firm teacher who will *neither* slap him down for being bumptious *nor* give way to his bids to run the class, be the most prominent, boss the projects, and so forth.

None of these three children is what one would call mainstream, although their types recur often enough in this age bracket. They are by no means fixed in their ways for life: so much depends on whether their home life changes, how intelligent they are, the friends they make and their experiences at school. But early habits acquired in dealing with others are often long-lasting, especially when encouraged by parents and when they reflect part of the parents' life style. Girls and boys are fast approaching the period when they are most likely to identify with their parents and accept them as models of what they should say and do. There are two parts to this: copying their parents and repeating those acts which seem to get parental approval.

When a child seems to be very disobedient, it is hard for a parent to accept the apparent paradox—that his child is trying to be like him. Identification is a two-way process. A child wants his parent to be close to him, to talk things over and to help to register interest and approval when he is doing something he believes to be in the family style. If he doesn't get this, he may devise ways of seizing attention, often at the expense of others in the family who seem to be getting in his way. If he is very frustrated, he will look for rewards outside the magic circle, doing things which express his annoyance in ways that are deliberately *not* those of his family. Even in these cases, however, it is interesting to note how something like aggressive independence may be partly modelled on a stand-offish father, or sometimes a mother. When the naughtiness takes on a physical aspect, such as attacks on other children, this is very often a reflection of parents' predilection for using force or physical punishment in the home.

Nursery school and play-group experiences are usually helpful in contriving social situations in an atmosphere where, on the one hand, there are turns and fair shares and, on the other, a watch is kept on the proceedings to make sure that children are helped or distracted if they have an unhappy encounter. Primary school is another matter altogether. Children will vary in the age they begin this important stage in their social progress, but most will be into it when they are six. What they meet there when they start is described in the next chapter.

Chapter seven

Primary school

When, some time in his sixth year, a child moves into a primary school, it usually means the end of one era in the family and the start of a new one. If he is one of many, of course, it may not be a new experience, but it inevitably means that his mother suddenly has a good deal more time in which she is by herself or able to concentrate more on the younger children. She sometimes looks forward to this change eagerly, but then finds herself regretting it and not knowing quite what to do with her freedom. Jealousy and suspicion of the teacher's role are not uncommon, although this passes with time as the inevitable truth is accepted that her child is now a *school-child*.

Many children sense a change in their status when they start school. Part of this comes from other, older children, who talk of it as something separate and superior. Part is the encouragement of parents who try to overcome a child's fears of what school will be like by giving him a feeling of importance. It is as well if parents do not fall victim to their own propaganda. Yes, their child is taking a step forward. But the sheer fact of this move does not make him any more mature on the day of his joining than the day preceding it. Treating him as if he were an animal who now had tusks and could therefore defend himself is a kind of wish-fulfilment. It would be pleasant if the transition could be immediate and painless. But it rarely is.

A few children go to boarding school at this age. This is hardly to be recommended, although sometimes family circumstances make it better that they should do so than not. These children are going to lose a lot of contact with their parents during a formative period, when talking to them, watching them and simply feeling that they are there is important. Some boarding schools accepting children at this age are extremely adept at helping children of different kinds who find themselves boarded out. Some are not. Institutionalization is not too strong a word to describe what happens to children who go to them. The problems and criteria for choosing between these schools are set out in *Children Apart* by Peter Rowlands (1973).

Most children will be day boys or day girls. Among them, a minority will be going to fee-paying schools, the rest to one of the local state primaries or to a specialized state school (e.g. children in delicate health). The problems of starting are identical in each. Also identical are the chances of finding insensitive teachers, who run the reception class with all the atmosphere of an army recruiting depot in war-time. In most cases, primary schools aim to make things easy for new children who are starting there. Arranging for a visit or two during the term before entry or during the holidays, when the school is quieter and less alarming, are tactics which can help establish the feeling that it is a pleasant place to visit. Similarly, a good school will take the trouble to find out which of the newcomers know each other already and which will need to be helped by introduction to two or three who could become friends, preferably living near each other so that this contact can be continued out of school hours.

Another approach that makes for a happy introduction is for teachers to follow the principle that all creatures, even young humans, have a basic need for defensible territory. Far better than being left to imagine that the whole building is a confused and noisy mess is to have a desk, or table space, and a locker allotted to *you*, personally, and perhaps a corner of a room in which you and a few others are encouraged to collect, every so often, as a kind of base. This base can become decorated, over a period of time, with personal insignia.

A large part of the psychology of settling in happily (whatever the place) is generally a sense of ownership of at least part of it. This is equivalent to establishing control. There are many analogies in adult life: the unease that people feel when in a boarding house with a common staircase and landing, used by the occupants of several rooms, and the gratifying sense of possession of a hotel when you are established in one room that you like and know well. Some primary school reception classes preserve the nursery school ritual of a rest after lunch, in which the children sit or recline on cushions or rugs and listen to a story. Occasionally they fall asleep. This is, in itself, a clear expression of a child's confidence in his control over a piece of 'territory'. Some teachers comment that the settling-in process for a new child at school often seems to date from the first moment that he relaxes, genuinely and drowsily, on the floor. This sounds rather like the advice given about cats and dogs: in a new home, keep them in until they have had a good sleep, a meal and have groomed themselves. Given that with children entering school we are dealing with fear and displacement—with very primitive effects on the mind—the parallel might not be too far-fetched.

What can be done to help a child reach the point of losing his anxiety about starting school?

(a) For a start, a mother must tone down her enthusiasm about the 'freedom' she now proposes to enjoy. It is easy to be tactless about this to an impressionable child, who imagines himself as a discarded millstone and his family life as a happy period which is now irrevocably lost. In this frame of mind, it is small wonder if he kicks and screams. 'How many years do I have to go to school?' a six-year-old sometimes asks. This is like asking, 'How long am I condemned to stay away from you?' This is the beginning of looking on school as a penitentiary. It is not much use talking about holidays: they are a long way off and beyond the time-scale over which he is capable of planning, anyway. To reassure him, he needs to be made to understand that school is a minor detail, compared to the love his parents feel for him and the pleasure they take in his company.

(b) Don't talk about it in advance as if it is a big change that will affect his whole life. If he is happy at home, he doesn't *want* a big change. Nor, if he is normal, will he be specially keen to pick up a challenge to his strength of personality—which is the picture some parents paint of it in a child's mind. Being told that he is expected to be tough-minded about going to school and 'not a *cry-baby*' serves to underline the terrors ahead and to raise doubts in his mind about being able to cope.

(c) Try to give the impression that school is *fun*; if in doubt about the truth of this yourself, take a closer look at the local primary school and compare the atmosphere with what you once confronted yourself. The school regime *is* less repressive nowadays, although of course it is still possible to find a rigid, task-orientated sweat-shop if you look for one. Recall the laughs you had, rather than the horrors of meeting a dragon of a school-teacher or the sarcasm you attracted when you forgot your homework. Your child is quite capable of expecting that those things might happen to him. Similarly, do not dwell on how *hard* things were to learn; he is no more anxious to face this kind of humiliation than you were.

(d) At the same time, do not oversell it. School is not one long birthday party. He will be less disappointed if he is expecting interesting things—'always something new at school'—rather than a land of delight.

(e) Go along in the company of one or more other children. If you don't know any other mother taking her child to school for the first time, ask the teachers for some names, get acquainted and arrange a joint expedition. This applies to bringing children to school *after* 'Day One' as well. Alarm about being left at school does not disappear after the first visit, and accompanying another child is an excellent distraction from fear.

(f) Take him up to the door yourself. Don't leave him to somebody else to take. School will be a happier place for him if he feels that it is part of your world, too. Most schools are relaxed about mothers going through with their child as far as the cloakroom (often darker and more anxiety-provoking than the classroom or the playground). If he feels that you, too, move into and out of the building, and if he sees you exchanging a greeting with the teacher, he is bound to feel more secure. Visits to see the school and the teacher before term begins have been mentioned already; they have the same effect.

(g) There will come a moment when you must decide to go. Tell him you will be back, when all the other mums come to collect their offspring, but do so *casually*—not, as can be seen sometimes, as if you were promising to bring relief to a gallant captain of a garrison soon to be surrounded by savages. Then *go*. Inevitably, some mothers betray hesitation. Hesitation implies concern. Concern arouses fear. Once afraid, the child seizes his mother by the legs and howls. Now there is trouble, all right. Don't criticize him for clinging; you do not want him to feel worse. Look for distractions, wait until he is quieter and then *go*. Tell yourself that teachers are not merely soothing parental nerves when they claim that 90 per cent of children who are soggy when their mothers leave, dry up miraculously when they are out of sight. One reason for this is often overlooked: a hesitant mother is much less of a calming influence than one who is kind but decided in what she does.

(h) At least in the first week, *don't be late* in coming to collect your child. There are few experiences so depressing as to watch all the other children meeting up with their mothers again and still there is no sight of your own mother returning. Imagination runs wild, suggesting lurid reasons for this. Afterwards, he will associate his unhappiness with the school itself.

Arguably, the best way to prepare a child for primary school must include choosing the best school for him. An opposite school of thought maintains that a parent's debt to society is greater than the obligation to his child to optimize his chances of a good education, and for that reason the concept of choice of school should be discouraged, since the health of society should gain from the principle of equality of opportunity being extended to early education. This is an argument, in short, for introducing all children, irrespective of background or talent, into the state system at five. Any parental desire to improve a child's education should therefore be channelled into taking an active interest in what is happening at the local state primary, in pressing for a stronger PTA, in keeping up a constructive dialogue with the staff about aims and methods, and in raising a strong voice for bigger state and local subsidies for education. All these activities are desirable, I believe, for parents to preserve with regard to *any* school.

This is not the book in which to further this argument, one way or the other. But this chapter deserves a comment on three points that are sometimes made by the most vehement proponents of state education for all:

(a) All state primary schools are comparable, in the opportunity they afford, to all children.

(b) Children of all abilities and of all temperaments are equally well served by what their local state primary can offer them.

(c) A child will fulfil his academic potential in the course of time just as well if he starts and sticks to the state system (irrespective of which school he is at) as if he goes anywhere else.

In my view, given the research that has been done and common-sense deductions from ordinary observation of the facts, none of these claims is justifiable at the time of writing. In the future, it may be different. Meanwhile, there are two other arguments from the same quarter, which are worth considering more seriously:

(d) Going to a fee-paying school, especially at the primary level, gives a child a false sense of distance from and superiority to most other children.

(e) This encourages him to have a sense of values in which too high a premium is put on academic success, a 'good' accent or any of the other indications that somebody has been to a similar school, when judging other people.

Here again, it is best to acknowledge that there is a basic dispute in society. Some parents are more anxious about preserving middle-class status for their children than they are about giving them a rounded view of life, and of all the people who contribute to it. They have their own priorities and that is their business. But it *is* important for them to reflect that they may be restricting their children's experience and outlook, if they insulate them against other accents and other ways of doing things, at primary school age. Later, their children may be alarmed by or defensive against children from other social class backgrounds. Their reactions will be interpreted as stand-offish—and in this way British social class consciousness perpetuates itself. There is little doubt that as the 1970s are developing, there is a greater advantage, year by year, in being able to communicate with all kinds of people from many different backgrounds.

Before primary school age, children are indiscriminate about whom they accept, talk to, avoid or play with. But this is a critical point where stereotypes about what others are like are liable to crystallize and take very firm hold. It is all too easy an age for teaching, or implying, that one only has dealings with other children in like uniforms, with well-brushed hair and narrow vowel sounds; that one discourages children from the noisy school where they don't have 'proper lessons', from families who live too close to the railway or from those of the opposite sex or of a different colour.

Some fee-paying schools accept the point that a restricted environment is not so much exclusive as impoverished. They follow a policy of mixing the sexes, the races and the backgrounds of the children who make up their numbers. It is worth finding out what is the policy of the schools you have in mind, and comparing them. A similar point has to be made about certain state primary schools. Impoverishment of the environment extends to schools where, say, four in five of the children are from immigrant families who do not speak English at home. A rich mixture is what is wanted for the benefit of *all* the children.

Sometimes it is very difficult to exercise any kind of choice between state schools. Local authorities tend to discourage parents from being fussy, which means administrative inconvenience. In practice, negotiation is usually possible, if there is a good reason for it.

Many parents are anxious about what their children are actually going to *learn*. 'Whatever happened to the three Rs?' is the *cri de cœur* that parents often make to each other on their way out from a visit to a primary school. What indeed? The last two decades have seen a large number of experiments, and there is still controversy over what the results have been. For instance, have disappointing results from using the ITA (Initial Teaching Alphabet) been due to the teachers or the system itself? Or to the fact that quicker children often know too much about how to read ordinary words when they enter school, so that results are based more on less-intelligent ones? Nobody will ever know for certain. In mathematics, arguments about set theory have spread right across Europe. Are children actually helped more by a verbal and pictorial approach to numerical concepts, or do they need an early introduction to arabic numerals and their use if they are to develop confidence in their control over them? (See Figure 3.) In West Germany, anxiety about the results of years of 'Mengenlehre' (set theory) has led to a situation where politicians who aspire to office at state level are increasingly required to declare their position on this question.

Amid the controversies, it is certain that one irreversible tendency has affected teaching in most kinds of school. This is the recognition of the fact that children who enjoy what they are doing have a much greater chance of learning subjects quickly and thoroughly than those who are forced to learn but hate it. Think back to the last time you prepared for an important examination; how much *detail* can you remember? And yet, you can still probably talk at length about those aspects of the subject that interested you and drew you into it. This is an example of the contrast between force-feeding and education. At some stage in any ordinary person's life, a measure of force-feeding will be necessary: practically everybody has to learn something, whether it be academic or something to do with business, that they find tedious. But the job of a primary school is not to anticipate this moment. It is to help children to get into the habit of looking into a wide range of subjects more closely, more co-operatively, more economically, more confidently and with pleasure, both in the process and in the success.

Few parents, I imagine, would take exception to such a programme. But they have problems on two counts: first, the timescale on which a 'modern' school operates and, second, the identification of ways and means. It may not concern the teacher of the reception class that a particular child does not start reading

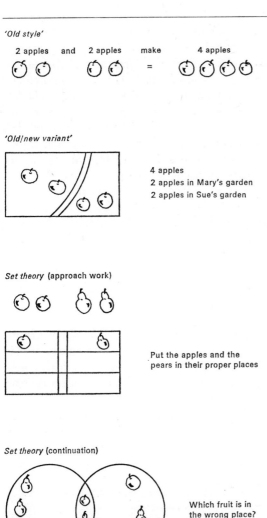

'Old style'

2 apples   and   2 apples   make   4 apples

'Old/new variant'

4 apples
2 apples in Mary's garden
2 apples in Sue's garden

Set theory (approach work)

Put the apples and the
pears in their proper places

Set theory (continuation)

Which fruit is in
the wrong place?

Figure 3 Numerical concepts

with any skill by the end of his first year. She knows that her children vary enormously both in natural ability for a subject and in natural curiosity about becoming able to master it. She can tease this curiosity, but better than forcing it is to encourage interest in what seems to hold his attention more easily. In this way, he will not develop a negative feeling about reading and he will gain in confidence from his other work. Identification of ways and means involves deciding what you want and distinguishing this from the ways it might be obtained. A more sophisticated aim than that of being able to recite times tables is to bring a child to the point where he can approach a mathematical problem intelligently. Knowing what 7×8 equals then becomes incidental. If a child knows how to look this up on a slide rule—or even from a printed card, for that matter—he is intelligently using the means available to anybody in a normal situation.

But the *use* of 7×8 in the course of problem-solving is a higher attainment. The means are useful, but not without a broader understanding of what you can do with them. A child of five or six is limited in the extent to which he can grasp hypothetical situations (as discussed in Chapter four). But by being given concrete problems to discuss and work at, they can begin to see how they can tackle different kinds of question or task, and how they can employ various means, such as a times table, to aid them.

Very roughly, this is what many teachers with whom parents get impatient are trying to do. Obviously, they vary enormously in their skill and their success, just as do teachers conducting conventional classes in the more traditional preparatory schools. They vary particularly in these ways:

(a) General understanding of children and sensitivity to individual attainment and needs.
(b) How far they believe in encouraging task-completion.
(c) Imagination in varying the children's diet attractively and putting ideas across.
(d) How far they feed an individual child's environment, so that he has something to progress to if he wants.
(e) Whether they have the leadership gift to contrive a happy, purposeful atmosphere without recourse to intimidation.

I suggest that when you watch your child's progress at school you keep these questions in your mind. They are more pertinent to future education than whether or not there is any rote-learning. Conditions are worth noting too: even the best teacher cannot struggle indefinitely with over-large classes or under-heated rooms. Then, discuss your feelings with the teacher and the head-teacher, as you think best. Your child only has one school-life to lead and a good start is important: therefore do not hesitate to come forward (provided it is not every week) and talk it over with the teachers. Statistics show that those parents who make contact with teaching staff have a far greater likelihood of their children doing well academically and acquiring a better-than-average emotional adjustment at school at the age of seven (see *From Birth to Seven* in the further reading section). This is for various reasons, but understanding and influencing what is being done at school must figure among them.

Mention has been made of children of 'all abilities'. In many schools, children will be given an intelligence test soon after their arrival. How far is this likely to be accurate? In most cases, the test will be administered individually, since many of the children cannot read instructions yet. An important part of the individual test is to check on the motivation and the emotional state of the child being tested. If either is suspect, the results are rightly suspect. The tester, therefore, needs skill at interpretation, not simply a calculation of figures. Reading ability enters into the test, but is not crucial to getting a high score, in most of the modern tests used. An understanding of simple, everyday situations, an ability to use words to describe them and a sense of special relations between objects are more to the point. A score is worked out in terms of the correct or appropriate answers the child gives, to arrive at the 'mental age'—i.e. the age at which *most* children would achieve the answers that the child has given. A simple sum then takes place, as shown below.

Calculating IQ (intelligence quotient) A child has just become a six-year-old. His answers are consistent with a mental age of six years six months.

$$\frac{6 \cdot 5 \text{ (mental age)} \times 100}{6 \text{ (chronological age)}} = IQ$$

$$= \frac{650}{6}$$

$$= 108 \cdot 3$$

Because the average mental age is depressed by children with a mental handicap, the average IQ for children in a reception class at primary school would be expected to be a little higher than 100. An extremely intelligent child might register an IQ of 135. This means a mental age of just over eight (assuming he is just six). You can never prove that an IQ calculation is an accurate assessment of your child's intelligence. But a low score, subsequently ratified by a trained psychologist, is an important indicator, because it signals the need for special help. The test shows, quite often, the *kind* of help that may be required. A very high score is usually a good prediction of high scores in the future: in these cases it seems probable that something exceptional by way of intelligence has been recorded. The scores of *most* six-year-olds will waver for a year or so until they can all read, and when they have got beyond the stage of misleading the unwary tester by taking more interest in him than in his test. There is no point in regarding IQ scores as irremediable facts, particularly with a young child. But it is well worth asking a competent tester for his assessment of the *ways in which* a child's intelligence may be unusual from that of others (musically, a difficulty with numbers, etc.), so that you have more understanding of his potential skills and potential problems. A tester will often also make a private assessment from observation of *how* a child goes about the test and of his 'emotional age'— which may be younger than the mental age in very bright children. This is well worth thinking about and discussing with his teacher, if his emotional age is low.

Some children settle down at primary school all right for a month or so, and then turn against it. There can be several reasons for this. One common one is that a younger brother or sister has obviously been profiting by the absence of the school-child, in increasing the attention and fun he is getting from his parents. This means using tact and redressing the balance. Sometimes what is needed is to take more interest in what is happening at school. If it does not pass off quickly, and there is clearly a strong fear or dislike in the child's mind, this may be a sign of tension between him and a particular teacher. When this happens, keep an open mind until you have talked to other parents about this teacher. The antipathy may be personal and temporary, possibly disappearing after you have talked with her. But it *may* be a situation where several children are coming away from school humiliated and frightened. Do not *hesitate*, in such cases, to air your feelings directly with the head-teacher. Because of staff shortages, this is bound to happen occasionally, even in good schools. Act decisively, when you feel the evidence is clear, and suggest to other parents that they do the same.

Chapter eight

Getting on with his parents

There can be no family in which there has never been any conflict of wills between the parents and their child. Where families differ is in the ways that they accommodate these conflicts, and whether they let them disturb the overall feeling of happiness and security that any home wants and needs.

Another point to remember is that no family is proof against frayed tempers: no parent should think that this problem is something that Fate has inflicted on his family alone, or that those other parents that seem so tranquil and so superior do not experience frictions of their own. Everybody slips below their own personal standards of tact and self-control occasionally, and there is no point in brooding guiltily over what a bad scene or difficult period might have done to relations within the family. It is much better for everybody to think in terms of today, and next week; how to get things better and how everyone can start enjoying life at home a bit more.

In his second year, a child is likely to have held out against his family at some point—to refuse to eat, to be stubborn about being changed, or dressed, or given a bath. Later he learns the word 'No' and finds it is rather fun to use. (Father and mother go through the 'No!' ritual, and there is no reason why he should not, either.) Throughout his third year, and to some extent his fourth, the child is liable to protest, cry and throw a tantrum if he does not get what he wants. Sometimes this is directed against the world at large, sometimes against his mother or some other person. One element in young behaviour is being cross with oneself, when tiredness, clumsiness, inability to cope or to express one's feelings becomes too strong. Tantrums decline during the fourth and fifth years, although when they *do* come they are stronger. Gradually, a child develops his own style with his parents, in which

4

avoidance of trouble plays a major part. Being close to his parents and getting what he wants (which means getting proof of their love more than satisfying curiosity or a desire to possess whatever is going) are key motivators. Meanwhile, he is becoming conscious of himself as an individual, so that any threats to his self-esteem are resented and feared. The basic 'style' that a child acquires depends for its effectiveness primarily on two things:

(a) How close he gets to his parents, and how often this is.
(b) The sensitivity and understanding between them, which depends on the personality and the intelligence of both; and on the parents' interest in their child.

The 'style' breaks down if there is a problem, real or imagined, that strikes at the root of closeness to parents or self-esteem.

For example, a brother and sister of six and five get along reasonably well with each other, most of the time, when playing by themselves. As it is the weekend, their father follows them into the garden, talks to them both and they show him what they are doing. There is an element of rivalry in this, but as he pays attention to each in turn, they each keep within the style of relating to him that they have found to work. He compliments both and walks off. Then Moira, the sister, remembers something. She jumps up and shouts, 'Hey, Daddy! Is it time for us to visit Grannie yet?' As she does so, she knocks accidentally into the edge of the palisade that Brian, her brother, is building round their 'house' under a tree. 'Oh no!' cries Brian, in a rage. 'You've spoilt it all, you stupid dum-dum!' he shouts at her. Moira attempts evasion, while giving him a hand at setting up the palings again. 'No I did *not*!' she maintains. This infuriates Brian further, and he then pushes her over, so that she falls and bursts into tears. We have now reached the critical point, because Moira rushes with a howl to her father's knees, while Brian informs him, 'Oh, Daddy, she's made it all a mess!'

This is a very good testing ground for the father. If he has a favourite between them, it will show in his reactions *now*. The child who is *not* the favourite will very likely be reminded of the fact and his (or her) behaviour will immediately become worse because of this reminder. If, on the other hand, the father takes no sides, and decides his children are appalling company just at the moment, he may stalk away gruffly, muttering, 'Sort it out between you. You're not very nice to know.'

This course has the merit of seeming fair, but has the big disadvantage of throwing children back on supposed resources that they obviously lack. They will be angry with each other all the more, if the result of their argument is withdrawal of interest and (in their eyes) love. Besides, he sets a poor example in co-operation if he shows that he walks away when there is trouble. The same can be said against him if he loses his temper with the children.

Father's role here is to be, alternately, comforter, judge, friend and peace corps official. On the palisade, he may need to be a construction engineer as well. His best hope is to hold out a friendly hand to Brian *while* he is putting his arm round Moira. A three-way hug is what they really want, to re-establish the happiness of five minutes ago.

Father has to watch his words rather carefully. Obviously there will be afternoons when he will feel cross and say, 'Oh do be quiet, please, both of you!', because he would scarcely be human if he did not behave like this sometimes. But most times (one hopes), he will be less edgy and more eager to restore a happy mood. If he tells Brian off severely for behaving badly, while comforting Moira, he will be shaming him, at the same time as demonstrating greater concern for Moira than for him. Brian may genuinely feel that he is being unfairly treated: this makes it worse for him, because he cannot express this feeling or marshal his defence adequately. He has several recourses, the most obvious being to burst into tears and hide somewhere in the garden, where he will linger until he is found and mollified. Other steps he can take are to appeal to his mother, which he may well do if it has worked before. Six is a good age for melodramatic exits too—swearing to die and never return. The mistake is to expect Brian to come back to being sweetly reasonable of his own accord. He has not the emotional sophistication to return and say, 'I'm sorry, Daddy. Let me give Moira a kiss. Can we be friends again now?' His self-respect has been shaken and the reconciliation needs to start from his parents.

If this is an argument for the father *not* expressing his displeasure, how can he prevent Brian from doing worse things in future to his sister, when he feels so moved? Possibly, she might have been seriously hurt this time. The answer lies in making it very clear that what Brian was doing was wrong, but not raising it to an explosive emotional plane which implies to Brian that he is evil, a disgrace and unloved. Telling a child that something is dangerous and that he must not do it is one thing. Wringing one's hands over what he *nearly* did, or what a terrible child he must be, is another. The second course succeeds in alarming him, but also— by implication—in making him feel thoroughly inadequate to control his actions. Brian, like all children, is secretly afraid of his own temper and the lack of control that a tantrum brings. If his parents can give him a feeling that some of his reactions are sensible, while others are dangerous or 'silly', he is far more likely to develop self-control, gradually, than if he is encouraged to be afraid of the monsters lurking in his breast.

A sharp telling-off is sometimes given by parents when they need to vent their feelings on someone. A six-year-old is too easy a target and a parent who treats one as such must feel incapable of normal achievements. Sometimes, however, it is given in the belief that it does a child good. It can achieve a purpose in the short term, i.e. stopping a child from doing something. However, the long-term messages are not so much a matter of generalized good behaviour, but the fact that *this* is how an adult acts; that *this* is how a stronger person treats a weaker one; that *this* is how somebody treats another that they love, every so often; that he himself is the kind who deserves to be treated in this way; and, if it goes on through childhood, that this is a parent with whom it is hard to communicate as one person to another and possibly someone with whom it is no fun communicating.

In the garden scene above, it is worth noting that a word to Moira would not be amiss. She accidentally knocked down Brian's wall of palings. Children of up to about eight or nine tend to have a very simple code: they judge each other by their actions, as opposed to their motives. In Brian's book she *destroyed* his wall. Brian would not be unusual in thinking this. (There is one interesting exception to this, when children of mixed abilities are playing together: most young children rapidly become remarkably patient and tolerant of breakages where handicapped children are concerned.) It can be argued that children are often closer to the truth than parents. Many 'accidents', as was shown long ago by Freud, are the results of promptings from part of the mind that is usually kept under control, and of which we are not normally conscious. Careful examination of 'accidents' shows that they are often expressions of dislike or envy. What is not consciously intentional is often unconsciously intentional. Not every incident is necessarily explained in this way, but there is no doubt that many are. Knocking down a wall, which may have been obviously more the work of her brother than of herself and which had just been admired by her father, could well come into this category. Moira did it just as she was claiming more attention for herself, which suggests she had some rivalry in her mind.

If her father silences Brian's protests with, 'Oh, shut up: it was only an accident!' Brian will feel hard done by, in terms of the justice that he, at his age, understands. It may encourage him to organize a few 'accidents' of his own. The message Moira will get is that accidents are legitimate. A meaningful look is usually enough to show that you realize that some accidents are more accidental than others, and that girls like Moira should appreciate this too. But blaming her roundly for the incident will be unfair in *her* terms. This is because the last act in the sequence was Brian pushing her over. *That* was clearly premeditated. Besides, it is the last event which is uppermost in a child's mind, and punishment related to something that has passed some time ago means very little to a child.

Perhaps all of this seems very complicated. So it is, with all human behaviour, when you stop to analyse it. Father, however, cannot spend all afternoon puffing at his pipe, making his mind up how to react. Nine times out of ten, being natural and following what they *feel* is right, is perfectly reasonable in most families. Stopping to reflect and gather a bit of calm can, however, produce a good effect on rioting children: a parent looking wise and rock-like is sometimes very much what they want most, while emotions are threatening to run away with them.

All parents like to feel that they are in contact with their children. This is how they benefit each other, after all—quite apart from the fact that discipline as such depends on it. Understanding people should come before understanding rules.

Children change over this period of time in the way that they expect parents to behave, in what they like their parents to be, and what they resent or fear most in their parents. Figure 4 shows some of the main features of this development. The information depends on children's own statements, which might not be fool-proof evidence, given that they vary so much in the extent to which they can talk or want to talk about these things. But it gains from having been collected by psychologists, who were prepared to interpret, as well as record, and to ask children in different emotional states.

It should be remembered that children see things very much through their *own* eyes until, approximately, the eighth year. This is borne out in both the points they appreciate in parents and those they do not. Most are expressions of things which parents do to them or ways in which they affect them. 'Possessions' indicates a further stage of thought, in which they are prepared to

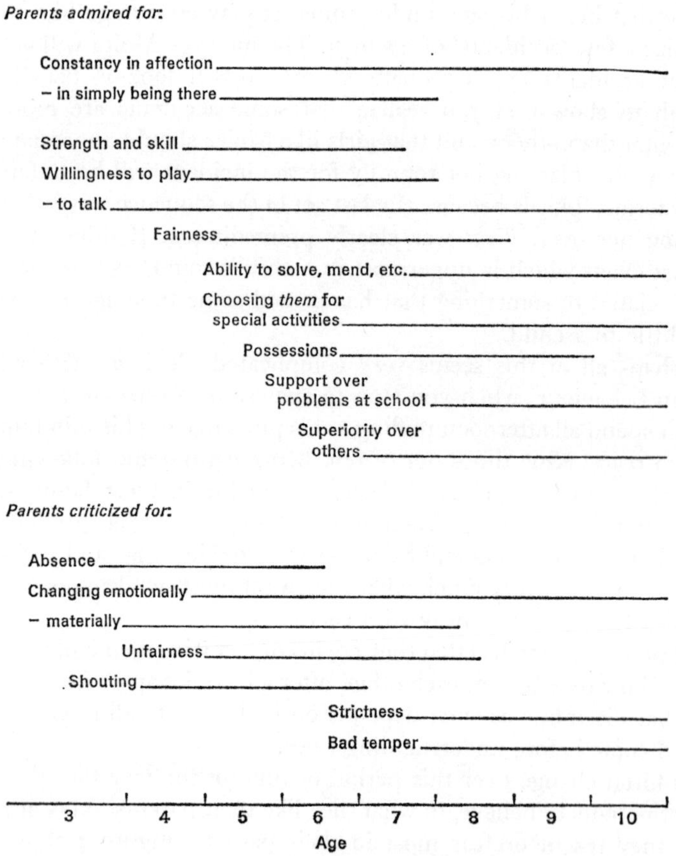

Parents admired for:

Constancy in affection _____

— in simply being there _____

Strength and skill _____

Willingness to play _____

— to talk _____

Fairness _____

Ability to solve, mend, etc. _____

Choosing *them* for
special activities _____

Possessions _____

Support over
problems at school _____

Superiority over
others _____

Parents criticized for:

Absence _____

Changing emotionally _____

— materially _____

Unfairness _____

. Shouting _____

Strictness _____

Bad temper _____

3	4	5	6	7	8	9	10

Age

Figure 4   What children admire and criticize in their parents, as they grow older

Notes
1 The position of each characteristic in the page gives a rough idea, against the time-scale, of the age at which that becomes salient in a child's mind.
2 The dots indicate the period over which a child notices each characteristic particularly. (This does *not* mean that when the dots stop, the characteristic ceases to apply at all.)
3 From four onwards, girls tend to resist their mothers more, boys their fathers.

consider people as characterized by certain things which they have and others do not. A 'possession' may be a pipe or a special chair, just as much as an Aston-Martin. But it would be sentimental to suppose that children are concerned about soul and character to the exclusion of material things. When they go on, later, to talk of 'strictness' or being prone to 'bad temper', they are making more sophisticated comments. These demand a measure of generalization and a sense of comparison with others, especially circumstances in other families. Seven and eight are notorious ages for children protesting 'But Billy's parents let him do that!' It is as well to know that children in both strict *and laissez-faire* homes are equally liable to come out with this comment.

There is a curious omission of anything to do with smacking in Figure 4. It seems to be a fact that big, sustained emotional changes are far more alarming, throughout childhood, than an occasional blow delivered in temper. This is not to condone the distribution of blows. The kind of comment that a child makes when he is really critical (in sorrow or in anger) of his parents is 'Sometimes she doesn't say anything at all and it goes on all day'. From six, sometimes seven, they introduce comparisons in time (whereas up till then one has to assume these from the words they use). For example, 'Last summer it was super and we played a lot together. Now when I come back from school they only pick up my little brother and leave me to eat by myself.'

Not all these 'changes', of course, have a clear basis in fact: the point is that this is the way the child sees them. Possibly the most important thing in his life is the way he fits into, and believes he fits into, his family and the warm atmosphere that this imparts. Any threat to this is, perhaps, the worst that his parents can do. A threat appears in the form of an emotional change that cannot be easily understood, and goes on for too long to seem consistent with his role in the family remaining secure. Besides that, a sore bottom is neither here nor there. But it is interesting that 'shouting', as opposed to 'smacking', occurs fairly high in the child's list of parental crimes. Possibly this is because a prolonged shout is an assault on the spirit, as opposed to the body, and as such it becomes criticized strongly at five and six, when a child is trying particularly hard to emerge into an individual personality, viable in himself.

Many psychologists admit that they have smacked their own children, occasionally. I number myself among them. None of us is, I imagine, particularly proud of this. The psychologist's defence has nothing to do with maintaining discipline or teaching an unruly child a lesson, because there are far better ways of doing both, while maintaining a better understanding. The points made are usually these:

(a) If it is natural to him and occurs within a flash of temper, it helps the parent to relieve his feelings in this way, and perhaps be a better parent afterwards.

(b) If it is within temper and immediately consequential on an act which has been expressly forbidden, it underlines that point and makes for consistency in attitude, which children appreciate.

It follows from these points that psychologists do not approve (or practise) premeditated physical punishment, or incorporate it into their basic pattern of parent–child relationship, or encourage it when parents are calm and in control of their feelings. They also tend to favour apologizing to the child afterwards. The idea of this is that if they do not say they are sorry, they are establishing an example that may find its way out in all kinds of ways later. Violence breeds violence. It is better to admit that one is *not* a perfect parent and that sometimes one's own standards, regrettably, slip below those of a civilized family—which, incidentally, are the standards one is trying to pass on.

But there is a difference between saying, quickly, 'I'm sorry, I didn't mean to hit you. But you made me so angry when you shook pepper over your sister that I felt I had to. You mustn't do that again', and having an emotional switch-back ride. This starts with a clout, then goes on to regret, remorse, and a massive Reconciliation Scene, with tears interspersed amid the hugs. A child really has no idea where he stands in those circumstances and is afraid of the great tides of emotion that sweep back and forth.

Reconciliation in itself is crucial. But it comes best when it is part and parcel of regaining emotional control on both sides—not of behaving as if a prodigal had returned.

This is worth remembering in those situations where a howling child is removed from the scene for a few minutes, for a cooling-down period. Opinions divide sharply on this, some maintaining that it is a suggestion to the child that love is being withdrawn from him. Apart from causing him anxiety, it may serve to convince him of one of the doubts in his mind which may have led to disturbed behaviour. But there is a difference between taking a child into his bedroom and leaving him there with instructions not to attempt to return before he is nice again, and picking him up and taking him into the garden, or on to the balcony, for a spell while holding him. The latter has the advantage of keeping close contact, while removing him from a stressful impasse which he is clearly not capable of getting through on his own. It also allows for explanation, or a running commentary on the events. Even if the child seems still to resent the fact that he is not getting his way, while a discussion of the reasons and everybody's feelings on the subject is being led by his mother or father, there is no question that at a deeper level he appreciates his parents taking the trouble to show that they are noticing and not just repressing him out of hand. But circumstances, generally in larger families, some-times make it necessary to adopt the first tactic. If you do this, don't let him linger indefinitely: as soon as you have a moment, go back and offer an olive branch. This is *not* a sign of weakness. It gives him something positive to which to respond.

Many a bad scene starts with a rebuff, or a refusal, or a feeling on the part of the parent that a particularly important custom of the house is being overturned. Take a cool, reappraising look at some of these customs, as time goes by. Some of them may be simply matters of administrative convenience and have nothing to do with the health of a child or respect for his parents.

Bed-time is a good example. There is nothing wrong in choosing a particular time at which baths should be taken and beds should be entered. Routine is more acceptable than an arbitrary decision every evening. But not all children are the same about the amount of sleep they need. Many have a lot of energy to kill before they drop off—even if they have been quietened down with a story or two. If these *want* to bounce around, laugh, read a book or what-ever, does it really matter? Children who are allowed to do this tend to be bright-eyed and wide-awake the next morning. Once they are in the right situation, they judge their sleep need very well. It is those who are not put into the right situation until too late who flop around miserably, getting more irritable as television or the party drags on, and attract their teacher's notice the next morning for looking pie-eyed and unresponsive. In their bed-rooms, they choose *à la carte* very sensibly. In Victorian times, a child was expected to fall asleep as soon as he was put to bed. To increase the chances of this with babies, laudanum was sometimes used. For older children, the gas-taps were sometimes turned on

4*

for a brief spell. Nowadays, the father is sometimes deputed to march upstairs, clap his hands loudly and cry, 'You be quiet in there! You're supposed to be asleep!' Sometimes it is a bit like asking a river to stop flowing: it *will*, when it is ready to, and the tide turns.

Watching television comes into this category, too, in some families. But forbidding indiscriminate watching is pointless unless a viable alternative is offered. This may mean playing with the children yourself. Children will accept that, but they abhor a vacuum. The point will come, once they have started school, at which certain TV shows are important to them: the others watch them, so why shouldn't *they*? Here again, ask yourself if the wrangle is really worth while, before digging in your heels. You may feel that a programme is downright bad for your child, in which case refuse stoutly. But you should realize that in doing so you are increasing its desirability for him. If he gets the chance, he may watch it at a friend's house. It might be better if he saw it in your home first, where you are able to discuss it together.

Forbidden fruit tastes sweeter. Most adults acknowledge this, particularly if they can look back objectively at any compulsions they had to do this or that, when they were exploring the world at six or seven. And yet it comes as a shock to those adults, more often than not, when they discover their own children in the grip of an overpowering desire to do what is not allowed in their home. The rule may be: no sweets except for one after lunch and one after tea. Then, in the middle of the afternoon, you suddenly discover, as you pass the window, a hitherto guileless child standing on a chair to reach the box on top of the fridge. A furtive face turns in alarm to greet your look, both cheeks puffed out with chocolate booty, hamster-wise.

'Why?' you ask yourself. He cannot be hungry. It isn't as though sweets were completely forbidden. You haven't had a row that day. He gets lots of love and attention, so what can he be compensating for? (Stealing sweets and other things is sometimes found among children who feel deprived of maternal comfort and regard, so that compensation is worth passing round your mind as a possible motive.) But the core of this problem with many children is merely a matter of their need to demonstrate that they are individuals, who can act independently from your system and your rules. Before you worry whether your child has some kleptomaniac streak, consider that all children want to express this essential difference that is themselves in some way or other. Some feel that the out-of-bounds sweet-box is a challenge, or a kind of dare. When they raid it, they are showing themselves that they can get into and handle objects which are hedged around with some adult taboos.

Be true to your word, by all means, when this happens, and tell him not to do it. Repeat the point about sweets making holes in the teeth, as an explanation for your concern in this. But don't act as if the moral world had suddenly crashed, because you then invest the whole incident with guilt: the association made is not simply between taking sweets and guilt, but between self-expression and guilt. Guilty children become more furtive. It also pays to suggest both in your reaction to the scene and in your comments on it (e.g. 'All that trouble for some sweets!') that this is not the kind of adventure that you personally respect as the mark of somebody who is forging ahead in individuality. This implies that it was a *silly* act, rather than an evil or an unnatural one, but like most hints it should not be overdone. Children sense the boundary between friendly commentary and moralizing very perceptively.

The smaller the space you live in and the less defensible territory each member of the family has inside it, the more opportunity there is for collision of interest and for rows to break out. This observation has been made by psychologists and social scientists at all stages of the scale between rats in cramped cages and families suffering from overcrowding. It is a fact that seems to apply right through the animal kingdom, and it affects man and his children just as much. Obviously it doesn't help to say to a harassed parent that he should have more money, so that he can buy a castle and dedicate one whole wing to his offspring. But it remains a fact that just as each part of a family needs to be able to rely on togetherness at certain times, they need to have the chance of spreading out from each other, too. This suggests that a high premium should be put on getting space, so that everybody has their own corner, and that, failing this, family sorties should be organized where everybody can run free for a while and feel untrammelled. Sometimes parents overorganize weekend sorties (e.g. 'at 3 o'clock we will reach the Victoria and Albert Museum. That will just give us time to see the costume section, the old glass and some Flemish pictures, before we go to Aunt Joanna's for a quick cup of tea, and then on to the theatre.'). Highly educational, but where is the opportunity for the children to run across the fields, choose a tree to climb or just wander? The tighter their living conditions, the more they need frequent space and the freedom to enjoy it as they wish.

Some parents nag. No parents ever admit that they nag. We hear them on trains and on buses. It is another kind of over-organization. It is also, in a sense, cramping the child. If you have the slightest suspicion that you issue the same instructions about eating up meat or doing up shoe-laces, many, many times in the same afternoon, consider two of the points made earlier in this chapter. One is that the rule may not, in fact, matter and that you have chosen the wrong ground on which to fight a battle. Second, that you are tending to confine your child within too small a space. He is not just 'being lazy', as you may suspect; he is being different. Difference will out. Realizing this makes for better relations. If you can *laugh* about the meat ('Well—if you *want* to look like an umbrella when you grow up!') and *laugh* about the shoe-laces ('If you put your foot in the river you might catch a fish on your laces!'), you show that this is not such a vital issue to you as enjoying life with him. Surprisingly, he may then conform. Another positive hint for naggers is to set yourself a rule: for every order you give, ask him one question. Ask for information, for his views on something or for what he would like—anything. But don't make it rhetorical or sarcastic. It makes a parent much better company if he shows he can be a good listener, too.

Parents with more than one child are often tempted to point to one or another and say, 'But Sally eats her meat!' or 'You never see Roger going round without his shoe-laces done up!' This sometimes works—in the short term. But it works because it increases the tension and rivalry between the children. They will pay each other back for it, sooner or later. They will pay you back, too, for implying that your admiration for one child over another is conditioned by the extent to which they conform to the house rules. But here again, few parents can avoid making comparisons altogether. This is a matter of degree, not of black and white.

Around six or seven, a child may shock his parents in another way, too. Although they may have been very enlightened over the question of children 'lying'—i.e. they accepted the fact that children imagine fantasies so strongly that they can express them as facts—they are unprepared for the kind of lie that drops another child, possibly a brother, deep into the mud. Somehow this seems heinous and out of all proportion to what has gone before. But the power of fantasy is still at work—'Wouldn't it be nice if he had smashed Mummy's vase and I hadn't?' leads to a confident assertion that this was the case. Rivalry may add colour to the story, but the origin of the slander may yet be comparatively innocent.

While it helps to understand why your child may do this, you cannot just let it go by. Telling lies against others can become a habit, usually in two circumstances: if a child gets away with it successfully *or* if he is caught out and punished for it in a way that makes him feel guilt-ridden, and more or less committed to ruses of this kind for getting back into favour or reversing a position of inferiority to his brother or sister. There has to be a middle way. This is a talk, in which the reason why this kind of lie is so unpleasant is explained. This kind of talk works best if it is a *two-way* discussion. No child is registering an explanation if he is nodding meekly and glancing hopefully at the telephone in case it might ring. He is simply feeling uncomfortable. Suggest that you act it all out, if that helps. Once you have got his wavelength, make it a good-humoured occasion.

Some parents feel that morality is a serious matter that needs to be approached in a spirit of deadly earnest. They probably succeed in inculcating a sense of right and wrong, but nobody really enjoys justice in that kind of atmosphere. Most of the morality ingested by children is gained incidentally anyway. It is example that gets taken in, rather than precept; this is because the process of identification throughout this age period is so strong. You can tell your child not to swear until you are blue in the face, but it is the indiscreet 'Oh, bugger!' when you drop a hammer on your toe that is assimilated. You cannot really blame a child for choosing between two standards, if you offer him both.

There is a lot to be said for making clear to children what you really believe in and being consistent. Part of the way in which children explore that individuality is to ride their wild horses right up to the border and see about crossing it. Very often they seem to want to make sure that your limits are such-and-such, and that if they go beyond a certain point you will stop them and become cross. A parent who knows that this is what his child is doing can afford to smile when he says, 'Oh no you don't, my bucko!' There is then an unspoken recognition on both sides that the border has been tested, and has been found to exist where it was. There need be no grimness about this, however. We like our own policemen to smile and pass the time of day: we criticize surly weapon-conscious militiamen in other countries. This is *not* a precise analogy, but there is enough of a parallel with the relationship between child and parent in the role of authority, to make it worth stating.

Humour can defuse many dangerous situations, when patience on either side is about to give way. Most parents realize this and suggest that there is something funny about how they, and their children, are getting het up. But sometimes they made the mistake of looking for humour in their child, as opposed to in the situation. A child on the verge of a tantrum may be diverted by something amusing, provided he does not feel that he himself is the butt of the humour. Few things are as humiliating as sarcasm, even if it is unintentional. A parent need not fear loss of respect at making *himself* the object of a good joke. Children *want* to be diverted; they *want* good relations with their parents and they will love and respect a parent all the more who can make a funny face and pretend to be a chimpanzee just when everything is looking black.

Chapter nine

What can go wrong?

Nobody really enjoys, I suspect, a chapter with this title. But it may be worth a glance in case there are signs of something that may need professional advice. Most parents are inclined to be defensive where their children are concerned. Even if they feel that something may be wrong with their child's development, whether this is on the physical, intellectual or emotional side, they draw back from asking for some help. It is as if disclosure of a problem reflected on the family. When someone who has been in this frame of mind at length approaches a doctor or a social worker, they may go in a spirit of resentment and suspicion of what they are going to be told—*before* they are told anything at all. This is usually a transfer of their feelings against the situation to the person they have to consult. Some of this is partly a result of being brought up not to make a fuss, while most is from a very real and understandable anxiety that all must go well with their children. But a great deal of the emotion could be siphoned off if it were more generally accepted that professionals are there to help, not to put a parent on trial. It is professional in a parent to go and see one when the signs suggest it.

The children who will be described in this chapter have all, with one exception, been helped to overcome their problems to a very large extent. The odd one out, Francis, has at least been given a happier time than seemed likely at first. All these improvements have depended primarily on parents, but parents working in conjunction with professional advisers.

Marie

At five, six and seven, Marie was one of the girls you were less likely to notice at the school playground. She was small, dumpy and rather plain-featured. She moved slowly and always seemed to be towards the back of a group of girls. If you approached the group, you could see that she did not instigate any conversation: she repeated what the others said or related to them in a passive way. If she started something herself, it was a catch-phrase or a piece of a chant or a song that was popular with them at the time.

Teachers at school took little notice of her at five, accepting her simply as one of the quieter ones. At six, she was noted to be slow at making progress at reading, which was taught by ITA. She opted to spend more time with paints or 'Plasticine', and sometimes was perfectly happy just to watch the others going about their business, while she twisted and untwisted the end of her dress, between her knees.

The school doctor, on his annual visit, felt that she had poor muscle tone and was physically weaker than the average. He pronounced her rather overweight, flat-footed and rather lacking in co-ordination. Her sight was perfectly normal, but the doctor was dubious about her hearing. He mentioned to the head-teacher that she did not respond as quickly as other children, and was not always clear about what she was being asked to do. Possibly this was a physical problem, possibly she was mentally slow to grasp the point of what was being said. On his recommendation Marie was taken to an audiology unit, where a specialist reported that her hearing was, in fact, normal.

She was now seven, and the gap between her work and that of the others, even in a large class, was beginning to show. She had another problem to contend with, too. Several other girls got into the habit of using Marie as a target for venting their feelings, poking fun at her and bullying her. Their 'game' consisted of calling Marie their 'servant girl', making her get little things for them at make-believe tea parties, and pulling her hair or forcing her on to all fours if she displeased them. Teachers intervened occasionally, but they could not make Marie popular, and they had too much to do to police the playground continually. (The girls who did the bullying had their *own* problems, too, which the school was largely unable to remedy.)

Dates were arranged with Marie's parents to discuss how best to plan her schooling, given that she was not making much progress or contributing to what was happening in class. But these were not convenient and the months slipped by. Her teacher noticed that Marie was more often away sick. She looked helpless when asked for letters explaining her absence and the point was not pressed.

Eventually, a policeman observed a man, who was on the local list of persons meriting special attention, walking with Marie in a park. The policeman wrote in his notebook that the man hurried away at his approach, that the time was half past eleven on Monday morning and that he ascertained that Marie had only just met him and was finishing a piece of chocolate he had given her. The policeman took her to his station, where she spent a very enjoyable hour with a woman officer, while telephone calls were made.

Marie's parents were shocked that she was a truant. They blamed the school, roundly. The head-teacher admits that Marie had not enjoyed school and that not much had been done to help her. Scrutiny of absence notes was tightened up. There would always be *some* bullying in any school, but it had gone too far and had to be stopped. She blamed the pressure on her staff, pointing out that teachers with little experience were being put in charge of classes of over thirty. Somehow Marie had 'slipped through the system'. She did not blame the parents directly, but implied that they cannot have had much close contact with their child or concern about her schooling. She also felt that Marie was out of place at her school—not that Marie was to be blamed for that.

At the local Child Guidance Clinic, a psychologist tested Marie's intelligence and estimated her IQ at 92. This suggested that a special school was probably needed. He reserved his judgment on just how accurate this could be: on the one hand, her use of words and her reading skill were behind now but might conceivably be waiting for some kind of breakthrough; while, on the other, there was the fact that explaining to her the nature of each question needed unusual care and patience. Emotionally, he found her a very passive child, lacking in drive, very suggestible and easily put off when confronted by a difficulty or a cross word. She liked listening to music, joining in singing games (provided they were not too complicated) and playing around with paints, sand and water. All her interests were pitched at a stage younger than her actual age. Significantly, Marie preferred the company of fours and fives, and it was noticed that she was naturally kind and understanding with younger children and toddlers, too.

Marie's parents have one other child, a boy who is two years older and doing very well at a public school. They are proud of him and admit that Marie is 'a disappointment' compared to Alan. But, they maintain, she is a 'nice' girl who 'is very quiet and doesn't mean any harm'. The incident in the park jolted them into taking a more active interest in her. The news spread round the neighbourhood, which alarmed them, possibly as much as the danger itself. They have refused to accept the fact that a child of theirs could be of lower than average intelligence. But they accepted the idea that she might go to a school that would allow her more individual attention and which would be a happier atmosphere for her. That would prevent the problem returning. The name of 'ESN school', however, nearly put them off. They resisted this, at first, but then they found that the only alternative places involved paying fees, and all school-fee expenditure had been ear-marked for Alan.

Marie has thrived, in fact, at her ESN school, although there were ups and downs. She had her difficulties with other children, but here the teachers knew what difficulties to look for; and they were able to build up her confidence, her sense of what she herself could do, could expect, could ask for and could insist on. The important factors here were:

(a) A close relationship with one of the teachers, who took a special interest in her.

(b) Increased contact with her parents, who were kept in touch with what she was doing and what could be expected in the future.

(c) More attention from her mother, once her brother Alan had gone to his boarding school. Marie is more a companion now, less a mobile piece of furniture.

(d) Help at getting to learn simple, useful things through the medium of activities that Marie enjoyed—e.g. drawing huge letters in finger-paints and decorating them was a happier, more successful path to finding her way round the alphabet than a formal approach; number work was practical, involving, for instance, calculations of how many glasses of milk she had to take to the younger children, whom she loved helping to look after.

(e) Making use of different senses to get understanding of something (e.g. textured numbers, in colours, etc.). This compensates for her slowness to grasp new ideas.

(f) Giving her confidence in her body with remedial physical training for a group of children with similar problems.

Although this is less obvious, another point that has helped Marie is that her parents have gradually come to terms with what she is—a slower girl, of lower intelligence than most, who is yet lovable and capable of contributing a great deal if she gets the help she needs.

Bradley

Bradley is *more* intelligent than the average. He is small for his age, but has alert eyes and looks wiry. When he was still in the uterus, his name was put down for a prep school and a public school, both of which his father had attended. He obligingly proved to be male; now all he needed to do was to follow the academic course planned for him.

In almost every way he showed himself equal to this task. He read early, enjoyed talking about stories and grappled with educational toys of varying degrees of complexity. He was presented with cuisenaire rods, to give him a good start with the principles of number work. His parents dedicated weekends to museum trips and historical rambles, and by way of birthday treats there were visits to concerts and theatres. None of this in itself did Bradley any harm. He enjoyed more than the usual share of parental attention, even for an only child. He gained greatly from this, too.

Where he lost out was in contact with other children of his own age. His parents were particular about his playmates and his mother did not encourage horseplay, even with eligible partners. He did not go to nursery school, because the local one did not measure up to his mother's standards. He was not popular with other children and when he started at prep school he had some hard lessons to learn.

Ingrained in his character was a belief that he was due to be the centre of attention, by a kind of natural right. He did well at lessons, but his 'pushiness' was resented by some of the others, who looked for opportunities to outsmart him. His classmates felt that he was selfish and that he 'showed off'. His attitude to them was disapproving, if not disdainful. Half-way through his first term, he was asked 'Do you like your school, Bradley?' and he answered, 'Oh yes. But the other boys are horrible.' He had found that they did things like snatching your cap off, for fun. If you 'couldn't take it', they laughed at you.

When he was seven, he was falling foul of some of the teachers, too. They disliked the way he assumed the right to ask questions at any time, or to claim that as he did not follow something, it had been badly taught. Although they supported him in his protests against unfair treatment, at least one regarded his classmates as fully justified in branding him a cry-baby and a sneak.

In what seemed a sudden development, he told his parents he

hated school and if they sent him back there he must surely die. His protests were politely brushed aside and his parents tried to cheer him up. They talked to his masters; they invited some of his 'friends' home for tea. But every week, for a while, there was a tearful scene. Then there was a quiet period again and his parents decided the phase had passed. But to their great alarm, the end-of-term report showed he had slipped from fourth to nineteenth place in English, and his other results were comparable. His form-master regretted Bradley's 'loss of appetite for work' and suggested he was 'taking a rest'.

In fact, Bradley had reached, at seven-and-a-half, a state not far removed from despair. He was automatically defensive towards anything that was put in front of him. He hated his existence, and made it bearable by switching off his expectations and avoiding situations that made him at all conspicuous in front of the others. Despite this, they still attacked him from time to time and called him 'Weed', a reference to his size and inadequacy at games.

His parents could only guess at this. They decided that the school was 'not a happy school', and much as they admired its record for getting scholarships to public schools, they seriously debated removing him. First, however, they engaged an educational psychologist to see Bradley and advise on his education.

This man was impressed by Bradley's IQ of 132 on Stanford-Binet, and a higher score on WISC. 'Yes,' he assured Bradley's parents, their boy was very intelligent and this was not limited to one or two specific talents. But emotionally, Bradley was behind his age group. Socially, he was very immature. (The psychologist got at this by showing some pictures of school scenes, starting a story about them and encouraging Bradley to comment on what was going on in his own words.) This made it very difficult to make friends, to avoid being bossy or critical in a way that invited reprisal. Other children, who were used to playing with others, to taking turns, to swapping toys, to keeping their boasts or their claims within a certain range, so as to impress but not antagonize each other, and who knew each other's lore, interests, catch-phrases and fears, these children soon rumbled Bradley as someone who was 'different'. An analogy is the comment made by more insular people, 'He has a very good accent, but you can tell he's not British.' 'Rather than change his school,' the psychologist summed up, 'I suggest you try to change his life style. . . .' He pointed out Bradley's worried look and his chewed nails (obviously not in his presence). His parents took most of this advice because they have a very genuine love for their son, which goes much further than his scholarship potential, and because they had been forcibly reminded of how much they had valued popularity when they had been at school.

You cannot undo a superiority complex in a few weeks. Nor can you buy back the years four, five and six, when getting a feeling for how to interact with others comes so easily. But you can try to make things better, and this Bradley's parents did. They sought out opportunities for him to meet and play with other children, of both sexes, both a bit older and a bit younger. Interestingly, it was the company of obliging ten-year-old children that he seemed to enjoy most. (This is sometimes the case with very intelligent children.) He has two good friends of his own age as well, now that he is nine. They form a group at school that is still at one side of the mainstream, but they are accepted as part of the scene, if a bit odd. Bradley also gained from finding a teacher who turned him on to geography in a big way. He has his enthusiasm back, is doing well, and is much happier and less nervous.

Rosemary

Rosemary had carrotty red hair and a charming smile. When she turned six, with her long legs and her confident look, she seemed a good bet to become a star actress in the future. Then a curious patch of sore skin appeared in the crook of her elbow. It received ointment, but failed to disappear. Further patches began to make tracks over her body, on her chest, on the insides of her thighs, under her arms and on her neck. With increasing alarm, her mother took Rosemary to the doctor and to the specialist in skin diseases at a nearby hospital. Tests revealed that these outbreaks of rash were not connected with any other physical condition from which she might be suffering. There were preparations which could contain the rash, and make it less uncomfortable and less unsightly, but they were unlikely to cure it completely. A child psychologist was asked in to talk to the mother and child, separately, and he confirmed the view that this was a psychosomatic ailment.

Rosemary's father had left home some months earlier. Her mother had been forced to find work and park her two children.

The onset of the rash coincided with a period during which Rosemary had been taken from one school to another, then to a relative's home, and was then shuttled among a sequence of acquaintances.

Skin problems in children are more often psychogenic (i.e. are symptoms of something wrong in the mind, rather than the body) than is commonly supposed. They are sometimes interpreted as appeals for attention or help. Accident-prone children, who are always burning themselves on stoves and coming in from the garden with bloody knees, are thought to fit into this category, too. What more dramatic than to show something raw and bleeding, to become the focal point of the family again?

In Rosemary's case, this kind of explanation seemed to fit well. She had lost those contacts which she valued above everything. Probing deeper, over a succession of visits, the psychologist suspected that within Rosemary lurked a terrible fear, that it was dislike of *her* that had driven her father away. The two had never been specially close, but his complete departure at a time in her life when a girl needs his approval was a profound shock. Her confusion came to the surface of her body as an alarm signal. A psychologist has to be very careful how to communicate his suspicions. Here, he simply talked about what might have been going on in her daughter's mind with Rosemary's mother, until she speculated on similar lines.

Then Rosemary was settled in with a friend of her mother's on an indefinite basis. At weekends, she saw her mother, who kept her younger child with her. She was treated as part of the family and was accepted. Once the regularity of this system became predictable and she became very fond of her foster-mother, the psychologist noticed at successive visits that Rosemary was much more like a normal child in her behaviour. That is, she talked about her interests; and while being regretful about not seeing her father, she could talk about her mother and seeing her mother, without getting anxious. Her understanding increased. Gradually her skin problems receded. They may not disappear altogether, but they look as if they may.

When a child 'produces' a symptom of this kind, anxiety about rejection by a parent, or guilt about something to do with a parent's illness or death, has often to be suspected. Other similar symptoms are legion. The reason for choice of a particular symptom is very often obscure, but sometimes it seems connected with what the child perceives is most likely to alarm or get sympathy *in his family*. Nobody knows exactly whether the psychosomatic problems tend to run through families for this reason, or because there is a physical predisposition handed down that makes one kind of reaction to stress more likely.

Asthma, allergies and migraine have been put into the psychosomatic category, but there are many arguments about these problems which are scarcely understood. *Some* allergies seem practically a straightforward physical equation. For example, whenever a particular child eats tomatoes, he is sick; therefore, simply keep tomatoes off his plate. But psychologists have pointed out that in many cases succumbing to allergies is strongest when there is the threat of attention-withdrawal, or fear of failure (e.g. asthma is often worse before exams).

If your child suffers from something of this kind, you must take obvious physical precautions and offer the right physical aids. There is no point whatever in worrying about the possibility of contributing to the problem through past neglect or anything like that. At the same time, it is always worth considering whether there may be certain factors in your child's mind (possibly with no reflection on yourself as a parent) which may be increasing the likelihood of his body making this kind of appeal.

Francis

Tall, strong and full of energy, Francis is the apple of his father's eye. His father is a prominent golfer, who glories in the fact that his son seems to be every inch an athlete. An early walker, an early runner, and able to leap to the ground from a height of four steps at the age of four, Francis seemed only to have one significant choice to make in his future life: which sport to enrich with his talent.

His mother found him to be 'quite a handful'. She declined, early on, to be 'a grass widow *and* a housewife as well', and employed a mother's help while she pursued her career. This did not protect her from having to deal with complaints about Francis's behaviour when at birthday parties or visiting other children's homes for the afternoon. For example:

'But I can't understand it. You're perfectly well behaved at home. Whatever happened?'
'Mr Gregory shouted at me, Mum.'

'Well, Mrs Gregory tells me he's sorry, but you'd pushed Tim Gregory into a cucumber frame and he's now in hospital.'
'Well . . . well . . . you see, Mum, we were having this game . . . .'

His mother told him off, but did not talk much about his less fortunate exploits. His father, who enjoyed the contrast between his virile son and the tameness of some of the others he saw on Sundays, would remark, in Francis's presence, 'Well, but Tim Gregory is such a little drip.'

When he was seven, Francis did not have quite the sports reputation his father wished, because although he was feared he was unpopular. This counted against him in team games. It was a black day when he had to admit at home that he was not in his class football team. Not long afterwards, two other children in his class noticed that he was transferring the contents of one mackintosh pocket into his own, in the school changing room. When one of them protested, Francis warned, 'I'll smash your face!' and thrust him hard against a wall. The other escaped and brought a teacher.

Francis's mother was confronted with a great deal at once. Many points about her son's behaviour, including his rudeness to teachers and his habit of distributing Kung Fu chops to boy and girl alike, were raised at the subsequent interview. The headteacher took the view that expulsion was an admission of failure with a young child, and that direct punishment relieved feelings and underlined school rules but did not guarantee the future. His staff, however, were beginning to protest that Francis was 'impossible' or 'needs a damn' good lesson'. When his mother told his father, with the comment, 'This is one for you, John, I can't cope with this', he was inclined to the latter view, too.

Francis is a boy who has not been greatly helped. He has undoubtedly suffered from not having much contact with his father, whose success at tournaments has taken him further and further from home. Neither parent has ever involved themselves to the point of making clear what kind of acts they believe to be right and wrong; they have contrived to give the impression that the other children are out there to be beaten—one way or another; they have never (so far as is known) expressed more than polite interest in the doings of any other children and have tended to criticize them; they have been at hand to note triumphs (mainly of the physical kind) and to come to the rescue when Francis has triggered off a social disaster, but they have not shared much ordinary life in between. The more they regarded him as a problem, the more he was inclined to interpret their lack of contact as a mark of disapproval.

Theft and aggression do not necessarily go together. But both are often a sign of being insufficiently understood or loved by a parent. The headmaster was right, in the sense that the cause has to be tackled, if the symptoms are not to recur. Meanwhile, other children have to be protected, and disapproval has to be registered so that *all* children learn what the rules are and feel they can rely on their teachers to prevent anarchy, in which the weakest will always lose.

Francis has been taken along to some golf tournaments, and his mother has organized outings with him and another child who was persuaded to join the party. She has, on the headmaster's advice, tried to talk more to Francis, especially about school and about the other children there. It helps, but it is obviously an effort. His parents pin their real hopes on getting him into X School, where they still respect athleticism as a good qualification for entry and where discipline is strict. 'That will sort him out all right,' they feel. It is not exactly like washing their hands, but clearly parenthood has taxed them more than they expected.

Francis is, in fact, likely to be pressed into a kind of conformity at public school, if he gets in; his aptitude for games and formal school work (which is fair) will be channelled. Very possibly, he will hate it at first and then enjoy it. But he may well fail to emerge as a normal human being, with human values, because by and large this is a family job. *Beneath* the conformity, what will there be?

Children who perceive, consistently, that their parents are interested in and benevolent towards others; that they have respect for each other's, their child's and other people's stronger wishes, and for their possessions; and that they have a social code, whereby some things are clearly wrong; these have a framework that makes aggression beyond a certain point, and stealing, much less likely. If those children also feel that they can count on being talked to and listened to regularly, without triumphs being expected of them, then the chances of aggression and stealing practically fade altogether.

In the meantime, it may help to note that an aggressive child can be helped towards more mature behaviour by being presented with a playmate of the opposite sex or by being asked to play with a younger child. The latter needs an effort of will, but for short periods it can do a lot of good. Be wary of situations, on the other hand, where he is left to cope by himself with two or more children of the same other family; they tend to gang up for protection and confirm his outlook, even if they win.

The last thing I want to do is to suggest that every mother who takes up a career is putting the health and development of her young child at risk. She may *have* to do this. She may *need* to do this, in the sense that if she does not she feels frustration and failure, and (at least subconsciously) blames her child, who then suffers most. Nor am I prejudiced against all itinerant golfers. The point of the last case history is that these behaviour patterns on the part of the parents were symptomatic of their basic lack of concern, and probably lack of confidence, in their position as parents. Nor did they devote much of their thought to their child *as a child*, who needs loving and helping.

There are many kinds of problem which have not been analysed here. Some are obvious and straightforward; e.g. a child has a sore throat and catarrh, followed by a rash and a temperature, a doctor is called and the diagnosis may be measles. Measles runs its course, and although the child may be held up in his schoolwork for a while and feel sorry for himself, recovery is usually quick and complete. Some are problems which only affect a minority, whereas Marie, Bradley, Rosemary and Francis represent difficulties that recur (sometimes not on the same scale or over the same time period) among many families.

Here are what a number of doctors and paediatricians believe are situations where parents' judgment is inclined to be mistaken, which leads to problems. Those I interviewed maintain that mothers of children in this age group are usually very good barometers of when the moment demands medical attention and help. Mothers can sense, much more easily than doctors, when a child is not reacting *quite* as he is used to behave. But here is where they may make mistakes:

(a) **Eyesight** With some children, shortsightedness gets worse after five, and help and understanding is required. They are active, and they are able to compensate for not being able to see more than a blur in the middle distance. Because they act normally, parents may not notice the problem until it is advanced, and causing problems at school. Whether it is picked up at school or not depends on the teacher, the size of classes and the regularity of testing by a doctor. Regular check-ups are the answer.

The same comments apply to hearing.

(b) **Convalescence** Sometimes 'Can I get up now?' is taken as a sign that a child has recovered fully. It means that he is recovering. There should be a period of pottering around before the imposition of the full routine. Otherwise, they feel worse and a relapse robs the child of more school-time than would have been the case. A child neither knows his own weakness, nor his own strength. 'Do you feel well enough to go to the party?' must get the answer 'Yes'.

(c) **After a sprain or a fracture** This is a similar point to (b). It is very hard to follow an active child around to make sure he does not overtax a limb or a joint that has suffered from an accident. But long-term weakening or distortion must be guarded against, and appointments for check-ups to make sure all is well should *not* be missed.

(d) **Teeth** When dentists pronounce that a lot of remedial work has to be done, parents are often taken aback. Surely, they reckon, they taught their child long ago to brush his teeth regularly. What went wrong? Lack of check-ups, most likely, plus midnight toffee feasts. (But see Chapter five for an analysis of what action *can* be taken.)

Chapter ten

Towards seven and eight

Much of the change apparent in six-year-olds moving towards the age of seven and eight is a matter of degree, rather than the emergence of completely new features. This will not be the case so much with a late developer, when many new achievements may seem to appear at once. But for most children, it is a question of building on what has already been started. Physically, they gain mastery over tasks they were beginning to understand at six. Thus, they run faster; they catch balls thrown at more difficult angles; the bicycle becomes easier to turn, to stop and to pedal at speed; if they have begun swimming or ski-ing, those sports become easier too. On the social side, they have started school and are now in the business of making the most of it. They examine the possibilities of new friendships within the class or in the neighbourhood, using for the most part the repertory of approaches that they have acquired, varying enthusiasm with caution as they see fit. A new brother or sister, of course, may interrupt their view of home, at any time; but if they have got used to living with one, they are by now in an easier relationship with them, looking for opportunities to have fun together, rather than ways of circumventing the opposition that prevents their being the favourite child. Emotionally, they are likely to have benefited from the rough-and-tumble of school and the administration of objective justice by teachers, so that they are more capable of accepting that there are times when they lose as well as win and give way as well as seize. They have learnt compensations for not getting what they want: they can change the subject, make up a joke, adopt the 'sour grapes' pose and wait for Fortune to turn her wheel. In all these developments, then, they are drawing heavily on the past.

Yet some developments are certainly dramatic and may be taken to be different in character from what has preceded. When six-year-olds linger hopefully on the edge of a hopscotch court and they are at last invited to take part, with some condescension, they do not usually hold the serious game up for long—unless, that is, they cry and demand a second turn. But a game between those of seven and eight is not nearly so predictable. Part of this stride forward may be put down to specific practice at the game itself. It is an interesting game, though, in that it brings together a number of skills that are typically the mark of a seven-year-old. These include:

(a) Hopping for a length of time on one leg.
(b) Hopping with control over direction.
(c) Balancing on one foot and grasping a small object.
(d) Throwing accurately, as opposed to hard, or simply to getting the direction right.
(e) Counting forwards *and* backwards with ease.

Also (in *some* games):

(f) Pursuing a complex competitive task single-mindedly, without being distracted by catcalls, false advice, attempts to make one laugh, etc.

Hopping demands strong leg muscles, an advanced sense of balance and what might be called 'eye-and-foot co-ordination', when it is directional. This is the difference between the accuracy demanded for the game and a short succession of hops in the form of staggers, that a child can manage at four or five. An accurate throw at hopscotch involves judgment of weight and of the kind of bounce afforded by the surface, as well as close co-operation between eye and hand. An intricate balancing act depends on the brain's ability to translate a wide range of minute signals, each indicating varying degrees of tension in each part of the body, into the right series of corrective movements that will make an unusual disposition of the limbs in space consistent with gravity. Although even two- or three-year-olds can be taught to repeat numbers parrot-fashion, counting as such does not mean a great deal to them. They cannot be said to have command over numbers. But a seven-year-old has grasped the *idea* of the cumulative sequence 1, 2, . . ., 12, and can count backwards as well as forwards, subtractively as well as additively. He needs this automatically at hopscotch, both when he reaches the 12 and has to return, and when he has to miss squares already occupied by others, on the outward or the inward passage.

Young children are very suggestible, particularly when they are allowed into an older children's game on sufferance. If they start doing well, they may be shouted at 'That's not the way to do it!' They lose concentration, put both feet on the ground, and demand, 'Why?' The older ones laugh, tell the younger one how easy he is to trick and continue with their turns. Cruel and unscrupulous to a sensitive onlooker, but not a bad warning about much that happens in life. This may be partly why there is a long-standing tradition in many areas of trying to distract other players at hopscotch in all kinds of ways. A seven-year-old has more assurance about what he is doing and is much harder to put off. He has become more goal-minded and less keen on participation for its own sake; and at the same time he is more confident about his position among the children he plays with. All these are more likely to be characteristic of a seven-year-old, although those who have fewer chances of playing freely with other children may go through until eight or nine before this is a fair description of them.

Next time you pass a game of hopscotch, stop and watch. It is a wonderful catalyst and demonstrates an enormous amount about children's physical and social development.

The brain itself plays a crucial role in even the apparently physical accomplishments of a successful hopscotch-player. Two processes have already been described in *How Children Grow, Book 1*: maturation, whereby the central nervous system (CNS) has to grow a certain length of *time* before it is capable of organizing more complex functions, and the growth of the brain after birth. At seven and eight, the last ninth or tenth of the brain is filling out, until it reaches what is nearly adult brain weight. 'Maturation' is a description of the process whereby the parts of the CNS gradually become ready, as they grow, for more superior and more precise functions. These include brain-controlled physical actions, such as picking up a shoe while balancing on one leg, just as much as making selective use of the items stored in the memory to see how a new problem might be solved.

Some boys will not be seen dead with a skipping rope. This is unfortunate, because it is a very instructive exercise for learning control of one's body in space and in different rhythms, as well as being enjoyable. But at seven, distinctions between what a boy and what a girl might do are beginning to prove too strong. Whether boys indulge in hopscotch varies by region or neighbourhood. Whether girls join in football games is locally determined, too.

But skipping often involves singing and dancing, and these are beginning to be suspect for many boys at this age. Girls, therefore, have to be relied on for showing one very significant advance—the change-over from a few energetic twists and leaps to a relaxed, authoritative use of the skipping rope, varying pace and style according to whim. It doesn't happen overnight, but once a child gets a craze for it, she perseveres doggedly and gets it much better, and it may seem as if it was just a knack that had to be acquired in one stage, like blowing one's nose.

Skipping develops a sense of what sort of body you have and what you can do with it. This is not tangible knowledge. But it is very much in evidence in the movements of any child who goes on to be good at a particular sport or any pursuit, such as dancing, which demands confident marshalling of all the body's resources if a high class of performance is going to be reached.

Swimming is another activity of this kind; it increases self-awareness, as well as being a useful, pleasurable end in itself and having the lure of a sport for some. Other such activities for both sexes are gradually becoming attractive. These include judo and yoga. Children of seven and eight can gain a lot from both of these. They help give confidence, because even those children who are relatively poorly co-ordinated and are clumsier than others can achieve *something*, from which they can learn and get satisfaction. They are open-ended activities; the expert still has a lot that he can explore, while, at the other extreme, there are some positions that a mildly spastic child can slowly master and feel the better for it. Judo and yoga are also partly competitive, but rivalry is or should be kept within bounds, and there is none of the fierce recrimination that sets the primary school's football pitch ablaze. Any parent who feels that his child is falling behind others in his physical development or is being disregarded at football or yard games demanding strength and fast running might well consider finding a judo class or a yoga group, to see if he takes to either. Both are easier to start when young, but must be properly taught. A seven-year-old may master a lotus position in one afternoon; an adolescent will take much longer. Part of the problem experienced by children who do not shine in the playground or the sports field, and who start to *believe* that they are less good at running, jumping or playing with a ball than others, is that they are intimidated by the moral strength and presumption of those who are by nature more eager rivals and are put off by the noise and bustle. Such children will prefer yoga and judo, and swimming and diving classes too, for the fact that the pace is controlled.

Even so, some children are simply not going to be athletes. They do not want to be. They can be tempted to run around a bit and go for walks, but they demonstrably prefer other things. There is no point in trying to insist on enthusiasm; that may be mirroring the kind of pressure they get at PE or during games periods at school. If father and mother do something physically active *themselves*, their children's interest is likely to move in the same direction. But it is important for a parent to distinguish whether 'I just don't like football (or netball)' means an active dislike of participating in games or sports, *or* 'I wish I were good at football (or netball), or something I could do well at and enjoy'. Try to find some substitutes, but do not force him to adopt a substitute.

Football is the *lingua franca* of children, linking nationalities, races, social class groups and (often) the sexes—at least until puberty. Watching seven- and eight-year-olds at the game, however, shows that they are much more mature for it physically than they are emotionally. There is a vital need to win and to distinguish oneself personally, that affects most little boys. 'It's only a game' has to be said to them, but is extremely difficult for them to believe. Every match on television is dominated by anxiety to win. Every encounter with an opposite number on the pitch is a duel. Every goal scored is a victory. When brothers play against each other on a makeshift pitch, with two sweaters for the goal, all their feelings of rivalry bubble up to the surface. They depend utterly on somebody else deciding what constitutes a 'foul', because they have none of the control necessary to be objective with each other. A seven-year-old player can be all eagerness one moment, positioning himself in the goal for the shot that another is going to take. Then he fails to stop the goal and hurls himself on the ground, saying 'Too high! Too close! Not fair! We're not counting that!' Then, equally suddenly, he gets up, rushes after the ball, shouting 'You're in goal now!' behind him, as he prepares to even the score.

This era during which parents shudder at their children's reactions to being worsted is vivid but short. They firmly believe that they have spawned the most unsportsmanlike creatures ever to howl 'I'm going to take my ball away now, and I'm never going to play again!', but, if they look around, they will see most young children doing the same. While they are eight, usually, a change in attitude sets in. They gulp down disappointment more easily; they take more pleasure in laying on passes so that others may score; and they apply a longer time-scale, enabling them to accept one reverse more equably, hoping to make it up later. Part of this comes from sheer experience of football, part is due to the fact that at eight there is a beginning in the understanding of other people's points of view.

The young child, as mentioned before, sees one world—his own. This is no longer entirely true of the eight-year-old. Gradually, he begins to pay more attention to what others think about a situation, to what those others are feeling and how those others will respond to him in different circumstances. He can distinguish several separate moods in other people's manner and in their facial expressions. This helps him to plan how he deals with them more carefully. A warning look means something different from simply stopping to smile.

Other people's motives are still rather difficult for him to disentangle from what they actually do. In the playground, he will be suspicious of a child he knows to be unfriendly, when approached and asked to let him see the compass he is showing round. If he is proud of his compass, he is caught in two minds. He wants to increase his prestige in the playground and feels that the request is reasonable; at the same time, he has known this other child to push him out of the way, and feels that he might disparage the compass, spoil it or run away with it. It is often amusing to watch children of this age showing things to each other, but clutching them tight, so that they may actually provoke the consequence they are trying to prevent. In this situation, they are reasonably accurate at sensing motives—when the motive and the act are likely to merge into one. But they have not, as a rule, any great insight into situations where the motive and the act diverge; for example, when a child has been teased and lashes out, despite wanting to play, or when somebody tries to help but succeeds in doing the opposite.

This implies that for the most part they cannot conceive of problems that might follow if they accept a stranger's offer of sweets or an invitation to go for a ride in his car. As seven- and eight-year-olds are given more freedom in making short journeys by themselves, they need reminding of the important rule that approaches from strangers are to be ignored or avoided. A direct and uncompromising rule must, unfortunately, be given to them: they are not ready to apply what we call 'judgment' to each individual in each situation. This is unfortunate, because it inhibits natural curiosity, but the possible results of *not* having such a rule make it vital.

Most six-year-olds are able to take off and put on again most of their clothes. This has a lot to do with living in the twentieth century. They often run into problems with buttons, however, and half of them cannot do up shoe-laces with a bow. Small finicky tasks for the fingers are a question of skill, at which children vary greatly. Temperament comes into it, as well as better or poorer co-ordination. Pressure, in the form of 'For God's sake get a move on—I've shown you how to do it!' or of the teacher drawing comparisons between the skilful and the rest, can hold up progress not *only* at tying up shoes but at any other activities that demand similar application. When they are seven, and sometimes eight, most of these problems in self-care disappear.

Table 3 shows the order in which most children master each of the tricks involved. Quite a few children will be slower, and they are by no means retarded. Perhaps the commonest reason for being slow is being confronted with impatience, and a mother who cannot resist saying 'Here! Give it to me' in a tone which sounds ironic but can disguise pleasure that he still needs his mother. Children in this situation find it easier to give up than to learn.

Even when a child can cope with his own teeth, hair and bath-time, it does not follow that he will perform each task well or with alacrity. It is worth remembering that those who seem, perversely, to be doing everything extremely slowly may be enjoying the fact that they are being independent, and therefore spin it out. As with many tasks, it usually pays to compliment a child on how he is succeeding at them and to slip in the encouragement to improve it, rather than correct him. For example, 'That's a good bit of brushing! Yes, indeed, right round the back, too . . .' rather than 'What a feeble effort! Can't you stretch right round inside?' A child will *obey* the latter, but he won't when you are not there. If he hears the former often enough, there is a better chance that he will incorporate correct brushing into his own way of doing things.

Notwithstanding this, it pays to be fairly natural with a seven- or eight-year-old, because he is now much sharper at detecting changes in your manner and ways of speaking. Strangers can

Table 3 Caring for themselves

Age at which children can do it

	One child in four		One child in two		Three children in four	
	(Years	Months)	(Years	Months)	(Years	Months)
Doing up easy buttons	2	9	3	1	3	10
Undressing	3	6	4	2	5	0
Dressing	3	11	4	7	5	8
Doing up shoe-buckles	3	11	4	7	5	8
Putting on Wellington boots (and removing)	5	6	6	3	7	0
Doing up shoe-laces	5	8	6	4	7	6
Putting on tie (and removing)	5	9	6	6	7	8
Doing up all buttons, toggles, etc.	5	9	6	7	7	10
Washing hands, face	3	5	4	6	5	6
Brushing teeth	4	2	5	1	5	9
Combing and tidying hair	4	4	6	0	7	2
Washing oneself completely in the bath	4	8	5	10	6	5

Notes
1 The categories 'Undressing' and 'Dressing' exclude hard buttons, shoe-laces, etc
2 The hair figures are influenced by hair type and style.

puzzle him, but he will be much more suspicious of anything phoney about you than he might have been before.

There are some standard achievements at seven which rarely fail to make a parent pleased. One is being able to write, not just his name, but a line or two on a post-card. Many primary schools have some kind of 'diary' system, in which children put down something that impressed them the previous day. Some need more help than others, obviously, and some are more ambitious than 'I got up. It was rening [*sic*]', which I remember my own daughter once producing as a record of the weekend. But parents do not often see these first attempts at authorship, except on open days. One painless and happy way of encouraging output without getting into the way of the teacher is to suggest that you write each other post-cards. It doesn't matter that you are not away from home or from each other. Receiving post-cards and seeing a mother or father enjoying what they have sent is a delight that few children can resist. Postage costs can mount up if it develops into a craze, but the added interest in reading (if you print carefully) and writing must outweigh them. Alternatively, you can leave each other messages round the house. 'You will find an apple under the bedroom table', etc., can do wonders to reading comprehension. It probably won't be replicated at school, either. For children who, for one reason or another, are backward at reading and writing, or to include younger brothers and sisters in the game, you can do both these things just using pictures. They will enjoy it and have a sense of written communication, too.

A seven-year-old may be a good reader. An eight-year-old has a strong probability of being a good reader. But there is about one child in four who, at the age of eight, must still be judged to be a long way off. Much research on children who are 'dyslectic' (literally = 'bad reader') shows that each has a rather different problem which is holding him up, although there are similarities between sub-groups. This is to emphasize that a child who is slow in this skill needs help, rather than a vague hope that he may catch up with the rest of the class. Perhaps the best evidence on this was produced by Clark, who studied 1,900 children progressively, from 1966 to 1969. When they were aged seven, about one in seven still needed help with simple reading. At eight, it was about one in seventeen. More boys needed help than girls.

Reading problems must be taken up with his school. Also, since part of his problem may be an emotional one, it is important not to radiate anxiety in his presence. Parents may (but not necessarily) need to come to terms with the fact that their child's education will be best if it is different from the academic idea of early mastery of letters. He may need encouragement about other things, instead of feeling despondent that the world of learning begins and ends with books. Later, he might reach a reading and

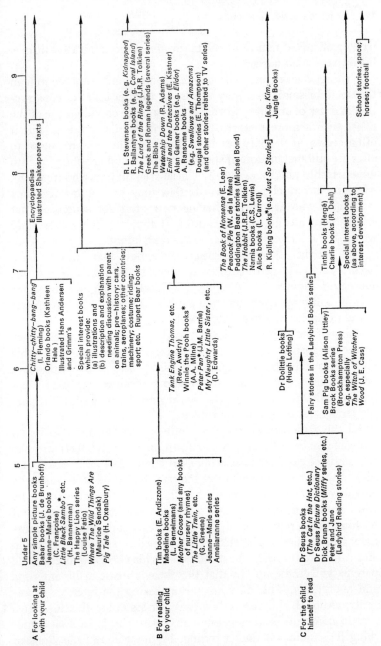

Figure 5 Stories and books for different ages

Note
Books have been listed in three categories: looking at with a child, reading to a child or being read by a child. Of course, the categories *and* the ages overlap, but this arbitrary grouping might help suggest what to move on to. The list is not exhaustive, but most popular types of book are included. Some publishers indicate the suggested age-group for their books. An asterisk (*) is by some books or authors who have been criticized on social grounds. Individual parents must decide about them.

writing standard that is adequate for *him*, although it may dismay his degree-laden parents.

Writing at seven and eight should be more and more accurate in the detail of small, everyday words; in a better sense of construction and use of auxiliary words; and in a more confident use of the page, with a more mature spread of his words across it. But it often seems to primary teachers that the children with more to offer are still making lots of spelling mistakes and are plunging into impenetrable jungles of words. These are children who innovate, who are introducing new words that they hear into what they write and who are always having new ideas for sentences that excite them but get out of control. If they are being constantly worried and driven into safe, neat constructions, they lose a lot of the delight of communication. Somehow there has to be a balance between getting them to want to be accurate and encouraging experiment. A child who really has got a taste for writing will most likely be showing it at this stage. It will appear in the words he uses to speak, as well as to write.

Many of the activities enjoyed together by parents and child are becoming suspect to this age bracket. It is unfortunate if this includes reading books together at night-time, because this is a powerful stimulant to interest in reading, writing, extending vocabulary and thinking about the world outside, as well as keeping the family ties close but enjoyable.

All the same, under the twin influence of the need to be an independent person and to conform to what he feels are the standards of his friends at school, an eight-year-old in particular revises what he will or will not tolerate. Bed-time stories may be cursorily dismissed as beneath his dignity. In the same spirit, he will feel embarrassment at being seen having his hair brushed off his forehead in public, or anything but the most discreet announcement being made of the state of his nostrils. '*Tell* me what to do and I'll see to it *myself*', he mutters, with his cheeks on fire. Astute parents will 'trade up', so that they keep abreast of his interests and his dignity. This does not mean sharing the interests necessarily, although this helps. It means not assuming that his tastes remain constant, or that because it is *you* who is reading something he should not find it boring. Figure 5 shows the kinds of books that usually have appeal at seven and eight, and how different they are from what goes before and what follows. However, it should be remembered that:

(a) While most five- and six-year-olds enjoy the same books, with a few differences between them, the individual differences in interest of those of seven and eight are much greater.

(b) The ideas of girls and boys of what makes an interesting story are now drifting a good deal further apart.

More physical involvement is demanded by these children now, too. Wasn't it convenient when they had tea, played for an hour, had a bath, had a reading and were tucked up quickly in bed? Now, between school and bed, mother and father find a human dynamo on their hands, just when they feel they need a quiet evening. In flats or when it rains, the problem is greater. The answer does not lie in heavy homework—this is too young to be programmed into a learning regime right through the day, whatever certain prep schools say. The same applies to heavy doses of television. Nor should it be solved by simply letting children run round out of doors in each other's company. Some of this unfettered play with friends is vital, but it is a matter of degree. It is all too easy to leave a child to take his energy outside, whenever it is inconvenient. But that is rather like running a hotel, not a home.

It is not easy finding the time or the energy to play football or hide-and-seek, or go for a walk even, after a full day's work. But there are many activities available which can partly involve the parents—from going swimming, to badminton clubs, cubs and brownie packs, charity work, music-making or hobbies like woodwork, painting or jewellery. There are jobs which children enjoy, too, provided they are not called 'chores' and the children are given increasing responsibility and encouragement. Cooking and gardening are examples.

An eight-year-old is already a marvellous companion. Somewhere he has lost a lot of the self-centredness that made his outlook less companionable when he was younger. He is more likely to have a particular friend, at school or near home. Now he is often curious about how his father manages for food when out at work during the day. He observes the good and bad times for making demands on his parents—not always accurately, but he watches for them, and is sympathetic and tries to help. He has enormous curiosity about all kinds of things and is easily stimulated to a new craze. Eight is a wonderful, open time of life, and doing things or simply talking a lot with a child of this age brings enormous rewards.

Chapter eleven

Eight years old and proud of it

It is often exasperating for parents of an eight-year-old to watch him change in a few short moments from an intelligent, sensible and assured character into someone who behaves in a way that they thought they had said good-bye to, a year or so before. They wonder if it is just *their* child who happens to be like this. Well, it isn't.

At eight years of age, no child is a complete miniature adult, unless he has been forced to suppress many of his natural instincts and to lose a great deal of his will power. In the past, breaking a child's will power, so that he was completely obedient, was regarded as an important feature of his education. John Wesley implored parents, from the pulpit, to do precisely that—'and your children will come to bless you for it'. But even in a thoroughly progressive household, in which parents attempt to stimulate a gradual acquisition of human values in an atmosphere of enjoyment and give-and-take, there is no reason why sensible children should not revert to a less civilized state from time to time.

Some things that an eight-year-old needs to do help to explain this. He needs to be an individual—which means not accepting *all* that his parents believe in culturally, educationally or morally. He needs to make his own mistakes—not in everything, just in some things. He has started to get glimpses of the world beyond his family, which intrigue him; other children do this, other families do that, and they talk about different things that they have seen and know about. Why *they* and not *him*?

He is making comparisons between what he sees of other families and his own. These comparisons, together with stories that he hears or reads about children being in a sad way and then rescued from misfortune, exercise his imagination. Particularly when he is prevented by his parents from joining in something

126

that he believes all his friends are doing (e.g. 'Well, I don't care who else is going, *you're* not going by yourself into the football stadium because it's too dangerous'), his imagination elaborates an alternative world which bills him as the hero of a kind of melodrama in a sentimental story. The details vary, according to what he has been reading or seeing on television. But some themes recur regularly.

One is the feeling that magic of some kind is, or might be, available to him. The idea of learning to fly seems a very real possibility. Becoming invisible or increasing one's size and strength by finding an elixir or a pattern of secret words, also enrich these children's fantasies. Some point out that these are all symbolic, in one way or another, of stages in the discovery of everything to do with the penis (owning it, in boys; lacking it, in girls), and with pleasure in stimulating the sexual organs, together with the knowledge that this is not encouraged in public and, possibly, in front of the family. But at another level they are all to do with ways of transcending the environment and of getting their own way to do the exciting things they know of, but are prevented, by age, circumstance or parental authority, from trying.

Another recurrent theme is that of the changeling. This is a fantasy that takes several forms, but adds up to a sense of being in the wrong family by accident. All problems are surmounted, provided the right family is found. Sometimes this involves removing the parent of the same sex—that is the one who is seen to be standing more in a child's way. Circumstances vary, but typically girls feel a need to outwit or remove their mothers, boys their fathers. Escape may be necessary, too; here bicycles may be invoked, or horses, or cars—whatever means that the child feels he is acquiring mastery over, or could, if he had the chance.

These fantasies sometimes inspire guilt in children (depending very much on how rigidly law and order is controlled in the household), but most of the time they provide a safety valve for coming to terms with frustration. Apart from this, they show what sort of frustrations a child feels. Every so often, he feels the need to shift from the situation of being responsible for his actions, from 'being a big boy now', and accepting the balance of power in the family. How pleasant it is, then, to go back a few years, to a time when being baby-like and irresponsible was accepted as reasonable for him at his age. One of the ways, after all, of avoiding the difficulties of life is to treat them as if they do not exist. Eight-year-olds

5*

occasionally can be seen forming little groups of 'babies', talking
to each other in baby language and imitating (often rather ineptly)
a toddler's behaviour. This regression can take less amusing forms
than a game when a child starts to whine and cry, and to complain
that nobody loves him or is fair to him.

Situations of excitement make great demands on the limited
sophistication in adult ways that an eight-year-old has. Games in
which their pride is at stake are a typical example. Eight is a
wonderful age to play 'Monopoly', for instance. The board, the
property and the money are all magic. But however much a child
is reminded at the start that everyone is friends and that this is
only a game, not to be taken seriously, his identification with the
token he is manœuvring round the board stimulates an enormous
lump in the throat when it is clear the game is being lost, and
makes it impossible not to argue tearfully and passionately when
something in the rules is ambiguous.

Getting lost, metaphorically, in an activity is another way the
eight-year-old has of avoiding difficulties. It might be called an
escape, but part of it is usually a need to be doing what the others
are doing. Fashions change fast at eight. One week, nobody in the
school playground is playing with marbles; the next week, everybody is. The same applies to the television programme that gets
discussed; the brand of sweets or chocolates that is most favoured;
and the need to possess a stamp collection, posters, guns, gramo-
phone records of a teeny-bopper idol or conkers. Being left behind
in a craze is tantamount, in a way, to unpopularity, because it
makes you an outsider. As more and more children at school
(especially the girls, but the boys also) start to have close liaisons
with particular friends, so unpopularity, whether real or imagined,
becomes a source of anxiety.

Very often, difficult behaviour at home, with regression and
tears interrupting the happy flow of communication between
parents and child, can be followed back to some difficulty at
adjusting with other children. The reverse is of course true as well,
and it is far worse for a child to be working out his home problems on unfortunate contacts in the playground. It is not easy for
a parent to help here, since he does not know exactly what goes
on and how far the unpopularity is substantiated. Teachers know
more about the facts and it is always worth discussing with them
which of the other children might be invited round for a visit or
two, to encourage friendship. The teacher may well have observed

which children have complementary interests, but of course he may not be accurate in identifying potential soulmates. Some trial-and-error may be needed before getting the right chemistry.

Parents sometimes expect too much consistency in an eight-year-old's friendships, alliances and dislikes. That *nice* little girl with whom your daughter played so charmingly in that *nice* family's garden that afternoon—how can your daughter now say she doesn't want to see her again? Any number of things might have happened to sour the relationship—jealousy over school work, or teacher interest, or saying something too sharply to each other and having a fight. Children have their own criteria, which are often mysterious to adults. One eight-year-old girl who invariably pulled another's pigtails at school, called her names and tried to range the others against her (although by nature a peaceable girl, not given to aggression) gave this explanation of her hatred: 'She sniffs so horribly.' Parents must accept that much of these, like their own relationships, are irrational. Eight-year-olds also admire, and even love, others, mainly older children, who may be superficially unpleasant to them, 'Because she rides so well', 'Because she's—well—because she's Monica!', etc.

Some children at this age fascinate others because they seem to be free from the rules that make life irksome. The wild one, who turns up at a party, refuses to treat any of the games seriously and invents a few of his own that break the local rules and seem to defy the authority of the adults, is a well-known phenomenon. He may be what is called 'hyperactive', moving with great energy from one interest to another, without getting a great deal out of any particular one, and seemingly unable to settle down to co-operate with anyone, or to accept help or instruction. But he has a great need of attention, hyperactive or not, and he delights in his own distraction value and in any anxiety evident among parents who try to re-impose control or a sense of direction on the party. Teachers know him well, for obvious reasons. Other children often adopt a double standard towards him: they laugh and copy what he does, because his spirit is infectious, but after he has gone home they join in the collective view that he is 'silly' or even that he 'spoilt the whole party'.

It is worth while noting, when you meet this kind of irrepressible extravert, that there, but for a difference in temperament and for his confidence in his place in your family, goes your own child. He, too, had his hyperactive moments at three or four. When children continue to be like this at eight, there is some evidence that suggests that they may well have been born prematurely, with some anoxia (lack of oxygen) at birth. They do *not* necessarily come from 'homes with no discipline'. Emotional problems may prolong their condition, but it seems often like a question of delayed maturation. Nor is the same child hyperactive in all circumstances.

When told that their child has been very unhappy or has provoked a scene, committing this or that social crime, parents are often very surprised. This is partly because children can be very different at home and away, unleashing all their tensions in a place and before an audience, when they feel it is safe. But parents' blindness to it is partly due to the practice of saying, 'It's been so nice having Edgar with us this afternoon; I do hope he can come again soon', irrespective of whether Edgar has behaved like a cherub or a fiend from hell. Some feel that politeness demands it, but it is not really fair on Edgar's mother to let her suppose all is well if all isn't well. Better to say, 'Well, we've had our problems, but I think we got through them and I hope he comes again.' Most mothers will accept the bait and ask what the problems were.

If your child has got social difficulties of this kind, it is not usually productive of better behaviour to issue dire warnings of what will happen if you hear of anything like it again. Many parents have tried 'They'll never ask you back again!', 'Everyone will know what an awful visitor you are!' and, more subtly, 'None of your friends will like you if you do that!' The point is that the child is trying to break loose, to behave in a way he cannot manage at home and to release feelings he is not able to express in his normal life. Try to attack the cause, rather than the symptom. Of course you must say, 'I don't like the way you were rude to Mrs Barker' or 'I was shocked that you hit that little girl'. But ask yourself, too, whether he has enough chances to let off steam at home, with his parents. Is he getting the worst of the bargain when choices are made between him and his brothers or sisters? Is everything so neat, tidy, quiet and regimented, that his energy gets dammed up? Are the pressures on him—to behave impeccably at home and to work hard at school—so strong that he is building up frustrations and a feeling that he has got to impose his individuality by force, if necessary?

It helps enormously if you can talk about such incidents with him *without* putting it in an emotional context, so that he just

hangs his head and nods meekly when you radiate indignation.
Talking freely and reaching a good-humoured agreement that he
had overstepped the mark, and that it might be a friendly gesture
to take some flowers from the garden across to Mrs Barker next
day, offers him a positive way out. Varying behaviour is much
easier than simply blocking out behaviour and putting nothing
in its place.

As an aid to feeling he is accepted by others of his age, groups
and organizations can be helpful. Some children are by nature
more in sympathy with loosely formed, informal groups. Others
prefer seeing an adult in charge and having a firm lead, and a safe,
reassuring framework within which to make contact with other
children. These can help, sometimes more than school, by increasing contact across social class brackets. But no child can be
made to like cubs or brownies, just because his parents did. The
ritual of these organizations means a great deal at eight. Parents
who laugh at it destroy the magic very quickly—often it cannot
stand up to strong light—and they can hardly be surprised if their
children then claim it is all beneath their dignity.

Listening to eight-year-olds talking to each other is fascinating,
because of the clarity with which different personalities distinguish
themselves and because of the rich mixture of near-adult phrases
and postures, on the one hand, and very simple child-like emo-
tionality, on the other. The following was a discussion between
Larry, Kevin, Prue and Sally, waiting outside their classroom
between lessons. Larry was just nine, the others eight. Sometimes
they were talking each to all, sometimes one to one, sometimes (to
use the Piaget term) there was just 'collective monologue'. Sometimes they were communicating or asking questions; sometimes
what they said seemed simply to be a kind of challenge or an
assertion about themselves.

Kevin (to Larry): 'Then he came out of the bushes, from behind, and
　　　 chopped this other man down—like this!' (Demonstrates with
　　　 side of hand; Larry feints.)
Larry: 'But he was a soldier. He must have had a gun.'
Kevin: 'He couldn't use his gun, because he was chopped, you see.
　　　 And he fell down—just like this....' (Pretends to fall,
　　　 deliberately bumping into the girls.)
Prue: 'Oh, Kevin! Can't you even stand up straight?' (They all laugh.)
Larry: 'What's that you've got, Sally?' (He tugs at a scrapbook she is
　　　 carrying.)

Sally: 'It couldn't interest you. It's about a horse.' (She won't let it go.)

Kevin: 'Oh no! Not *horses*!'

Prue: 'Sally's got the most super pictures of this horse she met on holiday. But she won't show *you*! He's black and he's white and he must be super to ride, mustn't he, Sally?'

Sally (solemnly, as if repeating a litany): 'Actually Augusta is a skewbald Connemara mare, fifteen hands high, and she—she goes like the wind.'

Kevin: 'Ha, ha! Which wind? The East wind or the West wind?'

Sally: 'You wouldn't understand, Kevin.'

Larry: 'Can I see your book, Sally?'

Prue: 'No, you can't understand either, can he, Sally?'

Kevin (mock Chinese accent): 'Me the King of Kung Fu! Me give you the death kick.' (He aims a blow with his foot at the wall between Larry and Sally, who ignore him.)

Sally: 'You can see the cover if you like.'

Prue: 'Oh! Isn't he a *lovely* horse!'

Sally: 'She!'

Larry: 'I like your horse. I've got a scrapbook at home. I'm going to bring mine in one day. It's got all the different machines in it you can get on a farm. I've got pictures of tractors and balers and seed drills and a walking drag-line....'

Prue: 'That sounds *horrible*!'

These are four very different personalities, each reflecting in one way or another the outlook of an eight-year-old. Sally has become entirely dedicated to studying horses and has had the advantage of some riding lessons. This makes her very self-sufficient, and she attracts some attention and admiration. She in turn gives attention and admiration to older girls at the stables. She has a good vocabulary and has acquired a complex conversational code. The degree of her commitment to horses is intense: she draws them, works about them, begs to own one, watches any television programmes that feature them, imitates them when running, and has long fantasies in which she escapes on a horse, or captures one and brings him home. Her fantasies have heavy romantic overtones, sometimes. She seems to work out the problems she meets through conflicts of will by means of control over this animal who is very real, but magic, too, in his associations with power, speed and a lovely partnership. Sometimes she is a bit lost to the others around her, and thus loses some of the contact and the popularity she might otherwise enjoy. She is very precise and corrects others—traits which are faithfully copied from home, but which are not always appreciated.

Prue is very dependent on the company of others. She sometimes tries to ferret into their souls and remain as close to them as she can. Her attempts at a close friendship with Sally tend to misfire, because admiration is not enough. She lacks genuine horse love and considers the scrapbook as a means to sharing a secret or a game that the others cannot join in. Friendship to her means an alliance. At home, she has a brother and a sister, and feels the need to reappraise and reform alliances fairly often. Being the odd sister out is what she cannot endure. Sally is not at a stage to reciprocate friendship, as opposed to acquaintance, but Prue cannot see this. Prue's command of language is less impressive than Sally's. She has not got any deep interests and is generally more pleased with things which sweep her up and entertain *her*, than with things she has to work at herself. She prefers pop music, exciting games like hide-and-seek and games with their own momentum and rhythm, like skipping or snap. She likes roller skates and her bicycle for similar reasons. But she also flits from one girl to another, and occasionally to boys, looking for someone with whom she can swear friendship and fight the world. Sometimes it works, but more often than not she is too intense and tries too hard.

Kevin is a boy for whom communication has got to be physical, as well as verbal. It is automatic for him, as for many children, to express what he feels more by touching, pulling, making funny faces and running around, as by choosing appropriate words and phrases. He is *not* non-verbal, but much of what he says is chanted, sung, shouted, distorted with funny voices and repeated with many variations. He rushes into things and delights in contests which are often physical, but usually good-natured. He is competitive, but does not bear rancour, and is happy to enjoy a game with someone he was fighting the previous day. He used to find concentration difficult in school and at home, but this is less of a problem now that he has a teacher he is anxious to impress. He is on a different wavelength from Sally, and for that matter from Larry. When his imagination is caught, he has to act on it, do it and impress it on others: it cannot just be a private thing, for oneself, one's fantasies and sometimes one's parents. He has no secrets. (If you ask him to keep one it is torture for him not to reveal it.) Though he likes the idea of guns and the martial arts, this is only to express his maleness and a certain desire to shock. He is more sensitive than most imagine, and does not attack or intend to hurt others so much as wanting to romp with them.

Larry is a quiet boy, by comparison. In his first year at school he was very shy and reserved. Gradually, he has got used to the rough and tumble of the playground, but he has gained from being kept back to be with children who are mostly a bit younger than the others. He reads better than they do and is clever with his hands at constructional jobs, whether making something from wood or putting together small pieces of machinery. It is tempting fate to leave him alone with a screwdriver and a clock. This side of him arouses the respect of many of the other children, who also know that he is stronger than most, despite not enjoying fighting. Larry is socially rather gauche: he was scarcely capable, for instance, of getting through to Sally. A strong verbal rebuff, like Prue's, will often put him off, but he can usually deal with Kevin and his like. He is less concerned about the male *versus* female battle than either Kevin or Prue, to whom it has become part of the framework of life.

None of these children is really exceptional—if, for Sally's horses, you substitute any of a number of interests (e.g. football, pop music, etc.) that can dominate a child's thinking for a time. But they share one thing, which puts them in a *minority* of children in the United Kingdom and increases their chances of academic success and the opportunities that stem from that; they all live in a middle-class suburb. There, the local state schools have teachers who stay longer; and they have extra equipment (in one case a swimming pool), paid for by the subscriptions and the fund-raising efforts of a strong Parent/Teacher Association. Where it is felt that a subject is weak, there is debate and consultation with the head-teachers. Moreover, the children have access to gardens, to more space in which to play and to more space that they can call their own, to build things, to work in or simply to enjoy controlling. Surveys indicate that their parents have the television on for less of the time; have a wider spectrum of interests, which they have the money and the connections to indulge; and have a greater likelihood of taking holidays abroad. This is not to extol the virtues of being middle class. (I should also point out that these families are also more likely to expect high standards of success, which often puts undue pressure on children of average intelligence. They also have anxieties about preserving the dif-

ferences between them and the rest of society, that lead to tensions
in the home.) But given all this, it is only realistic to note that a
great deal of children's potential development is bound up with
where and with what security a family can live.

A great deal, but not all! Here is another scene, from a very
different school. Fred, Shirley and Carol are all eight. It was
raining and they were sheltering in a corridor before school
started.

Shirley: 'You got a nerve! Get out of it!' (She has a magazine with
David Bowie's picture on the front. Fred has been trying to
read over her shoulder.)
Fred: 'I just want to see—ow! That hurt!' (Carol has stamped on his
toe. She has been reading the magazine with Shirley.)
Carol: 'Serve you right. If you want to read it, buy your own.'
Fred: 'It's not yours anyway.'
Shirley: 'Carol's my friend.' (She reads aloud a line or two,
pretending that she is not to be distracted. 'Ooh, there's Marc
Bolan. He's fab!')
Carol: 'Oh! He's too much!'

Fred imitated these phrases, and he did it so well that the girls
themselves laughed. Suddenly one of the girls asked Fred if his
father has got the car Fred had been claiming would be on the
way. He shook his head and kicked at the brickwork of the wall.
His father had had to stop work, because he had hurt his foot in an
accident, and now they probably couldn't afford it. Carol wanted to
know about the accident and Fred tried to describe it. This was
hard going for him, with his audience miraculously increasing to
eight children, each cocking an ear in his direction and making
comments and suggestions. '. . . he had this ladder,' Fred battled
on, 'only he wasn't up the ladder, he was standing on something
and the ladder hit him and he couldn't get out of the way. . . .'

Each was trying to visualize it; and so was I. Several wanted to
know what had happened to his foot. Was it broken? Would it get
better? Could he run? Would he ever be able to use his foot
again? Shirley looked very thoughtful and asked, 'If he can't use
his foot, he can't drive a car anyway, can he?'

This last comment is a very intelligent remark, on a different
plane entirely from a stereotyped adulation of a pop star. It demands a logical link between two pieces of information and a
hypothetical (what if . . . ?) deduction, which is well advanced for
an eight-year-old, certainly according to Piaget's analysis of the

stages of reasoning which children pass through as they grow older. I emphasize it, because despite a superficial look around the classrooms, it suggests that the children here, although performing at a lower level than Larry, Sally, etc., by no means lack intellectual capacity.

This volume has followed children through to this great divide, when the nation splits into two, possibly more, groups. Equalizing the opportunities of these groups, *without* lowering standards, is arguably one of the most important tasks facing the country.

Many of the features of the last scene were very similar to those in the middle-class school. There is the same chatter, punctuated by hushes and giggles when a teacher passes suddenly, and small shrieks from a group who were trying to stamp on each others' toes. They had various possessions that they showed off, and there were the same pretensions to indifference or to having something superior. Swaps and other bargains were being made. Football teams, plans and pop stars were being compared. The same snatches of pop music were whistled or sung. Contrary to prejudice, there were not so many more four-letter words flying around, although certain children here were using them casually and continuously, as if social life demanded it and they had no alternative.

Character types were distinguishable too, much as at the first school. There were the children who looked energetic and pent up because it was raining; the children who set the pace in conversation or argument; the children who followed on—some more, some less willingly; and the occasional rebels, who were outside the main groups; there were those who approached other children in an assured way and those who were hesitant, or self-effacing.

Differences between the two scenes were discussed with teachers who had experience of teaching eight- and nine-year-olds in different areas. We didn't agree on everything, but the main points seemed to be these. They are all matters of degree, rather than stark distinctions:

(a) A less confident approach to the teacher in the working-class school. These children found it harder to ask questions or to ask for help in what they were doing. Getting them to accept the teacher as a friendly source of ideas and knowledge—as opposed to an invigilator who is trying to get them to perform certain tasks —was tough going. Teachers were already being viewed as 'them' and not 'us'.

(b) Less encouragement to do well, either in the form of friendly interest from parents or in terms of example. Older brothers and sisters tended to scorn school efforts or achievements.

(c) More physical contact and less variation in patterns of verbal contact. They hug each other as well as fight each other more.

(d) A less rich background knowledge of stories, verses and fables that children of eight might be expected to have encountered. 'A lot has to be explained before starting' is how one teacher put the consequence of this.

(e) A more conservative view of rules and of what follows logically from what. The possibility of judgments such as 'guilty but provoked' is less easy for them to grasp. Partly this is due to verbal inflexibility, but they accept prejudices easily. Signs of inter-racial prejudices, presently coming down through the family, seem more common among them.

(f) More practical canniness—where things have to be mended, or money has to be hoarded before it is spent, or a bargain has to be made with another child.

(g) More awareness of some important features of adult life, sometimes including, for example, the need for 'overtime' to pay off HP debts. They are not shielded from arguments in the family as to whether Father should accept a certain job or continue to go down 'to the Labour'.

Most children at eight are asked at some time what they want to be when they grow up. The answers are sometimes amusing, but are beginning to reflect more of the pattern of interests that a child has developed, rather than a passing whim. Much is modelled on father's job or mother's. The answer may be different from one week to the next, but if a child imagines himself in something active, or constructive, or entertaining, or travelling, it will influence each answer. A very few children will have a cast-iron idea of what they intend to do, although for them it is not so much intention as conviction that their complete involvement in some pursuit will last through life. Some young musicians and some sportsmen are known to have been like this, and there are examples of children not knowing what it is, exactly, that their father does in law or in the city, but knowing that they must be like him. Following mother's footsteps is less well documented, since women's activities and opportunities have changed so much over the last decades.

While a lot can be understood about how a child is thinking when he is asked about what he will be, it is a mistake to interpret him too literally or to feel that some kind of choice has to be made soon. Exploring several possibilities is the only way to find out whether one has both an aptitude *and* a fascination for one of them. There are many young pianists, for example, who have the aptitude but not the fascination to make hard work, practice, examinations and performance a compulsive delight. There are parallels outside the arts, although anything demanding specialized physical skill comes to mind more quickly. A balance has to be struck to give a child of eight ample opportunity for pursuing interests and skills, without shutting the door behind him so firmly that he is programmed for a large part of his childhood.

Eight is a time when a child can be helped enormously, by his parents, to enjoy life now, and to prepare to enjoy it to the full in the future. Parents can help most by offering opportunities, not solutions. Plenty of opportunities arise for love, for shared activities, for changing the scenery every so often, for seeing how interesting it can be to study a subject really thoroughly, for seeing whether a real talent exists for this, or that, and for meeting different kinds of people. Opportunity to see examples of how to love, too, because, most importantly, that is what parents provide.

Research at Berkeley in the USA suggests that what a child is like at eight is a better predictor of what he is going to be like—in personality and in relationships with others—as an adult, than what he is like as an adolescent. So take a good look at him and enjoy him for what he is, rather than trying to turn him into something else.

Problems that are best ignored

Some frequent problems that cause parents a lot of anxiety are worth grouping together, because they are far better ignored, than made the subject of a fuss.

1 Eating too little   Parents sometimes feel that it is only their constant surveillance and pressure that stands between their children and death by starvation. They try a variety of tactics: telling the child brusquely to eat up and no nonsense, offering bribes, withholding pudding or sweets after the meal, drawing unpleasant comparisons between brother A who leaves a clean plate and sister B who nibbles like a mouse. Invariably, the more anxiety that parents show, the more unpleasant the meal-time, *and the food*, seems to the child. Children who are left to their own devices (with no special offerings of a separate menu) quickly gravitate towards a normal pattern. They will have their likes and dislikes—presumably *you* do, too—but for the age groups considered in this book a cafeteria system whereby children select or reject from what is on the table is most unlikely to prove harmful. It goes without saying that a sensible selection of proteins, vegetables and fruit should be made available on the table in the first place, without too much carbohydrate.

2 Bed-wetting   Of course this is a nuisance. Most children aged three (about three in four) are dry at night. For five-year-olds, the proportion rises to nine in ten. This is scant comfort to a mother who has to change and wash bed linen if she omits a nappy, and has worse problems if she omits the rubber sheet between the undersheet and the mattress. When children are seven, about nineteen will be dry at night for every one that isn't. But look at it from the point of view that in every primary school class there is likely to be at least one. There are more around than you think. If your child does seem exceptionally late, ask a doctor by all means if there might be a medical cause; but this is rare.

There are two kinds of bed-wetting. The first is of a child who has never, in fact, been consistently dry through the night. The second is when a child has been dry, but suddenly loses control of himself at night. It is no use worrying about the first kind, since some children are simply very slow to get bladder control. Part of the central nervous system is involved, and different parts of this mature at different rates for different children. (Similarly, some children at five find it easier to move their little fingers independently of the rest of the hand. But in the end, they all can.) Nagging at the child who wets his bed, or showing that you are anxious about it, may contribute to a psychological block which puts the day of control further off. The second kind of bed-wetting is almost invariably psychological; do not worry about the bed-wetting as such, but recognize that he is afraid, nervous or guilty, and needs basic reassurance that he is strongly loved and that there are no impending disasters. When he accepts this message thoroughly, the need to regress to an earlier stage of childhood will vanish and bed-wetting will stop.

3 Masturbation and exposure At three and four, most children have great curiosity about their genitals, and often this is extended to making comparisons of genital equipment and exploring the different feelings that can be derived from them. The terrible Victorian legacy of guilt and anxiety about masturbation is only just disappearing among some parts of our society. It is not always realized, even among more enlightened parents, that the child who does *not* masturbate may need more attention than others, who form the vast majority. Obviously, there is point in suggesting to children that many people do not like observing exposure or masturbation in public, and that they might 'keep it to themselves', but children are most unlikely to come to any harm.

4 Demonstrations of affection Some parents, particularly fathers, are embarrassed about displays of feeling between themselves and their children. They do not, they explain, want to make their children too 'soft' or dependent. But there is no better preparation for withstanding the rigours of life than knowledge and proof of continuous warmth among the family, in the background. Boys are the same in their need for this as girls.

Children differ, according to their personality, in the extent to which they continue to want cuddling as they grow older. *Pressing* affection on a child can be overdone, but there is no argument for refusing to join in a hug or a kiss when it is clear that this is what the child wants. Tired and irritable children are showing in one way that they want this. A hug can often restore temper more effectively than anything.

Nor does it matter if you feel that other parents and other children are not being demonstrative. They may be more rigorously Anglo-Saxon; but they are not happier for it. If you feel affection, show it.

5 Bad language; bad accent   Most children of five or six are exposed to far more words of four letters and their variations than many parents like to believe. But at this age, most of these words are meaningless, except possibly as vague terms of abuse. They enter a child's regular vocabulary usually under two conditions: if parents or teachers exhibit shock and horror, investing the words with more fascination than they deserve, *or* if the parents themselves (or other older members of the family) rely on these words. Over-reacting is self-defeating; telling a child that 'we don't like that word much' is simpler and much more effective than a threat. Similarly, you cannot preserve a double standard for long—saying what you feel yourself, but forbidding this to your children. Many children go through a phase of repeating one or two words that their schoolfriends are very fond of. This is best handled by showing mild disapproval only, and it will be found that the phase soon passes.

Primary school is also a good time for experimenting with accents. And why not? This is how languages are learned. Parents sometimes worry about the impression that their child makes among their friends of being *déclassé*, if he brings a nasal twang back from school, and they worry about the effect this may have at an interview with a public school headmaster. But most of these people know the score.

Although most children take after their parents when they speak, there is something very personal about speech which makes parental insistence on 'prunes and prisms' liable to be resented as a threat to individuality. Resentment grows if at school a child has to avoid being laughed at for maintaining too much of an Oxford accent. At a later age, a standard expression of revolt is to adopt a different accent from father's, or from what mother would like. This will be less likely when parents concentrate on giving an example, rather than nagging, and where they decide early on that within certain behaviour limits their child must be what he wants to be.

6 Thumb-sucking and nail-biting   If a child really wants to suck his thumb or bite his nails, there is very little a parent can do about it. At most, they can get cross when they see him at it, they can tug the offending hand away from the mouth and they can mutter warnings about deforming the teeth or being rejected by society. All this achieves, in fact, is an increase of tension between parents and child, and a sense of being prevented by one's parents from getting the kind of comfort a child sometimes feels that he needs when things go wrong.

Thumb-sucking is usually described as 'regressive'. That means, it is part of a younger pattern of behaviour into which a child retreats when he feels that he is missing out on love and attention, or that too many demands are being made of him as an older child. Nail-biting is usually a nervous reaction to stress. Some children say, 'It helps me to concentrate' and 'I have to do something with my hands': it is not unlike reasons given by some adults for smoking.

Chapter twelve

Coming into double figures

Most children feel that they are achieving something special, or at least becoming more important people, as they come up to the milestone of their tenth birthday. Double figures seem to be a significant advance on what birthdays have meant before. Reaching three figures seems very remote indeed, and rather unlikely. This helps make the age of ten seem rather an eventful point to reach.

They are now in an age group where many seem as if they are intent on rushing headlong into their teens. They are precocious in many ways that would startle most families of several decades ago. Their precociousness will be discussed more fully. But it would be a mistake to believe that any ten-year-old is different from previous ten-year-olds in emotional terms—for example so far as control over his feelings is concerned, or his need to feel part of a family, and to make friends.

A common Victorian mistake was to treat children as if they were miniature adults, rather than human beings who were neither mature nor experienced enough to appreciate how or why they were being spoken to, ordered around, or judged. Being children, they responded according to their feelings as to how they were treated. There is a certain danger nowadays, in being misled by the fact that ten-year-olds know much more through television, and wear or imitate teenage and adult fashions, into thinking that they should also behave like miniature adults. We sometimes come close to repeating the Victorian mistake.

A group of nines and tens going to a pop concert, or on their way to catch a glimpse of a teenybopper idol outside his aeroplane, or his hotel, is a rather fearsome sight. However extraordinary older people may feel that *teenagers* look when bound for a similar expedition, they are at least in some kind of uniform, by comparison with teenyboppers. The youngest fans can be at any stage of independence from what their parents want them to wear in their free time; some can borrow older brothers' and sisters' gear, while others cannot; some can afford to buy clothes, cosmetics and insignia of their devotion, while others sometimes adapt what they wear to school. This extraordinary mixture of dress, combined with the intense energy inside each small body, combines to alarm the onlooker when he sees them approach. They have a tremendous sense of purpose. But what *is* the purpose? This is a mystery—possibly as much to them as it is to us. Mystifying adults certainly gives the occasion part of its glory, in their eyes. But the chance to be totally committed in one direction is probably a more important part of the motivation. Getting completely involved in something, without any counter-balance in the form of self-criticism, or sensitivity to others' comments, is a sign of the age group.

Graham, Stephanie, Bill and Irene were jumping up and down on top of a wall beside the garden of a large London hotel when I first saw them. They were not alone: police estimates put the total who had turned up, hoping to see David Bowie install himself, at five hundred. It was difficult to find out, even afterwards, whether the singer was ever actually *at* the hotel. But in any case, his faithful five hundred were either at the wrong time or the wrong place. By the time this was communicated to them over loudspeakers, they had made a lot of noise, singing, shouting, turning up their transistors full blast whenever a cult song was being performed, and breaking out into impromptu games of football with empty cola cans. It was more than the doormen or the porters knew how to deal with, and the three policemen looked harassed and in need of reinforcements. Hotel guests were diverted somewhere to the rear, so that they could enter or leave by the door to the kitchens. But the only visible lasting results of the two-and-a-half hour siege were a few problems for the gardeners.

When they were convinced that they would have to see David Bowie another day, and before they joined up with others to start a trek back to the suburbs, there was a brief interval in which they could be talked with. 'Have you come a long way to see David Bowie?' I asked. Two of them told me where they were from, while Stephanie cried, 'I'd walk a hundred miles just to see David! He's the greatest!' She pointed to a safety pin on her T-shirt: the bulge underneath, she explained, was a picture of her idol worn right next to my heart'.

Not to be outdone, Irene told me about the scarf she was making at home, into which the name 'David' was being sewn, in red ribbon on white. She had hoped it might be ready to wear this evening, 'but I'm not much cop at sewing, see'.

I asked Bill how he felt, and he jumped up on the wall, shouting, 'Cor, David!' by way of an answer. He then jigged on the wall, playing a make-believe instrument, and singing a chorus from a pop song. Graham and the girls stopped up their ears, and told him to belt up.

They were all amazingly cheerful, despite the apparent failure of the expedition. They thought none the worse of their hero for not appearing. If they caught word of a Bowie concert the following week, they were all convinced they would turn up again. ('Do you know where he's going to be, then, mister?' Stephanie demanded shrewdly.) The Olympic ideal is that participation in the games, not winning, is important: this seemed to be a perfect example of putting such an ideal into practice. One moment Irene was proclaiming 'If David doesn't turn up soon, I'll *die!*' A few minutes later, she was agreeing that it had been fun. They argued as to which had got closest to the doorman, and which had dared to say what to the policemen. They enjoyed this arguing.

None of these children were eleven years old yet, except for Bill. They had first heard of the pop star's arrival through a circular, which Stephanie received regularly as a paid-up member of a fan club or a pop club. Later, it was confirmed for them by radio, and by a daily newspaper; one claimed it had been foretold on television, too. But word of mouth was the strongest influence. At school that morning, apparently, his likely destination had been mentioned—first in a cloakroom, then the playground, then everywhere. The previous day, he was known to be simply on the horizon, his date of arrival unknown. Then dramatically, everyone knew where and when. Since the other children round about were visibly unknown to the quartet, the same bush telegraph must have operated in several parts of London, and there must have been the same determination to find a route, get money for the fare, take provisions for the journey and set off.

Their parents had not been told exactly where they were going. It was not easy to tell how much their parents knew, but it was unlikely to be a great deal. Irene had told her mother 'the whole lot of us are going'. Bill maintained that his father 'knows where I am, all right', although he himself had not informed him. They did not expect serious trouble when they got home, although they had only a vague idea how long it might take to return. 'We can go to the underground station, and just ask for the right train,' said Irene, who sounded particularly practical.

Sometimes it is implied in press reports that pop fans are 'senseless'. Certainly when they are all rushing and screaming, in near hysteria, it is easy to conclude just that. But these four, in quieter mood, seemed very sensible and articulate. Bill may have been rather less intelligent than the others, although he may have been simply more shy. The others were certainly quick-witted, and they spoke and asked questions as would responsive children that any teacher would enjoy teaching.

It is very important that children who burrow deep into a craze of this kind are *not* assumed to be stupid. If they are continuously criticized for their enthusiasms, two things are liable to happen: they *accept* that they tend to think and to enjoy life at a lower level, and adopt a course of under-achievement both at school and later when thinking about careers; and they *separate* their ideas of pleasure from relations with their parents. At nine or ten, this can be a wedge which gradually produces a 'Generation Gap'.

This is not to imply that parents should pretend to share their children's feelings. If you dislike something, it is healthier to say so. But the way in which this is expressed can mean the difference between keeping communication open, and locking the child in into a defensive, self-perpetuating alienation system.

Another important question that arises from the description of the quartet's adventure above, is how far children of this age should be protected from the dangers of the world, and how far their self-reliance should be fed. It is a difficult tightrope to walk. While I am convinced that the quartet described above had parents with far too relaxed a view about what their children might be doing on their own, there are dangers in molly-coddling as well. If you show you doubt a child's abilities or common sense when in difficulty, he may appear more resentful than anything else, but he will begin to have doubts himself. Every child is different both in the degree to which they are cautious and 'sensible', and in their panic threshold. He is different in his experience, too.

Parents need to think, therefore, every now and then, if they are being too protective, or too optimistic where their own child is concerned. Just because another parent allows this, or that, does not mean that *you* should. When *you* are the complete exception, however, then it is time to re-appraise. Just because other children are going to join yours, it doesn't mean an excursion will be safe for all of them. Where an older, responsible child is in charge (it was not so with the fan club quartet) the argument that there is safety in numbers holds some water. But once a group starts to behave wildly, it is much less easy for any single child in the group to keep control of his emotions. Is my child ready for this? is the question which has to be considered, whenever a really new idea is put forward, whether it is travelling alone across a big city, going for a hike with a friend, going to a big football match, going to a family where the children are mostly older, or anything of this kind. The answer *may* be yes, or it may be no, at this age, depending very much on the child and on the circumstances.

The same individual appraisal has to be made when a proposal is put up to do something that is physically demanding, and possibly dangerous. Some parents only have a vague idea of the distance their child can swim; the length of walk he can undertake; the demands made on him by hill or mountain climbing; the skill he has with a bicycle, and how far he understands and practises road safety rules; whether he is sensible over money to the point of keeping his fare home. Yet each of them may have to be the basis for saying yes, or no, to an enthusiastic request. There are some precautions that every parent can take:

(a) Seeing their child is trained to take swimming proficiency tests.
(b) Seeing he is trained to take the police cycling proficiency test, and not allowing him to use a bicycle on the road by himself until this is passed.
(c) Making sure he understands how to use a public telephone box (even when he has to reverse the charges) and how to telephone a friend or relative if he can't reach you direct.
(d) Encouraging him to treat policemen as potential friends in need.

All of these increase both the child's confidence in himself, and the parent's confidence in that confidence.

Having decided what a ten-year-old may or may not be allowed, the problem is to communicate it. This is easier, if a parent has a good understanding of what is important to children at this time. Figure 6 shows some of the major influences on his behaviour. Each can have an effect on how he reacts to having his energy and his ideas held in check. For example, in the background are his relations with his parents. A boy is likely to have, by now, some conflicting ideas about his father. He admires him, and enjoys

Figure 6 Influences at nine and ten

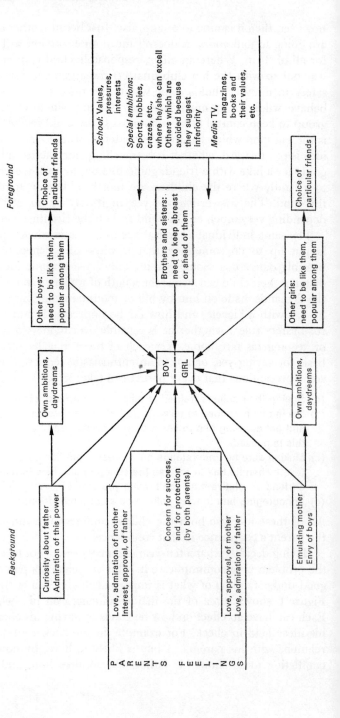

the idea of progressing until he can do what his father does. But he does not model himself so directly on his father as the younger boy would do. He is competitive with his father; and he is more anxious to be distinct from his father, in a way that others of his age group would envy and appreciate. He is anxious to please his mother, but in trying to excite her admiration he often succeeds in alarming or displeasing her. The core of his problem lies in trying to reconcile the need to be part of his family, and the need to be different.

Both these needs are important to remember when it seems difficult to understand why a child should be nice one day and very difficult the next. The chances are that on the first day, both needs are being satisfied in a balanced way; or, external stimulation —from school, from a hobby and from a new idea or game—is masking one need while the other is satisfied.

Success outside the home is one sign that a child is succeeding as an individual. How this affects social life at ten is discussed more fully in the next chapter. But not appearing to be the odd one out is, paradoxically, an important part of gaining acceptance as an individual at this age. Both boys and girls like to be seen sharing most of their contemporaries' interests, as well as knowing their jokes, their rituals and speaking a similar language. When girls need acceptance by a local group comprising both sexes, or other girls with tom-boy habits, this combines with a certain envy of boys and their ways to bring them in conflict with their mothers, as they suspend identification with their mothers' role.

Realizing that most children at this age detest and fear being shamed or even simply branded as 'different' in front of others helps a parent steer clear of tactlessness in refusals. They are sensitive to being seen by other children to be pampered or cocooned. Being laughed at is a torment. It may be necessary to ask a child to come in with you, away from his surrounding friends, before breaking the news that despite what the others may be doing, you do not want *him* to do it. Tactlessness in this area leads to considerable resentment over time.

A similar point, for those with more than one child, is how to pass judgment on whether a younger brother or sister may accompany an older one on an expedition. The biggest problems usually seem to come with younger children, who demand to be involved in what they see the older ones doing or planning to do. Automatically, the younger one seems rather young for it. Offering an alternative activity (especially if it is with father) can help allay the envy stirred by refusal. But in any event, tactful handling of the situation is needed to avoid one child smugly making capital out of his temporary advantage, or the other losing too much face.

At his age it is usually advisable to be clear-cut in the decision you make, whether you decide to allow both brothers to ride their bicycles to the shops on the High Street, or not. 'Well, I don't think so . . .' merely invites an argument, which may become bad-tempered. But this is different from allowing a discussion. Even if the verdict goes against them, most children want to know *why* they cannot do something; they are at a more logical stage of thought, now, where they can play with hypothetical situations in their minds—'If I were good enough to pass my cycling proficiency test, I would be able to cycle away with my sister to the shops' is more intelligible as a proposition now than it was at seven or eight.

This gives something for the child to *aim at*, which a tactful parent will try to provide for, when refusing permission.

'No you *can't* try to mend the television set.'

'Why not? I'm sure I know what's wrong with it.'

'Well I think you'll make it worse.'

'Oh, what can I *do* then? It's raining.'

'I don't know.'

This is a dreary cul-de-sac for anyone to find themselves in, whether they are ten or adult. You don't always have the time and energy to plan a ten-year-old's Saturday afternoons, but what he really wanted to do often gives a useful clue about something to suggest. In the case above, there is a chance that he might find a book about TV sets in the library, and enjoy learning more about them, about the principles involved, and how to use the knowledge in a practical way. It's not difficult nowadays to get started on making a radio, either. What he may be angling for, and what is not always recognizable, is an invitation to help you at what you are doing. At all events, he wants to be offered something rather than nothing. He may well sneer at your alternative at first—but if he gets down to it, it offers a way out of contemplating the deadlock.

A lot of the apparent coolness, of assumed self-sufficiency, in children at this age can be put down to the need to be seen to be an individual, so that trust becomes more automatic when it comes to a request to do something new and dangerous. The aloofness is only apparent however. No child at this age really wants to be cut off from his parents, unless they have done things that completely destroy his confidence in them.

On the physical side, children at this age often give a similarly misleading impression that they are indestructible. To get back to the early Victorians, briefly: at nine and ten, when children were strong enough, they were recruited for heavy labour that their energy was equal to in the short term, but for which their bodies were totally unprepared. The result was that although they managed to carry sacks of flour from the mill and although they successfully dragged tenders loaded with coal along narrow mine tunnels, this kind of effort took a terrible toll of their legs, their backs and their chests. Exhausted, they had less resistance to cold, or to disease. Unnaturally bent for long periods, they often developed spinal trouble that dogged them for life. None of this, at least in the United Kingdom, is seen today. But it is still a time during which regular checks need to be made, to make sure that nothing is beginning to go wrong now which might be more and more difficult to correct as the child grows older.

Avoiding overstrain is something which is much easier to advise than to practise. Both boys and girls enjoy seeing if they can impress each other, and their parents, by lifting heavy weights. The chances of their damaging their backs, by hauling on something and twisting, in such a way as to slip a disc, or allowing connecting tissues to weaken, so that two vertebrae are painfully squeezing what lies between them wherever the body bends, are in fact small. So is the risk of rupture of the stomach wall. But it still makes sense to teach a child how best to raise heavy things: they cannot be protected from raising them, but if they automatically go about this in a cautious way, so that they take a lot of the strain on their ankles and legs, they get a lesson which will be valuable to them for a very long time.

Posture is worth watching too. Bad posture is uncommon among younger children, except when they are very tired or if they affect it. If it is allowed to develop at nine or ten, however, it leads to curvature of the spine to a degree that will need remedial exercises later, if it is not to cause neck and back trouble when the child becomes an adult.

Nagging a child about his posture is notoriously unsuccessful. It helps a bit if he is told pointedly how much better he looks, especially among his friends, when he is standing or sitting upright. Good humour helps: most children are too amused to be

6

cross if they are told they 'look like a drunken frog', and they will be reminded of the basic message, whereas being told in a serious tone not to slouch merely gets them to erect a barrier of sourness. There is no reason, either, why children should not be told that this is more than a matter of interior decoration of the house, and they should be shown exactly why. If parents have a bad posture, they tend to be copied. It follows that parents will need to practise what they preach—if they are to avoid being labelled 'drunken frogs' themselves!

Other reasons for bad posture are copying their friends—over which you have no control—and too much study with little compensating exercise. Another factor can be short-sightedness, which can lead some children to peer forward, and to read books with the head bent. Sight tests are very important, together with at least one appointment with an oculist (as opposed to an optician), or with an eye specialist in a hospital department. During this period of life a tendency towards short-sightedness often gets worse. Both in the short term *and* the long term a child needs to get whatever help is right for his eyes. Obviously it is best to be making provision for this before he starts stooping. Unless he is very short-sighted indeed, or unless he plays a bit with older children who make comparisons of ability to discern objects and then discuss their conclusions, even a very intelligent child will not sense that he has this kind of problem. He assumes that *he* is the norm, except where it is proved to be otherwise. This goes for other ocular abnormalities too. Regular examination is therefore particularly important now.

Not long ago, there was never any problem about shoes at this age—apart, of course, from the fact that they wear out very quickly as a result of yard football or scuffing them in school corridors. The style of shoe was always, or nearly always, subordinate to the fit. But girls of ten now are more likely to want, and to get, shoes that are of a style that suit current fashion, or their idea of it. It is still less common for boys to have the peacock spirit at this age, but by no means unknown. Children of both sexes have the determination, by ten, to continue wearing shoes that they find uncomfortable, or even painful, provided that they fit with what the gang is wearing, or (better still) impress them. The harm that this can mean for feet that are still growing depends on the total amount of time that distorting shoes are worn, as opposed to regulation school shoes, training shoes, and going barefoot. It probably does little harm, according to some paediatricians, for a ten-year-old girl to spend a Saturday afternoon staggering after her older sister on platforms, if she badly wants to, but as a continued habit it may produce a deformity. Recently some footwear manufacturers have shown awareness of children's changing needs by producing shoes which are designed to attract them as well as to suiting the growth of their feet. Getting the correct width as well as the correct length of shoe is important, and not all manufacturers make a complete range of fittings available.

This review of physical problems should be counter-balanced by pointing out that at this age many of life's hazards are less likely to strike at children than before. They have acquired resistance to many illnesses and they can explain clearly what it is that is wrong with them when they have a pain. Provided their living conditions are satisfactory, provided that they get enough to eat, and are not exposed to continual cold and damp, there is every reason to suppose they will thrive. By ten, the average child has already had influenza, German measles, chicken pox and mumps. They are most unlikely to have caused any permanent harm. He may also have had measles, but other illnesses are less probable: if he meets any of the above now, given medical attention there is every chance he will take them in his stride. Appendicitis can still take parents by surprise (although it submits to treatment when diagnosed), particularly if they are over-suspicious of claims of stomach pains that could conveniently get a child off school.

This is a wonderful age at which to go abroad. Where before, all might have been sun, sea and the hotel swimming pool, a child going abroad at ten will be very curious about local life, about the languages spoken, about what people do, eat and think, and why this all should be so. The journey itself is something to contemplate, not just to endure. It may be rather too early for *most* children to relish being on the away leg of an exchange, and living for a week or so with people who are only moderately well known, and who are rather too persistent about talking German, or French. If the family is very well known to the child, and if he is socially mature, it may work well. Otherwise it is better to defer this very excellent means of learning about a country and a language until about twelve.

Accidents are the major reason for any child at this point in his life to fail to develop properly. Most accidents can be prevented. These include cases where

(a) Children have not been warned that something is dangerous; *or* the explanation was too vague.
(b) Parents have expected too much of their child, in terms of being able to take care of himself; *or* in terms of his withstanding temptation to try out dangerous things.

The great majority of accidents come into one or other of these categories. Road accidents sometimes, however, constitute a third one: when somebody drives dangerously, and even the best instructed child of the most careful parent falls victim to him. Everyone has to do their bit to restrict the chances of a serious accident occurring. But there is a point beyond which fortune takes control.

The more obvious parental tasks include *noticing* how a child crosses the road, as opposed to simply telling him how to do it safely, which should have been a lesson learned some time ago; *asking him* if he knows, or can remember, which of the plants in the garden are poisonous (e.g. laburnum, delphinium, foxgloves, etc.); and *talking to him about* electricity, and *how* certain jobs should be done while others are best left to electricians. Parents without much contact with their children do not notice what the chinks in their armour are. They forget, too, that country children may be at a loss with their bicycle in a busy city road; or that town children can get a false sense of freedom from traffic on country lanes. This is because such parents do not keep up their awareness of how their children's experience is growing, and where it is missing out. Over-protective parents, paradoxically, do the same thing: they only attend to their own fears, and their own needs to give instruction, so that they have little idea of how much is sinking in.

There can be few times at which it is more difficult to judge how far a child needs, and desires, more responsibility, and how far he needs to be protected against his over-ambitious ideas. The course is easier to steer if parents keep up contact, but there are sure to be difficult choices. It must be accepted that he is *bound* to want to make some mistakes for himself: the task is to advise and act in such a way that these are restricted to situations that are not so dangerous—e.g. let him jump from a tree if he wants to, but tell him not to leap out of a moving bus.

Over-protection is worse, long-term, than having a few bruises on the knees and having the experience of a fight or two. But, to revert to the point made at the beginning of this chapter, it makes little sense to deprive a child of part of his childhood prematurely by giving him too much responsibility and a sense of burden on his shoulders. Some are given this feeling because they are regularly put in the position of looking after younger brothers and sisters, 'or else'; others by being persuaded into an academic rat-race to the exclusion of most other pursuits by a process of moral blackmail—e.g. 'Think of the vast sums your mother and I are paying to send you to the H— school', or 'Your brother got into the grammar school after the 11 Plus: you won't let the family down, will you?' One other means of creating premature adults is to have a home atmosphere, or a boarding school, where the expression of emotion is firmly discouraged. Nines and tens do *not* gain in maturity by being urged always to disguise feelings of love, fear or disappointment. Prep school sang-froid is only superficial, and it often creates difficulties in relationships in later life, when people should be frank with others about how they really feel if they are to live together satisfactorily.

The Romans referred to children as 'liberi', or 'the free ones': free from adult care, from adult responsibility, and with a licence to speak and act as many adults would like, but dare not. They did not see this attitude as being at all incompatible with teaching children to have noble ideals and the like. Here they had an advantage over the Victorians, at least.

Chapter thirteen

Social contacts at nine and ten

It has already been pointed out that children become increasingly dependent for their happiness on being regarded favourably by others of the same age. The experiences that children have at this time hold a great deal of influence over the way in which they interact with others later in life. Whether they are basically out-going people (or 'extravert') who enjoy and need a lot of social contact, or whether they are more cautious about this ('introvert), keeping themselves to themselves, has in most cases been deter-mined a good deal earlier in childhood. But the way they come to terms with other people is still being determined.

Above all, there is observation going on all the time, of how a child's parents treat each other, their relatives, their friends, and strangers. Children do not necessarily reflect what they see their parents doing directly, and in some cases this would create im-possible difficulties. But what they see around them becomes the standard, which most feel inclined to reflect, sooner or later. Of course when children feel that part of their parents' behaviour is intolerable, they react against it, and consciously try to be dif-ferent. However, they usually betray some link with what they have seen: for example, a child who hates the way his parents shout at each other may show a preference for quieter friends, and may avoid arguments and fights, but when provoked beyond his endurance, he will shout in a very similar way to the one he knows but detests.

School is the next big influence, for most children. This is the real testing-ground, where they find out, often painfully, just how well they can get on with others, and fend for themselves. Up till about eight children tend, at school, to vary their friendships, exploring one companion, then another, without really developing any kind of deep long-term understanding of one particular friend.

This changes gradually. At eight, a child has a tighter network or repertoire of friends. Commitment to any particular one at any moment may be strongly maintained, but after a little time passes, that commitment may be abruptly transferred to another. The nine- and ten-year-old has a more mature concept of *regular* friends. Boys and girls tend to be somewhat different in this, girls valuing regular friends more highly. A lot depends on how much opportunity for contact outside school hours is possible, or is allowed. This does not mean to say that at ten a child is likely to be somebody's blood-brother for life. It means that the way they treat a friend on Monday is no longer simply related to immediate interest, pleasure or advantage: this is tempered by a sense that they would still like to be friends the following Monday too. Children are still very adaptable in their friendships, and can be ruthless when they change their criteria for what makes an interesting friend. But they are thinking of social contact over a *longer term.*

It helps to bear in mind what has been going on in a child's mind over this period, when trying to understand social development. These processes are particularly relevant:

(a) An increasing awareness that school, and the world outside the home, is not just a temporary retreat, but an arena in which many of the satisfactions of life have to be gained. Therefore it becomes more important to make one's mark there, to be recognized, to be popular, and to have friends.

(b) A better sense of how one is being regarded by other people. A seven-year-old may butter up a 'friend' in order to be included in a share out of sweets—quite shamelessly. A ten-year-old is more concerned about how such behaviour would be regarded by the 'friend', and by others.

(c) A better sense of time, and the value of maintaining close contact with certain friends over time.

(d) Understanding that what he *himself* may do to others is similar to what others may have done to him. This helps him to avoid (at least some) anti social acts, based on deduction from one's own experience.

(e) A broader social repertoire, including positive acts that are found by trial and error, and by watching parents' dealings with others, to be encouraging where friendship is concerned; and awareness of nuances between comments or tones of voice that indicate friendliness, warning, hostility, etc.

(f) Most children will have been curious for a long time about how things are managed in *other* families. By this stage, a large proportion go through phases of being fascinated by the atmosphere, or by what is done, in one particular family. The child identifies with one of the other children, or sometimes dreams his way into their midst. The effect is compounded if he finds the personality of one of the others particularly strong and appealing. This makes for an obvious need for closer friendship, although often he can only 'worship from afar'.

(g) Most children's stories, whether they are in smart, glossy publications that appear mainly in middle-class homes, or whether they are available to all through television, involve some kind of need for contact and friendship. Experiencing adventure together is one very satisfying aspect of the adventure. (Books like *Alice in Wonderland* are exceptions in this respect; while the Bobbsey Twins stories, and *Star Trek*, to give two very different examples, are mainstream in their demands of solidarity between two or more.) Children are very strongly impressed at least by some stories at this age, and live them out in fantasy and in their games: since they are being consistently fed the desirability of friendship in them, this must spill into their everyday lives and their aims.

Parents are sometimes very taken aback to find how strong the ties have suddenly become between their ten-year-old and somebody they have perhaps barely met. When they show their suspicion of this other child and ask 'Who *is* Roger, exactly? Where does he live?', this can often be taken as further evidence, by a sensitive child, of the repressive house rules that make home so uninteresting, and other families so enticing and desirable. The tie with Roger is automatically strengthened by thoughtless interrogations such as the one above. Children who feel a strong need to have a close friend outside the family sometimes defeat their own ends by being too intense—insisting that Roger, or whoever, repeats that he, too, is a friend for life, and protesting loudly at any actions or words that suggest that Roger has other friends, or that he need not share the same interests, or the same enemies. Girls are more likely to fall into this trap than boys, possibly because they are not taught to be inhibited about friendships, at least with other girls; possibly because they model the 'friendship' concept on the mother-and-child relationship, which of its nature rules out other influences. Whether or not a child is going to be consistent when he declares 'It's you and me against the rest, isn't it, Veronica!', it is a serious matter at this age; and laughing at some of the wilder expressions of it needs to be kept to a minimum, and out of sight.

Girls are often different from boys in the intensity with which they look for particular friends. They are liable to suffer much more from a sense of missing out on popularity. This can change overnight if they suddenly meet up with another girl with whom they feel they can share a secret, or simply be seen to be together. This last point is vital for most girls: at least half of their anxiety about *not* having a friend can usually be ascribed to the fact that they are being observed not to have one.

At this age, much of the business of making friends is centred round a common interest, or rather a consuming passion. Realization that they both share a common excitement about the performance of a local football team, or the chance of getting fishing equipment and trying it out on the same canal, makes for solidarity of feeling between boys. Girls who share the same dreams of owning a horse, or who enjoy the same dancing class or fan club, have the same advantage in making contact. This is one reason why close friendship at this age may become transient, as soon as a new enthusiasm takes over. It also results in a further separation of girls from boys in friendships as well as in day-to-day activities. Even though they attend the same schools, the kinds of sport and leisure which are encouraged for each sex become more and more distinct as they grow older.

Animals figure prominently in most children's social life, very often offering a means of getting compensation for lack of success, rather than a shared relationship that will be kept for long at the same level of feeling for its own sake. Many a child of nine or ten has been heard confiding to a cat or dog that this animal is the only 'person' they can really trust. The tendency to credit animals with complex understanding, and other human characteristics, is very strong. Sometimes a child is so carried away by his feeling of what an animal's response to him should be, that he loses control and does something unpleasant if the animal does not duly respond. Cruelty is usually brief, and fortunately most animals contrive to look after themselves. Most children repent 'rapidly' and enjoy 'making it up' with the now more suspicious pet.

The extent to which pets who die get mourned depends very much on whether the child is currently going through the process of transferring his social feelings towards it, and whether he is dependent on it for a friend. If not, children often sound remarkably

6*

callous, when they are simply being realistic about animals, applying what they have been taught about their life spans. For example, the whole of a certain class of nine-year-olds had been on very good terms with their teacher's terrier, who was frequently found in the school building. Some had fed it, some had cuddled it, all had petted it. The teacher was very sorrowful one morning, when she explained that Ricky had been run over at the week-end, and would not be seen again. The class took this news quietly; and then the following comments were made:

'Are you going to get another dog, Miss B—?'
'Are you going to get a *St Bernard*, next time?'
'You had him a long time, didn't you, Miss B—?'

There were many similar dispassionate comments. A few children, who were specially fond of Miss B—, and were also rather sensitive, expressed feelings like 'Poor Miss B—! It must have been terrible for you.'

'No one was actually sorry for my *dog*,' the teacher explained. Although she had felt rueful about this at the time, she agreed that the children were showing a healthier attitude and set of values than older but more sentimental people might have done. In fact, there were two boys who came up to her separately and tried to get details of what Ricky had been *like* when he was run over. But they, she reckoned, were making use of the occasion to find out about being run over, which (after a narrow escape) they needed to come to terms with. Ricky was Miss B—'s friend, not *theirs*. Moreover, they had not witnessed the demise, so that the pity of the moment was less likely to reach them through shock.

Human death, particularly if it is close to them, is liable to affect them much more. Here again, however, a child of this age is likely to be more realistic than his parents are prepared for, if he has not got on well with the dead person, e.g. 'Well she can't visit us again, can she!' and even 'I suppose that means one less Christmas present that I'm going to get'. It is tempting to shout something when a child talks like this, and it makes good sense to urge him to stop it, pointing out that he is making others unhappy. But you cannot expect or force children to have your own memories of someone, or to affect hypocritical grief. When you have a child saying 'What a terrible thing! We did all love her so, didn' t we?', there can be a tell-tale ring to the voice which suggests that a social lesson has been carefully learnt, and is being repeated. It can sound much less pleasant than tactless truth.

Children at this age are very anxious to be seen to be progressing quickly towards an adult conversational level—provided they have been given any encouragement, and if they have acquired a desire to be like, or to transcend their parents. (These two conditions often go closely together.) We have all seen them at this age, being allowed to stay up and being allowed to proffer nuts and crisps to visitors on condition they do not cause any trouble: they hover close to a group of adults, taking unnatural breaths every so often, determinedly angling for a chance to enter the action. Sometimes they feel they *have* to burst in, pushing a bowl of biscuits practically into a guest's face to grab the initiative. Sometimes, when they have at last got the ball in their court, they do not know what to do with it, eking out a long monologue that eventually has to be sawn off.

Striking a balance between helping them to feel more at home among older people and preventing guests becoming bored and infuriated is not easy. Visitors who gush can let success come too easily, so that a child, and his parents, are lulled into the belief that he has suddenly acquired poise, charm, wit and a sense of how to turn on the tap that says 'hospitality'. Parents need to watch for the pursing of lips that means that 'What a spoilt brat!' is their *real* reaction. But a balance has to be struck that is fair on the child in both ways.

Children need to have a lot of time with both parents if they are to get a feel for different kinds of social interaction, in different circumstances. Fathers who seek refuge in the pub at week-ends and mothers who say with relief 'Now he's ten, you can both go fishing and keep out of my hair at week-ends, can't you!' are reducing their opportunity. He is unlikely to be the best of company for *either* parent all week-end, and often he will declare a preference for his own friends and what they are doing. But most children in fact want to be drawn more often into what is going on, by mother and father. The balance of the two influences is important, on boys and girls.

It is very interesting to observe groups of children and see how they are composed. Earlier, with younger children, both the composition and the leadership of the groups tend to vary with the circumstances—with what the group is doing, and what the individuals in it are feeling like at that moment. With nine- or ten-year-olds it is harder to gain admittance to a group if you are an outsider; and the identity of the child who does most of the initiation remains constant, unless there is a major crisis within it. Children often seem to become more conservative, as they grow older, about whom to allow into a group. This shows that the group of children to which they belong—of course, it might be a series of groups, one at school, one near home, one further from home, and so on—is more and more important to him. Would-be entrants are sniffed out, partly in the suspicion that they might threaten the group and what it does, partly because the group structure and its hierarchy might change, which could be for the worse.

A group of six nine- and ten-year-olds are playing one afternoon in a communal garden, known as the 'court', consisting of grass patches, rock gardens, and disused tennis courts enclosed by a ring of Victorian apartment houses. These are used for meeting up regularly. Who is the chief among them is perfectly obvious to anyone who bothers to watch them for a few minutes, even from an upstairs balcony. This is Chris, who is ten, and big for his age. Chris says, 'Come on, go and get your roller skates out', or 'We'll play footer now, and Tony's got to be in goal on my side'—and although they may protest, they fall in with his ideas. If one of them makes a counter-suggestion, it is nearly always tinged with a sense of weakness, or a request, or a fatalistic sense that it will probably be turned down. Chris never has to enforce his ideas physically: he senses, although he would probably never think of it in these terms, that the majority will always be on his side, and that a rebel can most likely be 'frozen' into returning to the group. This makes him sound calculating. He is nothing of the kind. He glories, effortlessly and naturally, in his popularity, and takes pride in organizing games well, that everyone enjoys. He has become somebody who we say has 'leadership qualities': people can observe him and describe these qualities, but they will argue endlessly about why, precisely, he is like this, and not more like one of the others. He is in fact intelligent, although not astonishingly so; he looks strong, healthy and athletic, he is quick with his tongue, and can make jokes, as well as delivering rebukes which have a coating of humour; he is also full of information about things which are outside the court—about motor bicycles, about Heathrow airport, and the local sports teams; and he always has a lot of ideas about how they might spend the afternoon. Looking for the sources of his 'leadership', we might consider a range of different factors:

His positive, outgoing personality, partly inherited.
The confidence he has been given in dealing with others through his early experience with his mother and his father.
The ways in which he has watched his parents with others, and the extent to which he enjoys being like them.
His history of interactions with other children, the ways in which he has learnt that he pleased them best, and how he gets what he wants with his sister Janet who is a year younger.
Physical and mental make-up; what his family is perceived to be like, his and his parents' possessions, all of which add up to a total picture of someone that impresses other children, and makes them feel it would be nice to be more like him, and that a group with him in it must be fun.

The exact balance of these influences we will never know. But few of those with Chris's social flair are lacking in intelligence; in a confident relationship with their parents; or in a history of much early contact with children, with a good deal of rough-and-tumble. Nor, at this age, are leaders likely to be underprivileged in the physical sense; they can run and fight, although they do not have to show it. Of course there are some 'leaders' who have not got the benefit of some of these advantages but they are less common.

What of the others? Although they *look* like followers at first, it soon becomes clear that each has an individual way of contributing to the group.

David was born in the same week as Chris, but he seems younger, and less strong. He is the one that most of the group turn on from time to time, saying 'Oh, David! You nutter!' or 'It's *David* again!' For a while one wonders why he stays with the group, because he seems to derive very little from it, apart from insults. Even Archie, the youngest of the group, is expected to call him names and tease him, and he gets away with it. But far from leaving the group, or from keeping very quietly on the fringe, so as not to provoke attacks, he is actually courting trouble. However he sees his role, he enjoys it—even when it means rounding on the others in exasperation, and telling them he thinks they are horrible. It is the best group he knows.

Janet and Lesley are the two girls in the group. Sometimes they are alienated by what the boys are doing, or talking about. But they join in most things, football included. Janet, mentioned above, is Chris's sister. Lesley is Janet's particular friend. Chris is demonstrably less than affectionate towards his sister, and seems to go out of his way to show the rest of the group that he offers Janet no special favouritism. But although they insult each other from time to time, they never actually fight, or remain on opposite sides for long. Their relationship is different from those between other pairs in the group, because—if you watch them—they are obviously used to sharing ideas and feelings with a minimum of comment or explanations.

Chris is obviously rather 'soft' where Lesley is concerned, and never insults *her*. He doesn't express anything very positive towards her, except that he laughs, often, at what she says, and encourages her in games when she is losing. He admires her, but it is very unlikely that there is much desire, in any sexual sense. He looks slightly more clumsy than usual when he is close to her and the rest are at some distance. Lesley seems naturally coquettish, and at nine has an obvious flair for trading off her charm, although when it is necessary she will tackle and wrestle with any of them.

Sometimes Janet and Lesley detach themselves for a while from the rest of the group, and talk quietly to each other. It is as though they become briefly drawn towards a separate, female role, and have certain matters to discuss by themselves. They need this; but in terms of the time they spend inside and outside the larger group, they have a greater need to belong to that group. A larger group is less likely to become bored, although occasionally they will sit around on a low wall, simply discussing what they *might* do. Further than that, a larger group confess some kind of pride in belonging, that each of them can enjoy.

Also in the group is Richard, a shock-headed ten-year-old who has a distinctly different, lower-class accent than the others. He is very popular with them, and is regarded as partly a wit, partly a daredevil, partly a link with other kinds of family and other kinds of experience, and partly just as a friendly companion. He has a short temper, but the flare-ups die down quickly. The swear-words he uses are the same as those used by the others, and there is no reason to suppose that he taught them new expressions: but it is clear that the *freedom* with which Richard expresses himself is surprising, slightly shocking, and therefore apt to make the others giggle.

Nicky is the last of the six. He is smaller than the rest, and seems very neatly made, with pointed, but attractive features. He is partly of Indian extraction. In most of their joint activities he seems naturally very competitive with the others, and is anxious, possibly too anxious, to shine. The others know that they can tease him fairly easily by suggesting he is not doing as well as they are, and I have seen them reduce him very quickly to tears. Most times, however, they stop short of this.

If any of them could be said to challenge Chris for the leadership, it would probably be Nicky. He is liable to query suggestions for what the group should do that afternoon, or where they might go if it rains. 'Oh, listen! Why don't we . . .' is a frequent start to one of Nicky's remarks. This is part of his competitiveness, and it shows his need, as if were, to represent an alternative view, whatever the circumstances. He is squashed, over-ruled, derided sometimes, but often coaxed by Chris into putting his energy into a race, or into building a 'club-house'. Chris in fact seems to sense how to 'use' Nicky's instinct to compete in order both to keep the group intact, and to sharpen the intensity with which it does things. Eventually, Nicky may well want to have a group of his own. He has energy, skills, and he is clever enough to attract other children's attention. But he probably will not be a successful group leader, unless he avoids being competitive with others in his group. Children admire other children who seem to *transcend* competition, like Chris.

They all need each other. An interesting example of how cohesive they can be came one afternoon when morale seemed to be low. Two of them were kicking at a wall in a way they imagined to be like Kung Fu; the girls were arguing about something that had happened at school with David, who was exasperated with them; Chris talked about fishing, and felt they should all do some fishing somewhere, but it was too late to go. David's father emerged from a garden gate, marched up to David angrily and said, 'I thought I'd told you to come in by four o'clock. Come in at once.' David followed sheepishly, and the rest fell silent.

When conversation resumed they all debated, whisperingly, what was going to happen to David. Lesley thought they ought to go to David's father and explain that it wasn't David's fault. Chris was doubtful about the success of this move. 'What if we'd been holding him down?' said Richard. But 'We weren't, and he saw that, you idiot,' Nicky told him. They were led by Chris very quietly along the hedge until they were parallel to David's family's garden gate. They spent about ten minutes listening very carefully, Nicky in an advanced position by the gate itself, where he would be unseen from the windows above. Eventually they drifted away, when it seemed likely that David's family had left the house *en masse* at the front. 'He's all right, I expect,' Chris announced cheerfully, as they went back towards their wall.

Wishful thinking, perhaps. But they clearly needed to have, or even to fabricate, some grounds for re-assuring themselves about David, despite his being in many ways the target of the group's disdain. It is characteristic of most groups that when there is any kind of threat from the outside to one of their number, this automatically makes them tighter-knit. This might not go for something like a road accident to David, although they would each feel that strongly. The point about this incident is that David's father's angry appearance could have happened to *any* of them, and was in effect an implied criticism of the group: had the group not existed, David might not have got into trouble.

Experiences of group activities and group reactions of this kind are an important foundation for feeling one's way into more complex teenage and adult groups later on. There is an obvious point that the extent to which adults tolerate tightly disciplined organizations links up with the patterns of social interaction they became used to, and in which their needs for belonging to a group were satisfied, when they were younger. Less obviously, acquiring a sense of how people have to fit in with each other's needs, and what kinds of informal rules are necessary for the group to remain intact and content, paves the way towards being able to fit in with others in, for example, a work situation later on. Everyone recognizes the phenomenon of the person who joins a firm and never becomes integrated with even a sub-group in that firm, because however many contacts he has, and however successful he may be, his anxiety for personal positioning and personal satisfaction puts him at odds with those round about him. Another way of putting this is that he is socially immature, or lacking in a feeling for successful group interactions. Life is usually harder for such a person.

The more loosely a group is organized, the easier, in most cases, it is to join it. When Chris's gang were younger, it would have been easier for Eric, who is new to the 'court', to latch on to what one or two of them were doing, and be playing with them before there was any kind of formal acceptance. But at nine and ten newcomers are apt to be scrutinized before admission, almost as closely as those presenting themselves as candidates to join an exclusive upper-class club.

Eric observed the group carefully from a ledge in the corner of his back garden. It might have been easier for him if he had been less cautious by nature: some children would have rushed into the 'court', announced something like, 'Hey! I know a terrific thing we can do! We must take all those branches they've cut down and make a camp!' and ignored all rebuffs until they were entirely on the inside. They are less common, however, than children like Eric, who is very anxious to be accepted, but is very worried about making a wrong move which might subject him to ridicule.

One of the first manœuvres was enacted when the group were running down the edge of the court, past Eric's garden wall. Lesley and Janet were at the rear, and stopped parallel to Eric, instead of running on. Lesley looked at Eric and murmured something to Janet, who was not interested, and soon picked up speed again. But Lesley stood stock still, and stared up at Eric. He returned her look at first, but pretended to be doing something with the leaves on the top of the wall. The staring match lasted only a few seconds. Eric gathered up the leaves from the wall, and retreated down from the ledge. He continued his pretence of busying himself with them even after he knew that Lesley must be some distance away. He was showing *himself* that the incident was utterly unimportant, and that he had his own things to attend to. Not very convincing to the onlooker. But a good example of the comparative strength that belonging to a group can give to a child like Lesley, and the disadvantage that an Eric has by virtue of *not* belonging to it. When we go abroad, it is common to get a feeling that the local people look at us that much more confidently, than we do at them. This gives an idea of Eric's situation. He was a visitor to a foreign country, where *they* had the right to stare.

A little later, he equipped himself with a wooden bat that had a rubber ball attached, and climbed back on the ledge. It was perhaps the most inconvenient place for playing it, trying to keep the ball bouncing high, without dropping down, but he chose it just the same. Lesley and Nicky stopped by him, and watched. The ball trailed down by the wall, and Eric said to them, 'It's not so easy up here.' His words can be understood in about half a dozen different ways. But basically they contain an appeal; and a measure of self-defence.

Lesley laughed. Nicky said, 'Why don't you come down, then?' They looked as if they were more curious about him than unwelcoming—but they didn't want to make it too easy. Chris ran up just as Eric appeared in the court itself, and said, 'Hi, what's *your* name?' Leader talk. Eric showed he had a sense of how to fit into a group by visibly deferring to the leader. In fact, he was accepted very quickly, and five minutes later they were all playing hide-and-seek.

Two points had to be established about the newcomer, and they so organized it that both emerged clearly in the course of the afternoon. The first was to make sure whom he was likely to be stronger than, and whom he would lose to in a fight; and the second was how fast he could run. It would not necessarily have made things impossible for Chris had Eric proved to be the best at both, but it would have certainly posed a threat to his leadership. Further, he had to be weighed up against each of the others. The other major query about him, as in all groups, was whether he accepted the same rules for games, the same arbitrating principles in disputes, and the same taboos. But this takes longer to assess.

Eric was moderately quick at finding an entry and gaining acceptance. Others are not so successful. Partly it is their personality, and their previous experience at getting on with others. The group itself, however, can be more or less welcoming. Strictly authoritarian groups (whether of children or adults) are traditionally the least welcoming of anyone who may be suspected of not conforming, or not being like them. Had Chris been a vindictive despot, and had there been a rigid pecking order, Eric would have had a more difficult time of it. There might have been a complex initiation ceremony. But happy, confident groups, where each can be a relaxed individual as well as acting together, are relatively open to newcomers.

Parents are responsible for a great deal of the exclusivity of groups at this age, and the effects of learning and applying social divisions during this period cast a long shadow. Sometimes children are taught not to play with others of a different colour, or religion or accent or income bracket. The teaching is not necessarily expressed directly: it may take the form of jokes made with other adults against other people, and the implications are readily picked up by the children. The lessons are not easy to undo later because they have formed part of this very important early social experience.

The chances are high that at some point around nine or ten, a child will come into contact with death, or with parents who separate, and with some kind of act (like a bomb incident) which seems to strike at the root of normal relations between human adults. If he does not meet any of these personally he will hear about them from at least one of his friends, and from other sources too. The strongest tendency that parents have here is to protect their children from being alarmed by any of these events.

Certainly it does not help a child to draw him into conflicts, or unnecessary contact with violent feelings, or to feed him with information that he does not ask for, and that will shock him. But it is possible to go too far in this direction, so that his questions are avoided, and he is left in mystery. It can be very painful to talk about such things with children. However, if they are to develop a sense of perspective about the different kinds of things that can happen, and to feel confident about how they themselves will cope with what life throws in their path, then it pays to answer the questions simply, and honestly.

Should you suspect that a child is worried about something which makes social contact difficult—a family problem, or a conviction that the other children are hostile—it is worth talking this over with his teacher. An outsider can often be more objective about a child's reactions. And if there is something in the background threatening him, teachers usually want to know something about this so that they can be on the watch for trouble, and help where necessary. But *assuming* that a child who may be less gregarious than others is socially backward, or traumatized, does him no good at all. Indeed this can intensify a suspicion that he might be different from the rest.

Chapter fourteen

From primary to secondary school

Some of the children whose parents read this book will be making a choice of secondary school for their children to move on to at eleven or twelve. These may be destined to pass from prep schools to public schools, while some girls may be making a simple transition from the junior part of their fee-paying school to the senior section. There are many other permutations possible, including a move to a special school for children with a disability, or a particular gift. The great majority, however, will be moving from the junior part of their primary school into the local comprehensive.

Whichever the direction of the move, parents often have to re-assess during this period just what they believe is going to be best for their child. While it may be true to say that most children are likely to thrive at many of today's comprehensive schools, this does not allow for exceptions: there are both exceptions among children, and among comprehensive schools. There is no substitute for exploring the secondary schools that are available in your vicinity and making a personal assessment. Those which are unwelcoming (you can still see notices, occasionally, saying 'No parents may proceed beyond this point', and there are still headteachers who refuse as a matter of principle to let parents visit their school during a working day) may be automatically downrated. It is almost certainly symptomatic of a gulf maintained between the school, as represented by the staff, and the parents: this is not in your interests one scrap. Find out, also, what experiences other parents have had, whose children have been to the local schools. This gives you a better understanding of what might be expected. If your child can visit the school he is going to attend, so much the better. The more he knows about it in advance, the more natural it will feel to him that he is going on to it.

Sometimes the transition can be very difficult, especially for children who are leaving a school where there was little or no formal class work, and arrive in a room where everyone sits in straight rows facing the teacher and silence is expected. There are secondary teachers who vary their practice in order to make it easier for those coming in from a different atmosphere, but others won't. Parents can help by finding out about such differences, talking about them (but not warningly) to their children, and introducing them to others who crossed over safely.

Secondary school ought to be fun. It often is, although it usually falls somewhat short of the popular notion of 'the happiest days of your life'. It is a great mistake to look on it as a means to an end, if you are a parent, or as that terrible millstone which grinds more and more money out of you every term. Both these feelings are easily communicated to a child, who then wonders how quickly he can get out of it and the emotional pressures it brings.

This is a time during which a child passes from a creature who explores the world simply by making catalogues, or by trial-and-error, and starts to act on hypothesis. It is the final stage of the sequence that Piaget observed in his experiments on the growth of logic and reasoning among children. It does not come all at once. Some children may, in fact, have been acting on this principle, occasionally, at a more precocious age. But the idea of studying something by trying to fix on a rule, and then arranging everything so that a fair test of the rule can be made, starts to appeal, typically, to a twelve-year-old.

There are certain board games which illustrate this way of thinking rather well: 'Master Mind' and 'Cluedo' are good examples. In both these games, the winner beats the other(s) at making logical deductions from what he sees and is told, to see whether parts of his theory are correct, and then combines these parts into the winning answer. If you use trial-and-error you take much longer. You *can* be very lucky, of course, and this is usually unfortunate when it happens to an immature player, because he expects to be lucky in subsequent games. In 'Cluedo', the principle of checking which of a sequence of possible interpretations of the information available is consistent, by first holding one element 'constant' in your mind—e.g. 'Now what happens if *Colonel Mustard* was the murderer; which of the other details must be wrong?' etc.—and then another, is very clear-cut. It is always worth observing the *way* that children play games, to see which stage of reasoning they are at: is it wild trial-and-error; trial-and-error according to a pattern; are they making hypotheses, and if so are they testing them objectively, or inaccurately? Of course, when they are tired, or feel frustrated, they 'regress' to an earlier stage.

This is the background to advanced learning at school. It should be exciting, and very rewarding. There is also the prospect of a new set of relationships with other children, some of which will be very enduring. There is an enormous potential for humour at secondary school, too. Few jokes please anybody as much as the maddeningly repetitive riddles that delight twelve-year-olds, and get repeated endlessly. The scope for having a good laugh at somebody's classroom antics, or at the sudden deflation of a teacher's pomposity, is endless too. Even those who were picked on, or subjected to a strict regime, will remember, if they are honest with themselves, the good laughs.

At first children try to explain at home some of the mix-ups, the oddities, the funny things that have happened to them at school. Very often they only succeed in confusing their parents, who begin to wonder how much 'school must have changed since we were there'. This kind of enjoyment is uncommunicable: even if the parents get the gist, they often do not see why it could have been so impressive, or so funny.

The school diet is much more likely to be varied, now, than in the days when most able children took 'ordinary lessons', while it was the least able who were allowed to indulge in something like 'current affairs' or 'art'. Schools try to be much more of a window on the world than a passage in a library. They have a great deal to offer, and they do so at a point in their lives when, on entering, children are most likely to have unbridled curiosity about a wide range of subjects, and at the same time to have mastered the use of the basic tools with which to approach them—i.e. they can read about them, write down their impressions, make calculations about them.

It is a wonderful point in time. Many children take up at least some of the opportunities offered at school, finding at least one teacher who inspires interest and a desire to work hard at a preferred subject. With these, nobody asks any questions. Everyone expects it to occur naturally. It is the same when, as in most cases, a child fits into his class, liking some, suspicious of others, exchanging ideas and occasionally punches, but essentially swimming with the tide. What is less intelligible is when all this does *not* happen.

Most children undergo a crisis at school, often early in their second term, when most novelty has worn off, and there is a realization that a long stretch of routine and demand lies ahead. This makes parents ask themselves, 'What's going wrong?' or '*Is* it such a terrible school?' But the phase passes. Again, for most children, there are too many positive things to do, by themselves or with others, for a black mood to last for long.

Again, it is the exceptions who are worrying. This is why a great deal of this chapter is devoted to 'problems'. A few children have serious problems, while most have at least one of those described on the following pages at some stage in their school life. It is worth considering the main problems, so that they can be recognized. But this is, or should be for most, a happy and a fruitful time.

One of the main changes affecting the schooling and the peace of mind of children of eleven and twelve over the past decade has been the gradual disappearance of the '11 Plus' examination. For many families this used to be a kind of ordeal-by-fire-and-water that put everyone under severe pressure until it was past. Arguably, the worst aspect of it was a categorization of children into those who were likely or unlikely to succeed, leaving them to play out their school lives according to this role, being taught by teachers who were often too realistic or fatalistic about their school to strive to change the perspective. Now, there is comprehensive education within the reach of the vast majority of children, and there is no stigma attached to being at a comprehensive school *as such*.

There is still a certain selection process going on, however. Children who are placed by their parents into independent schools sometimes start taking proficiency tests, in order to justify selection from an overcrowded waiting list, at five or six years old. Those transferring from infants' schools to prep schools face similar testing at eight or nine. Those who are at prep school at eleven and twelve, plus some others from state junior schools, face common entrance or scholarship examinations. A large proportion of young society, then, either confronts or hears of others confronting selection procedures, according to which 'higher' or 'lower' levels of education (in *their* perception) are being meted out. This has a number of effects on what children expect from education, and how they view themselves by contrast with others.

It is pointless to deny, too, that there is also a great deal of selection within comprehensive schools. At least it is unlikely to be once-and-for-all. But streaming, or at least division by ability into sets for different subjects, is fairly common. Sometimes the 'streaming' may operate only for part of the day, and go by a different name. But tests are given, and notice is taken both of children who clearly show they have special learning problems, and those who show greater than average potential. The educational diet for children in the same class can then be varied, according to the need and ability, either as a matter of school policy or by a teacher taking the initiative.

'Children *know* they are being tested. They soon have a pretty good idea who the brilliant ones are, and where they stand themselves. Sometimes they have a good laugh at the slower ones, and this demoralizes them. . . . The main thing is to try to help those who show *some* kind of response . . . and to stop them getting into a complacent rut. If they know what you expect of them, more or less, very often they just stick there, unless you're prepared to broaden their horizons a bit.'

The above words were spoken to me by a deputy head-teacher of a large comprehensive school near London. They sum up very well the problem of 'psychological 11 Plus' that can affect children in today's comprehensive schools, unless it is guarded against.

Parents can get a good idea of whether their child is likely to be settling into a 'complacent rut' or not by talking to his teacher, and by listening out for comments about what is going on at school. Direct questions, especially of the '*Haven't* you been doing *anything* new or interesting lately?' variety, simply get evasion. But it is often worth talking about one aspect of a subject, and observing the *kind* of response that a child makes: for example, a historical play on television offers the chance to make a number of comments about whether they should see it, whether it's an interesting part of history, what the characterization is like, and so forth. The point to watch for is whether there is a kind of resignation on the child's part that means 'I've stopped believing I can do history, anyway'. Once he *believes* this, he is perfectly right: he can't. It is then a question of building up confidence again; finding out what has been putting him off at school; and looking for ways of renewing interest.

The other side of this coin is to regard children in a lower stream, or in other schools, to which entrance is automatic, and not the result of competition, as 'inferior'. Children at secondary school are fully aware of the economic and academic differences that separate them from others. They would be unnatural if they did not take some pride in their achievement. The difficulty lies in keeping this within bounds, so that they do not get into the habit of denigrating others: if they do, they are ill-equipped for today's, or tomorrow's society, and are in for rude shocks. When I asked Geoffrey, who is thirteen, fresh-faced but keen-eyed, and a scholar at his public school, why he and his friends referred to the boys at the old-established grammar school in the next road as 'village idiots', he screwed up his face and said, 'It's just an expression we use. But we're a long way ahead of them, and we work much harder through the evenings than they do.' Geoffrey is right about the last bit. He rarely does less than three hours' homework. At some level in his mind is the thought that since he has had to earn his position laboriously, he is entitled to glorying a little in his achievements. The strength of this feeling shows in the fact that he spoke edgily when answering my question. When glorying, it is natural to make comparisons with others. But he is wrong when he says, 'It's just an expression'. It is an attitude which may well tinge his relations with others for a long time ahead.

Most parents become anxious, at some stage, about their children's education. It is comparatively rare for a child's progress to be successful and unruffled from start to finish. Usually the anxiety is focused on one of two questions—whether the education is good enough for the child, *or* whether the child is good enough for the education. The list of possible reasons for poor performance at school, in Table 4, shows that there is a wide range of factors that may be at work. Before committing oneself to a fixed viewpoint (e.g. 'Everything was perfectly all right until he joined Mr Smith's class. That man ought not to be allowed!'), it is worth while running one's mind over the other possibilities. Several of the points in Table 4 may be operating in combination: this would mean, perhaps, that the simpler ideas for solving a child's problem, such as a change of subject, or a change of school, might be insufficient to be of real help.

It is also worth noting that some of the factors are 'internal', in the sense that they are more a question of how a particular child is reacting to the elements in his educational surroundings, while

Table 4 Reasons for poor work at school

Internal factors
Nervousness
Other emotional problems
Low motivation: disinterest
                policy of under-achievement
Sense of inadequacy
Physical problems: poor eyesight
                poor hearing
                tension, pain (e.g. over periods)
                ulcers, etc.
Pre-occupations: love ('a crush')
                other interests
                day-dreaming
Specific academic blockage (e.g. 'dyslexia')
Intelligence too low for the standard required

External factors
No encouragement from parents
Pressure from parents; expectations too high
Tension at home (real or imagined)
Bad relations with other children (e.g. bullying)
Bad relations with teachers
Subjects boring; boringly taught
Routine too demanding: therefore fatigue
Brother/sister/classmates discouragingly clever/over-praised
School friends opposed to schoolwork
Changes of school; curriculum; expected achievements
Bad preparation for examinations

others are 'external', i.e. factors with which the child himself has very little to do. In practice, it is more often than not a case of *both* internal and external factors being influential. It is not easy to separate them out, which is usually a task for an educational psychologist, who knows local schools, who has seen a lot of children, and who can be completely objective. The value of making the distinction between internal and external factors lies in making sure—if you consider both sets of possibilities—that you will neither be expecting too much, nor too little from a child, in a given set of circumstances.

Low down the 'internal' list comes 'intelligence too low for the standard required'. This is often a very hard one for parents, especially those who have had some academic success, to accept. The word 'intelligence' is used here to mean the kind of intellectual ability that is reflected in academic work. Obviously there are other ways in which people can be intelligent.

As should be clear from the remarks made above about the 11 Plus examination, this moment in life may be too early for many, for them to be gauged accurately in terms of 'intelligence' or academic potential. At this age, *some* will be obviously very bright, others obviously not. But by the age of thirteen, most children will have given some indication that they might be capable of the standards required in order to study satisfactorily at 'A' Level, and to be seriously considered for further education. This does *not* mean that they will be shining at everything. Far from it. It means that at least in one area, they will have shown a response reflecting both enthusiasm and ability. If this has appeared once, there is every possibility that it may happen again. If it has not, the chances are that any pressure that goes beyond gentle encouragement and tactful indication of other options will cause lasting resentment, because at root it is unfair.

Looking back at Table 4, it is worth paying attention to some of the *less* obvious factors. These are the ones that are most likely to take parents by surprise when they are pointed out by teachers, or later, by the child himself. One situation to which parents are often blind is the one where treatment of a brother or a sister as an academic hero is consistently sapping the will of a child who may only be marginally less intelligent, or intelligent in another way. Physical problems should be noted—at least by the school, if not by the parents. But it is remarkable how many of these are allowed to develop unnoticed. It should be remembered that the more intelligent a child is, the more skilful will be the way in which he compensates for short-sightedness, or deafness, for example.

Testing for sight is very important throughout this age period. Some children become more short-sighted until they are about thirteen or fourteen, when it levels out. Tests in the USA show that academically successful children are often more prone to sight problems than others: they cannot *all* have been reading in their beds by flickering candlelight! Some of this must be due to neglect. Even very clever children have little insight into the relative efficiency of their senses, until they are shown that they are different.

Bullying is, of its very nature, something that happens to minorities. But it is a very unpleasant ordeal for the minority. Both parents and teachers have to play a part in bad cases. It is quite possible that bullying has been encountered earlier than when a child is at his secondary school: typically, victims are singled out early on, and even when they move home or change schools, they are liable to similar experiences. But it is at the secondary school that it is often at its worst, partly because of the increase in the level of the violence that can afflict an older playground, and partly because the 'code' of silence, and the difficulties adolescents go through about communication in general, increase the victim's loneliness.

It is not often recognized that the victim and his bully (who are found quite as much among girls as among boys) are very similar in certain ways. Both feel anxious about being able to get on with others, both feel inadequate in the way they mix socially, and both lack a sense of perspective.

On the other hand, bullies find others who are similarly inclined, while victims don't. Many victims are only children; over-protected by parents who suggest in their manner that reason and cleanliness are the cardinal virtues; better off than their attackers; physically different in some way that sets them apart (smaller, taller, fatter, etc.); and sometimes gifted academically, or in art or sport. Most children who were bullied point to one moment when they surprised themselves and hit back. Others say what a relief it was when they moved up into the sixth form while the bullies left school to take up jobs. All have found difficulties later in getting on with others, however, since the sense of being an outcast, who cannot cope with attackers, leaves a long-term scar.

Parents can help, by noticing when children who normally enjoy school are nervous about going, or sprout physical symptoms to duck out of school: a talk with a teacher is justified. Teachers can help by organizing patrols and getting victims introduced into groups who are less aggressive. The task is not just to isolate the victim and keep him from harm, but to start to make him feel more like getting in with others again.

All schools have some sense of 'code'; it is all the more powerful for not being written down. Children sense that they should not 'sneak' on another child, even if they have been robbed or struck by him. Less dramatically (but no less effectively) there is often a sense of 'stint', whereby children belonging to a particular set work at what is close to the pace of the slowest, so as not to show him up. This is similar to what happens in some factories, where young enthusiasts are quickly made to realize that they should not show up the older, less capable men in the shop. 'How much have *you* written?' is an accusatory question which warns a child that he deviates from the party norm at the risk of prejudicing acceptance among the group. Often there are several groups in classes, so that children can perceive themselves as working in a way that is consistent with one, or with another group. It is by no means uncommon for a very gifted child, coming in the top 2 per cent of the population when assessed individually by a psychologist, to 'under-achieve', consistently, in his classwork. Very largely this is because he needs very badly to be part of a group, and he may worry about talking and thinking differently from them. Sometimes, however, there is a history of a teacher resenting his precociousness as vaguely threatening, or impertinent.

The strength of the desire to conform to the group, then, is a key factor. With many children, the strength of this desire ebbs and flows, much as if they need to reassure themselves every so often that they are, or can be, fairly popular. A few are always at odds with the others, and life is quite hard for them sometimes. These can include children with an inner drive to look for alternatives, to query the premise of somebody's question rather than try to answer it, and to demand why certain rules or conventions should exist. They may be creative, or simply rebellious and confused. They have a hard time at disciplinarian public schools. But there is also a large proportion of children who are totally committed to their group, or to a small number of others. These have very often a sense of loss, or of grievance as far as their parents are concerned, and the group aims and ethics becomes an alternative system to developing a life style based on the parents, and on one's regard for them. Frequently, they encourage each other to follow personalities or ideas which they feel are particularly different from, or opposed to, the expectation and values of parents and of those they associate with their parents' system— e.g. teachers, or the police. This need not be so dramatic as this sounds: it may stop short at the level of deciding that school work is a waste of effort, and that they have little time for anything but their own exclusive enthusiasms.

Teachers sometimes observe that they have more 'distress symptoms' to deal with nowadays among recent entrants to school.

These are important to note, and to find out more about, since they indicate that a child is very unhappy about some aspect of his home life, or his school life, or both. One obvious symptom is simply not wanting to come to school. At eleven and twelve this is more likely to be a sign of anxiety, although for older children there is evidence that sheer boredom can be a prime cause. Tics and skin problems, migraine and asthma are often mentioned as being more common, especially among boys. There is a never-ending argument about these so-called 'psychosomatic illnesses'—how far are they best thought of as physical, how far as the physical results of a mental state? But there is no question that they are at their worst before examinations, or when children are being ex-posed to family rows, or are anxious about their relationship with their parents. Sometimes skin problems are self-induced. At most schools there are a few 'hand-biters', and occasionally a school's younger forms will have a craze for 'hand-rubbing': here certain children, usually the less well-adjusted, will gently but persistently rub parts of their hands or arms (sometimes each others' arms), until sore patches appear. None of these things should be ignored, in the vague hope that they will pass away. If something is done to reduce the underlying mental worry, then they *will* pass.

Against all this, it is worth remembering that children are very resilient in this age group, and can take a few knocks without last-ing effects. They can put themselves into others' positions, now, whereas before they tended to see other people and their circum-stances exclusively through their own eyes. This means that they can have problems explained to them with greater certainty that they will appreciate at least part of both sides' arguments. When there are family problems it pays to talk to them more frankly (although not necessarily *fully*) since they appreciate any gesture that helps clear the air, or explains the situation, when a home passes through an unhappy period. It is uncertainty, and unpre-dictable changes of mood, that worry them most. Provided they are not leaned on heavily for emotional support, they respond well, and sensitively, as companions.

Most children will be laying the foundations for a lot of future learning during this time. They will enjoy this, too; even when they grumble, because it is a very deeply-rooted tradition for school-children to grumble. Parents ought to *expect* that there will be at least some grousing and groaning about how horrible lessons are, how slavishly they have to work, how like a dragon is Mr X or Miss Y, and how nauseous is the food. This is simply being true to type. It can often be distinguished from a serious problem by noticing how often it recurs—if your child tells you each week that he is dead bored, he probably is—and whether there is a certain satisfaction, almost a pleasure, in joining in a group ritual. Grumbling about school *is* a ritual, and joining in gives a sense of fitting in with the group. When a child is clearly nervous or frightened when talking about Mr X or Miss Y, then they may well deserve their 'dragon' reputation, and it is worth checking up.

In industry, it is generally observed that a workforce is at its most productive when it is reasonably contented about the working conditions, where a mutual respect exists between workers and management, and where everyone believes they have a worthwhile goal to aim at. School, of course, is not an exact parallel, but the principles are similar. Some children take to boarding, some do not. Some will enter confidently into whatever seems interesting and concentrate happily despite large, sometimes noisy classes, while others have a greater need for sympathetic individual attention from a teacher. Some will enjoy a routine that has a strong orientation to team games, while others regard what is supposedly recreation as a pain to be endured. All this means that there is very little point in nagging at a child that he must do better at school, or trying to make him feel guilty about under-achieving. Looking for root causes of problems is far more practical, as well as fair. Sometimes a change for the better can be organized in the short term, sometimes only in the medium term—and here a parent *must* swallow his impatience.

It is far better for a child as a growing individual to be helped to enjoy these years, than to gain a lot of skills and distinctions. Most academic gaps can be filled in later. Loss of the chance to develop a confident personality among others of a like age is irreparable. And if a child learns to hate lessons, as a cause of trouble, then this lesson is often learnt for all time.

Some questions that parents ask

1 My child is going abroad for the first time: will he be all right?
Depending a bit on where 'abroad' exactly is, the trip is not likely to
be any more dangerous than a visit to London for the first time.

By nine, most children are sturdy enough to be resistant to most
of the germs they will meet, and to recover quickly from any effects
left by others. It is the less usual illnesses against which protection
is needed. It is important to find out, for example, whether smallpox
injections, or a typhoid injection, is needed before travelling to, or
via, the country concerned. Any ABTA travel agent is likely to know;
and the leader of a school party certainly ought to know.

Apart from this, teach your child to follow the common-sense rules
that *you* would follow: e.g. not drinking the local water, but asking for
a bottle of mineral water with a meal, or to keep in the room; not eating
too much fruit; never to go swimming where the local people do not
swim themselves. And explain carefully that the traffic is *on the right*.

Children vary a great deal on how early in life they are ready for a
trip abroad separate from their parents. With a group, most children
at nine or ten are quite capable of tackling a week away without
feeling very homesick. But an exchange with a family is better at eleven
or twelve—unless the child knows that family well already.

**2 He has started smoking, and I don't know how much he
does it. How can we stop him?** For a start, he cannot be
stopped entirely. The great majority of children are impelled to
experiment with smoking in their early teens, if not sooner. It seems
so much an 'adult' thing to do that it must be tried. Few enjoy their
first draws on a cigarette. But because of the fear of appearing naïve,
many claim to do so, especially if they have been dared to try it. Even
so, they may not stick with it.

Smoking *is* dangerous to health. Several exhaustive investigations
point to this conclusion. The connection between heavy smoking
and lung cancer is established. Many also believe that tar deposits,

left in the inner throat, damage the tissues, making infections like
bronchitis more likely.

Acquiring the habit of cigarette smoking is common enough among
the young. It is both physically and socially addictive. Parents should
ask, and watch, how much their children are smoking. They should
also discourage it: but subtlety is required. They should talk frankly
about cigarettes with them, not so much in a threatening, but a
reasoning way. That smoking is stupid is usually a stronger argument
than that it is dangerous. (Many like the idea of courting danger.)
It can then become aspirational *not* to smoke. Another effective line
is that smoking lessens one's desirability among members of the
opposite sex—e.g. because of yellowing fingers, bad breath, etc.
Economic restraints are a help; but once a child has got the habit,
he will find ways of paying for it. If parents *themselves* avoid smoking,
it makes their arguments all the stronger.

3 He is very moody at times and refuses to do or enjoy anything. How can we shake him out of it? Will it pass?

One of the characteristics that are spotted regularly among children
at or around puberty is moodiness. When it first comes up, and there
seems no obvious reason for it, parents are often puzzled. Twelve,
for example, seems young to have pre-menstrual tension—but if a
girl's mother has it, why shouldn't *she*?

Most children go through phases of being more than usually
prone to moods. But if these moods get really 'black', and if they
get worse and more frequent, something has to be done. Such
children often want to talk, although they feel unable to do so
properly. They are usually uncertain about what is happening inside
them; about what is waiting for them in life; about the friends they
might have; about who to rely on. They are proud but unsure about
asking for help—a difficult combination. In some cases, they may be
sensing that something is wrong in their home, possibly between
their parents, possibly in the difference between the way brothers
or sisters are treated. All these are examples of being faced with
problems that are too great to find an easy way round; and too
delicate to talk about bluntly with father or mother.

Those children who have close friends usually recover from
moods much more quickly. But those who can talk reasonably freely
with their parents as well—*without* being told they are being stupid—
are in the best situation. A sense of humour helps a lot too. But
parents have to be very perceptive about when and how to appeal
to this without seeming to laugh at their children.

When children clearly do not respond to any of the normal
distractions, like hobbies, or trips, or the cinema or TV, their
moodiness may have a deep-seated cause which will have to be

7

investigated carefully before the symptoms can be affected. They may be afraid, very afraid of something that they cannot properly put into words. There is no stigma attached nowadays to asking for a psychiatrist's help; or to seeking an appointment with a social worker at the local Child Guidance Clinic.

4 He never eats properly: what should I do about it?   Parents are often surprised to find that other parents' concepts of what 'proper eating' ought to be are vastly different from their own. In any event, when children move into their teens, there can never be complete control over their diet. Some will gorge themselves if they really want to; others will diet in absurd ways.

What parents can do is to note how their children's weight, and shape, is developing. In most cases if something is getting out of proportion weight control is going to be needed, not extra food. Too many children eat too much. They need to be told about the dangers of over-eating, and encouraged to cut down between meals. The meals themselves need to be balanced, and interesting enough not to make the child long for suet puddings again, or chocolate bars. Obviously, school meals are a law unto themselves, but more and more schools recognize the need for low-calorie alternatives now, such as salads. It often only needs some extra parental pressure to get this started. Some children are going to need special diets. There are plenty of good books offering advice on this: but make sure you choose one that is appropriate to the age group, and check with a doctor if necessary. Finally, remember that it is counter-productive to offer round a bag of sweets in full view of a child who is supposed to be off them.

When very thin children do not eat 'properly', it is worth varying the diet to find out what is going to prove tempting by way of main meals. If they *still* do not eat much, they may have fear or a strong revulsion connected with food. A doctor, then a psychiatrist may need to be seen. This condition, known as anorexia, is more common than had previously been supposed, and needs attention before the child becomes physically weakened.

5 He is always getting into fights. Why? What can we do?
Some children seem to get into fights whenever they possibly can. They never know exactly *how* a particular fight started—it always just happened.

Being easily drawn into a rough-and-tumble need not go with wanting to hurt others. It can be a sign of several things: having a lot of energy, and not knowing what to do with it; finding it hard to get on with the group-structure of other children in the playground, or district; needing to show that one is as tough or as good as the others; desire for attention. Fighters often seem frustrated, and there is a theory that they are looking for physical contact at any price, because they are missing it at home or with close friends. This is a speculative argument, but it certainly seems to be true that they are less pugnacious when they are given affection rather than punishment. To ignore such a child, as a punishment, can have the worst effect.

Eventually most children come to the conclusion that it is rather childish, and below their dignity, to go in for fights. They work off their energy and some of their aggressive feelings on the football field, or at lacrosse. But there is another kind of fighter who does not know when to stop, and tries to inflict some kind of pain whenever he is crossed, or his temper runs out. There is a high correlation between being this way inclined and receiving harsh physical punishment at home. These children need a basic change in the way they are being taught to treat other people.

There are always some children who are suspected of being eager fighters, when in reality they find themselves being picked on at school for belonging to a minority group, possibly with a poor knowledge of English. When this is felt to be the case, it must be taken up with the school authorities at once.

Chapter fifteen

Puberty: understanding the physical changes

Puberty *happens*. There is nothing whatever that can be done about it. Some parents wish that somehow it could be arrested, although few would like it stopped altogether. But nature is against them, because both the onset of puberty itself, and the mental shift that urges children to do something about it, have been getting younger all the time. So the target has to be to help children to take it in their stride, rather than be overwhelmed by it.

Here are some recent accounts of children who *have* been overwhelmed, in one way or another. Their experiences are not restricted to any particular social background.

Judith

Judith, aged eleven, went to see a teacher in whom she felt she could confide, to tell her, tearfully, that she had a disease which she felt was 'probably cancer'. What she wanted to do was to be allowed to occupy a quiet corner of the sick-room where she could inconspicuously die. She is an impressionable, intelligent child, who has had a comparatively sheltered upbringing. Her school work, and her interest in school life, had deteriorated badly. She had interpreted her first period as a sign that she was diseased, in an area that was never discussed, and was a matter of shame, in her family. Her aunt had in fact died of cancer, and she knew that that was an unmentionable subject too. The teacher, with the school doctor, gave her some basic reassurance and advice. This was in due course resented by Judith's mother, who doubted the story, and objected to her daughter being instructed in these things prematurely and by others.

Philip

Philip, aged fifteen, is the probable father of twins. (No one will ever be quite sure, but the evidence points in his direction, rather than anyone else's.) It is a matter of good fortune (certainly not of planning) that he has not fathered more children yet. He lives in an average middle-class London suburb. As I write, he is preparing to take six 'O' Levels, and he is expected to pass each one without difficulty. He entered wholeheartedly into all the activities which his elder brother enjoyed—discotheques, drinking, parties with little or no light—including the urge to make love. His sexual activity reached the ears of pained but disbelieving teachers, until Jenny's parents arrived one black day to sort the whole thing out with the head-teacher. Philip had been told a bit about the 'facts of life' by his father, and had learnt considerably more about sexual practice from his brother, and from various books. No one had told him anything about responsibility for children, or about contraception, or about risks of venereal disease in promiscuity, or about how young girls feel when they become pregnant.

Doreen

Doreen, aged sixteen, is very grateful to her sixth-form teacher for being let off all kinds of school activities, and for being smuggled quietly into classrooms and into examination rooms to be able to sit her 'O' Levels, despite advanced pregnancy. She had slept with boys since her fourteenth birthday, and had always discounted the chances that pregnancy could happen to *her*. No one had explained that with frequent intercourse the chances rise rapidly, or that measures might be taken to avoid pregnancy. This is *despite* having basic information given to her by her mother at puberty; and *despite* having had many books offered her to read, both at school and at Sunday school. One comment she made to her teacher, however, was perhaps revealing about her mentality: 'Sometimes I thought, well, I like children, anyway. . . .'

Doreen's parents seem to have a good understanding with her now. Her baby has been adopted. She is working hard for 'A' Levels, and will probably get into university.

Jack

Jack, aged fourteen, was discovered by a teacher after school, preparing two younger boys for sexual activities. He was aware that he was doing something 'naughty', and he said he was sorry. The younger boys were excited but alarmed. Jack evidently had very little sense that he was organizing anything worse than, say, smoking a cigarette and passing it round. It was just—fun. Investigations showed that the ideas had been copied from the examples and suggestions of another teacher at the school, who later confessed to taking some of the boys home for 'extra physical training sessions'.

It is worth noting that in this case some parents had actually been told about this—perhaps not in complete detail—quite some time before this teacher's colleagues found out. They referred to him freely as a 'queer', but had not considered that it was really their business to interfere. So nothing was done.

It is doubtful whether Jack, or the others mentioned here, are going to be permanently handicapped by their experiences. But they have each been deeply affected. It may be some time before Jack attains a normal perspective on sexual relations. Yet he is lucky in this sense—that in the past he might have been severely punished, and left with a load of guilt, but no understanding.

There are many other children whose encounters with sex and puberty have much less dramatic potential, but who have still been made needlessly unhappy, or recklessly overstimulated. Helping a child take things in his stride needs positive action, not just sitting back and hoping for the best. It should start with giving access to information whenever a child seems to need it. There is no point in loading him up with information that he does not want, or is unprepared for, but there should always be an open door, so that he can feel confident about discussing anything with his parents. The other major task is somehow to give sexual matters a sense of perspective—natural, and desirable, but only a part of life, and not worth rushing. Parents impart this by example, by not sounding defensive or secretive, or alarmed when the subject arises, and by being cheerfully objective when sexual morals are queried, rather than hypocritical at one extreme, or salacious at the other. But first, it is a question of getting the facts right.

The start of puberty is clear-cut in the case of a girl, less so in the case of a boy. The first menstruation is a perfectly obvious sign that a girl has begun to ovulate, and is capable of having an egg fertilized in her womb—in other words, of becoming pregnant. This event is usually known to the girl's mother, who may have

Figure 7 Puberty and associated development—a typical boy and a typical girl

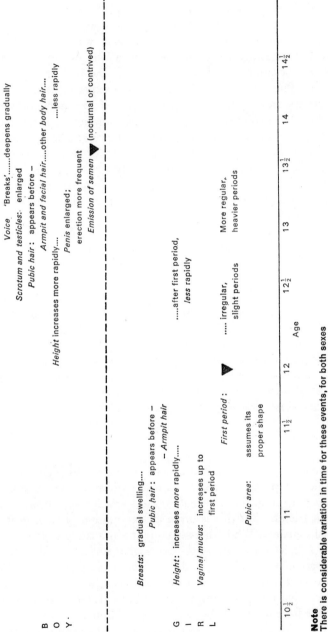

Note
There is considerable variation in time for these events, for both sexes

advised her daughter to look out for and report on the characteristic discomfort, and the small release of menstrual matter that follows. Preparation for the event helps from a practical point of view, as well as to protect morale. A boy may suddenly experience his first orgasm during the night, in a 'wet dream', which may attract the attention of whoever makes the bed or changes the sheets. But a boy is likely to be more experimental, and more secretive, and his family may not know if he has begun to have nocturnal emissions, or to give himself orgasms by masturbation.

Figure 7 shows the order of events, for girls and boys, in puberty. The age of puberty has been getting lower for years. Some calculations suggest that over the past seventy years, the average age at which a girl will be menstruating has become younger by about four years. The exact reasons for this are mysterious, but improved diet must be a big factor.

Earlier puberty has two important results. First, mothers are still likely to be surprised when it happens to their daughters, and are then forced to make up for lost time in explaining to them what is happening to their bodies, and why, and how to protect themselves against embarrassment and excessive discomfort.

Second, the ability to bear children reaches girls at an age when, with few exceptions, they have not got the understanding or emotional development that allows them to come to terms with their physical maturity. They need help, and the opportunity to talk about anything that disturbs them, both from the physical point of view, and with regard to the sexual role they have been given. Most girls want to know more about what boys are like, too, and it pays not to be impatient with perfectly natural curiosity.

Some girls seem to adjust rapidly, and completely, later priding themselves on being unlike others 'who make such a fuss over it'. Some also pride themselves on being self-sufficient, claiming that they can get all the information they actually want from books or from friends. But this is often an assumption of superiority that cloaks anxiety. While there is no point in foisting conversation on this subject on to any girl—bearing in mind that she may find aspects of it genuinely, and understandably distasteful—there is no excuse whatever from running away from questions about it and taking refuge behind the latest book. Literature is not a substitute for parents talking with their children, although it may be a help. Refusal to talk is direct provocation of a generation gap: it is encouraging a child to believe that he and his friends are essentially different from their parents on this whole subject.

There are a lot of 'secondary sex characteristics' that usually appear in a child just before, or during, puberty. But the timing and the combination of these characteristics is an individual matter that allows for much variation. This fact must be borne in mind when studying the 'time-table' in Figure 7.

In the example given, the boy is roughly two years behind the girl in terms of puberty. This is normal. But he may not be two years behind in all of the points in the Figure. Voice development may start early, with a distinct 'break' that makes a boy undependable in a choir; then the voice may be stuck as it were, between treble and tenor, and only gradually deepen until it settles into a recognizable range.

Usually the first sign of puberty for a boy is enlargement of the scrotum, or the sac that contains the testicles. The testicles themselves are enlarged, and are said to 'descend' when they spread downwards into the bigger sac.

Pubic hair first appears about this time, usually a little after the testicles have 'descended'. Gradually more and more hair appears, usually in the order—face, armpit, body. On the face, it is traditionally a soft down on the upper lip at first, and a faint suggestion of sideburns. Some boys, impatient for adult status, will deliberately encourage this growth by clipping this hair surreptitiously with nail scissors, or even by 'borrowing' their father's razor. Other boys are embarrassed by their hair, especially in the pubic area, and some word that this is normal, too, may be appreciated. Males vary considerably in the amount of body hair they eventually develop. Chest hair may take several years to spread around in virile fashion. Hormone preparations *can* be taken by young adults dissatisfied with their appearance on the beach—if they really feel badly about it. But during the teens, it makes more sense simply to wait. Body hair is a hereditary matter; tendencies to being hirsute run through families.

The penis grows in size for several months before the first emission.

One reason for saying above that earlier puberty is connected with better nutrition is that there is a connection between gain in height and puberty. Increase in height is faster for a year or so *before* puberty, and the rate slows down after that. Better-fed children tend to grow taller, too.

7*

With girls, there is a very gradual swelling of the breasts, which can be discernible up to two years before the first period. The breasts are unlikely to reach full size, even then; their development is a complex matter involving nutrition, subsequent hormone activity, exercise, and of course other events such as going on the pill, or pregnancy. It is not at all uncommon for one breast to grow at a faster rate than the other, but this can alarm both a girl and her mother. When one breast remains obstinately larger, this may be a family trait. But usually they are close to each other in size, eventually.

As with boys, a girl's pubic hair makes its appearance, as a rule, before hair reaches her armpits. Also as with boys, there is a spurt in upwards growth for a year or so preceding the first period, and a slowing-down afterwards.

For some time before the first period there may be an increase in vaginal mucus, which may give a false impression of puberty being imminent when it escapes from the vagina and causes staining. This is perfectly normal.

The first period itself may be slight in volume, and have a more watery-looking colour than that of a mature woman. Thereafter, for several months, possibly more than a year, periods can be variable, sometimes appearing on time, sometimes not, and sometimes not appearing at all. In the end, the rhythm becomes more regular, and periods become heavier. Some women athletes take hormone preparations to delay or suspend ovulation (and therefore periods), when they can calculate that they would otherwise risk being off form, or unable to play in a championship. Sometimes it is found that a contraceptive pill performs a similar function, longer-term. But it would be most unwise for any young girl to go in for anything of this kind without medical advice.

It should be clear that the development of the hormones is central to the whole process. Figures 8 and 9 are included to help explain where they come from, and what their functions are. Not everything is understood about hormones, which are difficult to study because they often act jointly, and sometimes have several different effects, depending on the stage reached in the life cycle.

Figure 8 is limited to a consideration of how female sex hormones combine to produce the effects necessary for reproduction. This is complicated enough. For the sake of space and clarity, no mention is made of the effects of Oestrogen on the secondary sex characteristics. It should also be borne in mind that the inter-

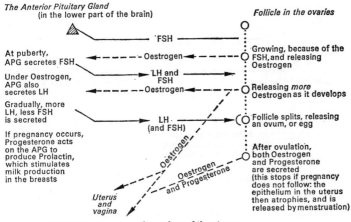

The hormones prepare the surface of the uterus

Figure 8   Female sex hormones

Notes: FSH = follicle stimulating hormone
LH = luteinizing hormone

actions between the Anterior Pituitary Gland and the ovaries do not happen just once, in perfect form, at puberty: there has been a gradual build-up to the point where the stimulation of the follicle can take the course prescribed in Figure 8.

The follicle is in the ovaries, the place where a woman's ova, or eggs, are produced. Note that hormones have to travel in two directions, so that both the APG and the follicle are stimulated by each other's secretions, before ovulation can take place. When this happens, an egg is released into the Fallopian tube. Here it may be fertilized or not, depending on whether male sperm reaches it, during or after intercourse. Two of the hormones (Oestrogen and Progesterone) have been acting on the uterus (womb) to produce a change in its epithelium (lining), so that this becomes the right kind of tissue structure to receive the fertilized egg, and to service it during pregnancy (as the placenta). The first menstruation occurs when the first egg has been launched into the tube and lost through non-fertilization, so that as no more hormones are produced to keep the epithelium going in the state it has reached, the body rejects it. It is largely because the hormones have not reached the point of preparing everything perfectly for reproduction, that menstruation is slight and variable during puberty.

The chart for male sex hormones, in Figure 9, is relatively

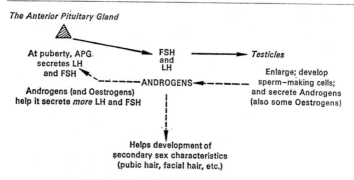

The Anterior Pituitary Gland

At puberty, APG. secretes LH and FSH

Androgens (and Oestrogens) help it secrete *more* LH and FSH

FSH and LH

ANDROGENS

Testicles

Enlarge; develop sperm–making cells; and secrete Androgens (also some Oestrogens)

Helps development of secondary sex characteristics (pubic hair, facial hair, etc.)

Figure 9   Male sex hormones

straightforward. For completeness' sake, it should be mentioned that there are several types of 'Androgens', which have differing functions.

If your child is particularly early on any of these points, it is simply a manifestion of earlier maturation nowadays. This affects boys as well as girls, although the evidence is neither so clear, nor so dramatic. But where there is a long *delay* in the appearance of secondary sex characteristics, or in menstruation, it is worth asking a doctor to make a check-up to see if there is some reason for it. It is important *not* to make the girl or boy feel that they are in any way peculiar about this. They are probably making comparisons among themselves at school, anyway, and adding to their sense of missing out may be a blow to their self-esteem. In some cases, resentment of one's sexual role, and subsequent nervousness and bitterness about it, can be traced to suspicions that one's body is not developing true to form.

Sometimes a girl may acquire some of the secondary sex charac-teristics of the opposite sex—to her annoyance, if she is anxious to be pretty. Body hair, including a thin moustache, can be embar-rassing. On the male side, some boys may experience slight swelling of *their* breasts, at fourteen or fifteen; this may affect, temporarily, as many as one in three. Both of these problems are examples of the fact that everyone has a certain amount of male and female in them. The balance is individual, and the pattern of maleness and femaleness is individual, too. A boy who does not need to shave may still be entirely capable of paternity. This dual sexuality, which everybody has, is best explained by another reference to the sex hormones. Male and female alike have each got those parts of the body which are typical of their sex, and *also* counterparts of the physical characteristics of the opposite sex. Normally, the latter are undeveloped, and remain so. The most obvious 'counterparts' are male nipples and the female clitoris. But the principle extends to men having a certain amount of female hormones, mainly Oestrogens, and women having some of the Androgens in their system. Since each person has a variable amount of the opposite sex hormones, and since hormones usually act jointly, or effect chain reactions, it is clear that there must be certain times of life when the hormones are stimulating the production of secondary sex characteristics of the opposite sex. This may be short-term; or there may be a longer-term imbalance, where a specialist's help and advice will be needed.

Chapter sixteen

Puberty: parents and their children

If parents are managing to preserve a matter-of-fact but sympathetic relationship with their children during and after puberty, most problems that their children are likely to have during this period will come to light quickly and naturally, and will be short-lived. But parents who *do* find themselves worrying, tend to have one or two broad categories of problem on their minds. There are some who suspect, to put it briefly, that their children may want, or be drawn into fulfilling, their sex role too quickly; and there are others who suspect that their children may not be growing up in a way that ensures eventual fulfilment of that role. In other words —too much too rapidly; or, too little.

To take the first problem first: some feel that their children are displaying precocious sexual interest, have too high a consciousness of their own sexuality, a determination to know more, and a will to experiment. Usually they place the blame for this on other children, on suggestive magazines and television programmes, on the loss of old-fashioned moral restraints—on anything or anyone rather than their own children. It is more realistic to suppose that, while blame may often be placed very fairly on outside influences, there is a certain curiosity about sex which will arise spontaneously, to some degree, in *most* people.

Having said this, there is no doubt that nowadays, young minds are teased by a great deal of sexually stimulating material, directed at them by most media. Some of it bounces off harmlessly enough; but some of it exercises the mind in a confusing way. Much of the tone of this material makes implicit assumptions about the interest in sex that it is 'normal' for a young person to have. Arguably, it is these assumptions, rather than the material in itself, which are more likely to influence attitudes towards sexual activity. How far this influence goes depends very much on the home background, and how far the child feels confident and happy about being part of it.

Parents have a difficult course to steer. Forbidding anything outright, by way of reading material, or shows, is virtually pointless, partly because it increases their desirability, and a feeling that the sign 'For Adults Only' really means what it says, and partly because it is more or less unenforceable. Making it clear what your attitude is towards this sort of thing is another matter. This is *your* natural response towards it, and it brings the issue more out into the open. Children like to know where the family stands on anything, and they respect consistency, provided it is not entirely joyless. It is important not to register too much shock, however, so much as a pitying disregard for the mentality behind, say, a magazine you are startled to see brought home. (This may mean a partial disguise of your feelings, but it will still be within the bounds of an honest response.) Shock stimulates a child's curiosity just as much as a prohibition, because it shows the material has *power*. Disdain puts it into its place.

You may worry about having a double standard, i.e. not letting them read what you read. In fact, it is very much part of human nature to derive some personal amusement out of stimulating material, and at the same time try to protect youngsters' minds from too much direct contact with it. William Faulkner's novel *Sanctuary* is a good example, perhaps; it is a strong, memorable book which few would deny had considerable literary merit, but most parents would feel that the rape scene, in particular, was not a good idea for a young teenager's reading-list. Most parents probably have some book or magazine that they prefer to put under a cushion. But what is important to realize is that sooner or later the double standard will become apparent to any intelligent child; and while most children are indulgent towards parental embarrassment, they do not easily forgive hypocrisy when they are in their teens.

One strong school of thought is that children are best helped when they are encouraged to treat sex in an entirely open way. The argument is that they will be more natural about it, and obtain more pleasure out of it eventually, while keeping a sense of proportion, if their parents are completely frank about sexual relations and sexual problems, their own and other people's, and if the parents and children can enjoy together jokes based on sex or sexual aberrations, explaining them where necessary. This view is sometimes (not always) combined with a feeling that children today ought to be brought up to assume sexual freedom, and equal rights between men and women in the question of sexual independence, while recognizing certain responsibilities, mainly towards children, or in the avoidance of pregnancy, or the spread of VD.

An opposing school of thought might approve the frankness, but claim that this is carrying things too far; that a clearer moral lead needs to be given to children in their own interests, so that up to the time when they have greater emotional maturity they will not become too easy a prey to unscrupulous people outside the family.

This is not a book on morality. Parents will have their own views on how far traditional codes should be maintained, both in and out of the context of sexual behaviour. Here are merely three points worth stressing, which have been reflected very clearly in social and clinical studies:

(a) Children are helped most, in the long term, when they are not made to feel guilty about interest in sex, or about pleasure derived from sexual stimulation.

(b) Children appreciate being given evidence that there are some basic rules to which the family adheres, for protecting each member against strong emotions—in others or in oneself. A completely *laissez-faire* system, because of the strength of the feelings involved, can provoke anxiety, and make for a confused person.

(c) Parents are entirely justified in deciding that certain books, films, parties, company or behaviour are undesirable, given the age of their child. If they have rules, they should *apply* them: but they must be prepared to discuss the rules, so that it does not appear to the child that the rules are organizing the people, rather than the other way round. A young person will only respect rules from which he is given to understand that, directly or indirectly, he actually benefits.

Another point about rules is that they need to be revised as the children get older. Parents have to realize that in most cases they are not preventing sexual stimulation and experimentation, but merely postponing its becoming obvious, when they are being restrictive. They cannot blame their children for this either. Curiosity, as stated above, is natural. Postponement in itself is a justifiable aim, provided it is not bought at the price of a severe break between parents and child at a later date, when the child decides he has had enough of restriction.

In his early teens, a child is hard put to it to come to terms with his new physical equipment. That, and the influence of the media, outstrip a child's capacity for understanding the mental effects of sexual relations, or seeing what might lie beyond body contact. For a while they need rules, and protection.

Pregnancy at fourteen, or even earlier, is a phenomenon of our times. It receives comparatively little publicity, partly for humane reasons, and partly because society has not really decided what should be done about it. Very young fathers receive even less publicity, although they too are very much in need of understanding and help. The duty of preventing children from reaching these situations must lie with their parents.

Offering advice on contraception to someone under the legal age of consent (i.e. sixteen) seems abhorrent to many parents. This is because it seems very much like condoning sexual behaviour in a child, and actually encouraging the male partner to engage in an illegal act. But if it is clear that, say, a girl of fifteen is likely to be having sexual intercourse, and that even if a particular opportunity is stopped, the next one will be avidly seized, then two courses of action should come to mind. The first course is to have a matter-of-fact talk with the child about the principle of conception, and how it might apply to her. (Often children do not immediately grasp this last part of the message.) The second course is— assuming that adequate precautions are not being taken—to talk about contraception, and make it possible for her to have what is required. The same principle applies to boys. This may sound revolutionary, and an encitement to break the law. What would they say at the local family planning clinic? Would the local GP co-operate? In point of fact, it depends on the clinic and on the GP. But the difficulty of suggesting anything of this kind is simply another sign that society has not learnt or decided what to do about a very real problem.

It is worth commenting here that many teenagers *reject* contraceptive methods. They complain about their being unnatural, and destructive of spontaneity in love-making. But part of their antagonism towards using them (apart from the cost) seems to stem from having been advised to use them rather sternly, e.g. 'Well, if you must be so depraved, at least take one of these.'

Obviously this kind of recommendation is entirely self-defeating, since it builds the wrong associations with the product.

Clinical studies have suggested that errors made by parents are often based on misconceptions of how their children actually think. Boys are frequently told nothing about the dangers of premature paternity, either because it is assumed that they are going to have greater knowledge about sex, or because the location of any subsequent 'disgrace' will be outside the family anyway. Boys at this stage of their life are spending less time thinking or fantasizing about starting a family than girls. They need discussions about family life, as well as about sex, and in particular they need some introduction to the principle of joint responsibility where producing an infant is concerned. In Scandinavian countries this need is recognized, and classes on family life are organized in many of their schools.

Another false assumption is that young people who have intercourse are necessarily promiscuous. Research among youth clubs in the north of England showed that it was comparatively rare for a young person of between fifteen and eighteen, male or female, to have sexual relations with more than one partner over the space of three months. Pairing, in fact, was much more common than 'sleeping around'. Talking to a child, then, as if he were promiscuous by nature, as opposed to feeling a close attachment to somebody, is making a false assumption that undermines communication.

Another misconception, of course, is that because others in the same class are sexually precocious, a particular child is going to be like them. They influence each other, but not to that extent. Many young teenagers talk about being urged to be like others, and enjoy sexual experience straight away. They would not talk in these terms if they did not see themselves as having a different viewpoint that was coming under pressure. It is important not to *add* to this pressure by assuming that youth today is automatically permissive. Lectures in schools about VD sometimes run the risk of going too far in this direction. It is only reasonable to warn children that it exists, how it is contracted, and how it is connected with promiscuity. But trying to put a child off sex completely by using VD as a bogey may serve the opposite effect: simply because the child identifies not with the communicators, but with those that they seem to be attacking.

If a child *does* become pregnant—what then? There are several possibilities. As society is constituted, none of them is entirely satisfactory. Abortion is one. Here there are moral issues, which are questions of ethical argument. From a physical point of view, it can be argued that abortion suspends a process, for which a young body may not be fully prepared: in some cases this will be so, but it depends on the body. Mentally and socially, a young woman is going to lose a large proportion of her childhood through pregnancy, including educational opportunity. On the other hand, she may suffer a deep sense of loss if a baby is removed from her for adoption. Not enough is known as to whether this feeling might be all the greater if the mother is very young and immature; nor is it really known how it affects future relationships. Abortion prevents this from affecting her. Some spokesmen for adoption societies play down the distress of a young mother 'who has made a mistake', and the closeness she may feel to her baby. But this is very much a matter of the individual personality of the mother. 'She'll get over it,' is a wish-fulfilling overclaim. She *may* get over it would be more accurate. For this result, she needs a balanced personality, lots of help, and strong relationships with others. Abortion removes the gamble element in this. The point that a baby in these circumstances is unlikely to have a very satisfactory upbringing could be used in favour of adoption as the escape route, just as much as for abortion. It cannot be guaranteed that a baby will fit into a grandparental home perfectly happily, although there are more cases of this than is supposed. A final argument for abortion is put forward by those who believe that the need to control world population is paramount: therefore, *any* unplanned baby should be aborted.

Against abortion, it is no longer possible to claim that permanent physical damage is likely to be done to the mother, assuming that a competent specialist, in a competent hospital, is in charge. Care has to be taken not to induce the abortion too late. A very young pregnant girl may be very hazy about dates, and a doctor has to exercise his own judgment. The big issue, however, is mental, not physical. It is a strange preparation for mature sexual response, and eventually becoming a wife and mother, to be operated on, with no little discomfort, for the removal of that which has developed completely naturally, as a result of making love. Investigation of the after-effects of early abortion on the capacity to respond sexually is limited to relatively few clinical studies, and needs more thorough research. What evidence there is suggests that if abortion is contemplated, it should not be undertaken with a young person except with psychiatric help, before and after the event.

The reader will notice that a lot has been made of pregnancy in children: this is because it is a problem of our time, and because there are no easy answers. The problem admits many individual views, but a personal conclusion is that the least permanent harm may be done by telling young people about contraception, and about how they can get it. Ideally, the family and school atmosphere would conspire to help young teenagers to approach sex more cautiously, and at a pace more consistent with their emotional development. But we are not in an ideal world.

The second area of major concern to parents is about children who do not seem to be developing naturally. Is there any risk of their child becoming homosexual, as opposed to heterosexual? This is far more likely to enter their minds today, when the subject of homosexuality is freely discussed. It should be noted that children at school know much more about it, in the average comprehensive school, than used to be the case. Parents may also have seen reports in newspapers that one man in twenty is an actual, or a potential homosexual, as is one woman in fifty. Estimates vary; the more dramatic ones are usually based on special samples, e.g. students. But homosexuals are clearly a significant minority. The Gay Liberation Movement, and other groups, champion their rights. Their standpoint is that parents should accept homosexuality in their children as an unusual, but perfectly acceptable trait, rather like being left-handed. This is still, however, a rather extreme view. Most parents want to think that their child will be sexually 'normal'.

Certain worries should be discounted. It does *not* make a boy more effeminate if his father has kissed him a lot as a child, and shows affection for him as he grows older. There is no correlation whatever between this and male children becoming homosexual. Then there are worries about 'crushes', the special friendships, sometimes unreciprocated, that young teenagers often have for older children of the same sex at school. It is probably the rule, rather than the exception, that children should first go through a kind of homosexual stage (often only taking the form of worshipping from afar), before adopting members of the opposite sex as love objects.

But what makes some people halt at this homosexual stage, and proceed no further? Assaults, intimidations, or seductions by older boys have often been singled out as the most likely reasons. In some cases, these factors have certainly played a part. But many children have been sexually assaulted and have *not* turned homosexual. Constitutional factors, and personality factors that reflect early pressures in the family, are needed to explain other cases, where homosexuals have become adult before understanding properly what they are like, and without having met anyone who has made any kind of homosexual declaration to them. Constitutionally, tests comparing male homosexuals and heterosexuals have shown that more homosexuals have physical features that suggest more than usual activity on the part of the female sex hormones. Clinical studies, on the other hand, have shown that there is very often a fear of woman, of having intercourse with a woman, in the homosexual's mind. In these cases, some prefer to identify themselves with a woman rather than with a man, and it has been suggested that they feel 'safer' that way. The fear may have started in a number of ways. Homosexuals are more likely to have had a shy, passive father, and a dominant mother; there is also some evidence linking harsh repression of sexual curiosity about one's mother, or about women in general, with later homosexuality.

Homosexuals are often heard protesting that there is nothing 'wrong' with them: that they simply prefer being what they are. Certainly many of them are in a happier state now than in the days when society hounded them. But they are often unhappy (irrespective of whether this is their fault or society's), and parents who feel that their child may have homosexual tendencies that go beyond a brief phase, have every right to ask for a consultation with a psychiatrist. *Not* that psychiatric help will necessarily make him heterosexual, or happy to act in a heterosexual way. But such a child may need to have help in coming to terms with his own feelings. He may need to overcome a strong sense of guilt, of inadequacy, and possibly of persecution, real or imaginary. Homosexual or not—and many people change during their life-time—it makes sense to face the situation as a family, with the benefit of an objective, confidential adviser who has seen many similar problems.

In fact, up to the age of fifteen it is unlikely that many of those who are going to be homosexual, whether boys or girls, are recognized as such by their parents. Failure to show great interest in the opposite sex may be greeted with relief, rather than as an odd sign. And, of course, it is hard to say whether someone is merely being slow, or secretive. Children with homosexual leanings may well have ceased to communicate, except at a superficial level, with their parent of the same sex. This, too, makes it hard to analyse feelings.

Most homosexual girls do not realize what their tendency is until they are fully adult. They can often be divided into those who seem to want to be similar to men; and those who, while preferring the attention of other women, have great femininity and a need for protection possibly based on failure to develop the confidence of a normal adult capable of looking after her own affairs. Both types commonly have a genuine fear of relations with men, and may find them abhorrent. But many 'lesbians' are not so neatly categorized.

It cannot be stressed too strongly that just because a girl is a tom-boy up to, and some way past, puberty, this is no reason for worrying that she may be destined to become the first, or 'virile' kind of female homosexual. She is, temporarily, fighting against the role that she perceives to be woman's destiny, and is resentful of the good fortune that local boys, and perhaps her brother, seem to have. She may feel, also, that she has somehow 'missed out' by not being equipped with more conspicuous genitals, or simply by not having a boy's strength. Countless girls go through such a stage, particularly if they see that their father approves and admires their brothers' male pursuits, or spends more time watching soccer on TV than talking to his daughter. They intensify their efforts if they feel they are being dragooned into female ways. But if they are treated more patiently and sympathetically, they adapt over time. In most cases, a whole complex of factors—e.g. interest in sports or hobbies that are common to both sexes, like music, and evidence from her father that he finds her pretty in a particular dress—divert the tom-boy gradually towards a middle path, and subsequently a female path.

She may still maintain strong interests in what used traditionally to be male pursuits, but—whether it seems right in a 'liberated' age or not—the great majority of girls tend in time to develop overt femininity.

Most girls have a 'crush' at some time, too. When the crush is on the gym mistress, as opposed to an older girl, and when it is protracted, parents sometimes worry (assuming they ever know about it) as to the effect it might have. But usually the object of the crush has her power over her admirers by virtue of representing an ideal. She is, or seems to be, the embodiment of all the wonderful talents and achievements that her admirers wish for; if only they were more athletic, more beautiful, etc. Once a certain threshold of familiarity is reached, the idol seems too much like flesh and blood. It is usually pointless to look for the roots of lesbianism in this kind of school situation, except in rather rare cases where a teacher is actively encouraging this kind of relationship. Even then, a girl is probably only influenced by this in the long term if certain other factors apply. These may include fear and shame where boys are concerned; a sense of alienation from the process of bringing up a family, as she knows it in her own home; usually low confidence in herself as a person who can go out and organize her own life; and some unusual constitutional differences.

I have avoided making any mention so far of single-sex schools, and whether they contribute towards homosexual tendencies. In the past, when a number of boarding schools had unenviable reputations for bullying with a distinctly sexual tinge, and homosexual teachers actively proselytized in them, such a contribution was frankly undeniable. Now, it is much more difficult to make a judgment, and there is not much by way of research evidence. (The finding, for example, that proportionally more male homosexuals went to public schools, may simply mask a socio-economic difference.) Single-sex boarding schools do create conditions, however, in which sexual exploration is far more easily directed towards one's own sex; by reducing contact with the other sex they may magnify fears, apprehensions, prejudices. But they may still only be a contributory factor. The holidays should provide opportunities for bridging the gap between the sexes. And a child who is to become homosexually inclined at this kind of school may be different from the majority anyway; he may have the misfortune to come under certain influences, in a particular part of the school, before being mature enough to cope with them.

Several aspects of modern life alarm fathers, in particular, so that they warn their sons not to be effeminate, pointing out that they looked very different when *they* were boys. It does not help a boy one scrap to tell him this. It attacks his confidence, and drives the wedge between the generations that much deeper.

Boys need to be accepted by their friends: if the norm is for longer hair, for a greater interest in clothes and toiletry products, and to a closer imitation of the life style of pop-music stars rather than sportsmen, it is natural for a boy to move towards these symbols that his friends will acknowledge. They do not necessarily make him any more effeminate in the long term.

There are other problems, too, that parents face when their children reach puberty, and pass through it. Some of these are picked up in Chapter 17, on teenagers. But two are more relevant in the context of relations between the sexes.

Not to display any interest at all in the opposite sex may be perfectly common at thirteen or fourteen, although it may be becoming less normal. If it persists at fifteen it is considerably less usual. In most cases this is a question of a young person keeping his thoughts to himself; or sharing them secretly with one or two friends of the same sex. Parents may wait in vain for any sign of enjoyment of a visit from somebody of the opposite sex, and may note that at groups, or in gatherings, he or she does not mingle easily, and is rather forbidding when approached. This can be worrying; but far more likely than a homosexual explanation is a lack of self-confidence, and a strong fear of rebuff or ridicule. It can affect both sexes, but is usually worse with boys. They are aware of the fact that, traditionally, they should be dominant, and make the first approach, but they cannot cope with this role just yet. Many are also aware that girls nowadays are expected to be more forward—possibly even 'liberated'—and they are uncertain whether to be relieved or alarmed by this change and what it might mean. They have a problem of adjusting to a girl as to a thinking and a responding human being—especially if they have been to a single-sex school—since most of the jokes, songs and folk-lore that they enjoy with other boys treat women more as sexual objects, things to be used, rather than to be drawn into friendship.

Girls, of course, may be just as shy, particularly if they suspect they do not measure up to the standards of attractiveness they perceive are desirable from films and magazines. In general, though, teachers tend to agree that girls have more *savoir-faire* when meeting boys than the other way round. Both sexes are likely to be nervous of the possible results of their own feelings being strongly aroused. This kind of feeling is another disincentive towards easy mixing.

It is better for parents to accept that there may be such an anti-social phase, for a time, and to wait for it to pass. This is better than looking for suitable young partners, and parties, to strew in their children's path. They should also avoid hinting that not being sociable with the other sex is immature, or abnormal. Informal gatherings of both sexes, especially those where there is no parent observing in the background, may be more attractive to such a child: a positive step, therefore, can be to find if there is some mixed group, e.g. a swimming club, which he might join ostensibly because he is interested in the activity to which that group is devoted.

Then there is the problem of *un*suitable partners. Parents are naturally apprehensive when they see someone they imagine to be far more mature and self-confident bearing down on their seemingly defenceless offspring. They are also anxious if they feel a particular companion, or a group, is hell-bent on a degenerate plunge, again involving their child. If a parent feels strongly that the ideals and way of life represented by this threatening outsider are totally opposed to what the family believes in, he needs to broach the subject, and try to talk it out, openly, with his son or daughter. But this needs to be done very carefully. Children react strongly against what they read as class prejudice, or a suggestion that *they* don't know what they are doing. Preaching about the danger and depravity of others only makes them more interesting, and possibly desirable. Discussion, not preaching, is the best thing that can be done; and the discussion has to be two-way. That is, parents must be prepared to listen to their children's comments about others, and signify that they take their point, even if they are not persuaded, from time to time. Those parents who have maintained communication, and regularly talk about everything under the sun with their children, have an obvious advantage.

It is often the children who have been over-protected against possibly damaging contacts outside the family, who are most likely to be struck forcibly by an unexpected social success they have made with the local wolf, or nymphomaniac. The fact that fathers usually worry more about the young men around their daughters, while mothers are particularly protective towards their sons, suggests in itself that a great deal of anxiety on the part of parents has prejudice, rather than objectivity, as its base. But there is always the exceptional circumstance.

Unfortunately, there can be no rule of thumb. Sometimes, it

will be very important to prevent an impressionable young person from getting too closely involved with, say, a group of heroin fanciers, or somebody with a drinking or a gambling compulsion. Occasionally it might be worthwhile pointing out that someone does not seem at all the kind who might reciprocate romantic feelings with any depth. But advice of this kind is very often entirely wasted. It can have the opposite effect: it can put a child in the frame of mind where he is *looking* for evidence that contradicts his parents, so that his own natural judgment is clouded. In any event, hard luck stories in early love are two a penny. Everybody is likely to want to make his own mistakes, and is going to be hurt some time. The best that a parent can do is to have helped to give a child confidence, and objectivity, and a feeling for some basic rules of behaviour and responsibility. Further than that, he can maintain friendship, which encourages free discussion, and a feeling that there is a friendly home to which to return, without recriminations. This does not prevent a child from getting hurt; but it makes getting badly or permanently hurt much less likely.

Chapter seventeen

What makes a teenager?

'Everything you've ever heard about having a teenage daughter is absolutely true,' a father confided in me gloomily. 'Teenagers shouldn't be allowed.'

In his case, adjustment was hard. There was a sudden change from having a daughter who delighted in traditional family pleasures, to seeing her hunger for new and threatening experiences. No longer the automatic assumption that everyone enjoys long muddy walks at week-ends with the dog, or family holidays, or Christmas parties at home; and no longer the feeling of sharing a common-sense attitude towards school, clothes, diet, bed-times, and the difference between the way *they* did things, and other people's silly habits. Now there was a numbing sense of cold war whenever money for toiletries, cosmetics, or for any clothes other than schoolwear, or functional underwear, was discussed between mother and daughter. And the flag of revolt was flown whenever visits to Grandma, jobs round the house, homework, or the dubious character of two older boys in black flying jackets were mentioned by father. To do them credit, the parents concerned had expected something of the kind, at some stage. But not at fourteen and a half. And not all at once. What made it worse for them, in a way, was that their elder child, a boy, was already sixteen, and had shown virtually no signs of teenage spirit or restlessness, and he regarded the scenes with his sister with detached amusement.

These are the first points to bear in mind, then: the *pace* of change towards what might be called 'teenage', or 'pre-teen' interests is increasing; and that it is a very *selective* matter. Some parents may, from their experience, regard most of the problems outlined here as very minor indeed, compared with what *can* happen. Others will wonder what all the fuss is about, and query whether this book is really talking about normal families. The viewpoint of one's own experience colours most attitudes towards teenagers. Teachers describe what they see in the older classes of their schools. The police, and some social workers, tend to see the results of the work of the more extreme versions of teenager, in their more extreme moments. Some youth club leaders, by contrast, and some charity organizers, are more struck by the greater social consciousness that they see among teenagers today: they see evenings and week-ends given over to teaching handicapped children to swim, or to visiting the unvisited in hospital, or to decorating old people's homes. They see the best side, and give a correspondingly rosy picture.

Society in general is two-faced about teenagers. People are shocked when they read of things like drug orgies, muggings and vandalism, because they suggest the break-up of civilization. And yet many rather enjoy these reports, at the same time. (Otherwise, why are they given so many opportunities to read and hear about this kind of news, while comparatively little action in terms of time or money is taken to do much about the causes of it?) The reasons for this enjoyment are complex. Part of it comes from the resentment felt by older people towards younger people, who have so much of their energy, and their life, before them. There is satisfaction in getting confirmation that today's teenagers are a 'bad lot'. But there is also a certain *admiration* for these very same teenagers, too. It is indisputable that young people today do not suffer from the same constraints as in former times. They have more chances of education, travel, communication, entertainment. . . . The chances are still not evenly spread, but there are more of them there. Society envies and admires today's teenagers. When they read about teenage excesses, many people note that 'young people don't seem very appreciative'. But society helps to mould its own teenagers; and it may be justly said that every society gets the teenagers it deserves. Our society has given them more freedom and more opportunities; has confused them by alternately depriving them of former ideals and standards, of behaviour, and then blaming them for not living up to those ideals and standards. We set them bad examples, too. We give them the chance of spending a lot of money, and treat them as a special corps of consumers for the purpose of making bigger profits, through marketing and advertising specially geared to their needs. To say that society—which then reproaches them for conspicuous over-spending—is two-faced towards teenagers may therefore be something of an underestimate.

This introductory passage is needed because, by and large, the development of children up to this point has been mainly one of response to their own physical nature, their personality, and their interactions with the rest of the family and at school. From fourteen onwards, a young person has far more points of contact with society at large, and with influences which may be very different to what he has met so far.

This period of life, up to adulthood, is very much a time in which to experiment with new influences, and new ideas, before the point of becoming committed to a particular life style. There is imitation of adults; but there is also a desire to try and do things differently from the adults one can see. Previous historical times and new or unusual philosophical movements are idealized, and taken over as patterns for behaviour. Media and the entertainment industry are quick to exploit such trends in thought, and rapidly make them seem more widespread, and sometimes more authoritative.

Nowadays, the teenager has a more distinct identity. But this really only goes as far as a convenient label for *other* people to use when describing young people. Someone who is fourteen or fifteen tends to be instantly suspicious when asked if he considers himself a teenager. He suspects that he is being categorized, and resents it. His individuality is important to him, even if he is not keen to appear eccentric. He resents any impression that he can be lumped indiscriminately with certain groups of his own age, or (which fills him with horror) with groups that are just a bit younger. Teenagers are aspirational, in a way that is individual to today, and is difficult for adults who did not follow the same progression to understand.

Figure 10 shows the difference between typical age-group aspirations now, and the simpler patterns they followed in the past. The models that children take after now are usually a year, possibly two years older than they are themselves. Of course there has always been, and always will be, a certain envy of older boys and girls, but this has tended to be based on a desire to be further along the road towards the position and the opportunities of an adult, with all the maturity, confidence and power that that suggested. The elder brother or sister had more status within the family, and represented the next approximation to the main target. But now that

Figure 10 Age aspiration patterns in teenagers

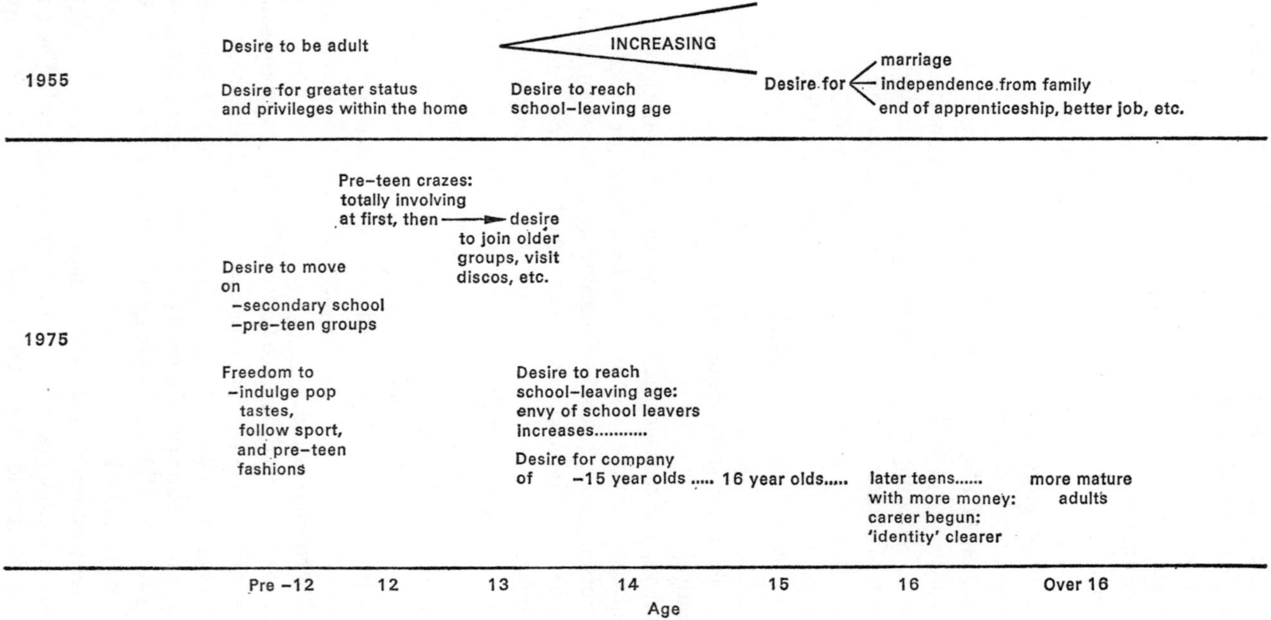

1955

Desire to be adult

Desire for greater status
and privileges within the home

Desire.for marriage
independence from family
end of apprenticeship, better job, etc.

INCREASING

Desire to reach
school–leaving age

Pre–teen crazes:
totally involving
at first, then ——→ desire
to join older
groups, visit
discos, etc.

Desire to move
on
–secondary school
–pre–teen groups

1975

Freedom to
–indulge pop
tastes,
follow sport,
and pre–teen
fashions

Desire to reach
school–leaving age:
envy of school leavers
increases..........

Desire for company
of –15 year olds ..... 16 year olds.....

later teens......
with more money;
career begun:
'identity' clearer

more mature
adults

| Pre –12 | 12 | 13 | 14 | 15 | 16 | Over 16 |

Age

Note
The more sheltered, family–oriented or academically inclined the child, the more he
inclines to a 1955 pattern—*until* a reaction sets in.

there seem to be far more wonderful objects of fantasy and wish-fulfilment among the age group that is only just around the corner, the immediate target is to join, be accepted by, or form a unit that corresponds closely to what that age group is doing, and is like. There are usually 'leaders' in these units who formulate policy on what to copy, what to enthuse over, and what to do. These are often acting as interpreters of what the slightly higher age group is about, and what its heroes are doing.

There is a 'pre-teen' phase which for a while seems more self-sufficient, that is, not so dependent on aspirations up the age-scale. The timing of this varies from one part of a city, or a social bracket, to another, but the average age given on the chart is intended to be twelve and a half. This is when the first big, totally committed concentration of energy and attention outside the family motivates the lives of these children. The strength of the emotions may swallow them alive, for a while. The external idol that acts as a pivot for their grouping may be a pop star, a footballer, the local riding teacher—or a combination of people who seem to be doing exciting things; all the more so if they are presented by press and television as greater than normal human beings, with intense magnetism. Nowadays, there are many young people of thirteen or so who are glorious (in the strict sense of the word) and command big followings. The Osmond success story is based partly on *demonstrating* that children can also be stars. Success is attainable, even for a pre-teen, is the message. It is a situation, where all the wishes to be loved and to be popular that affect normal children to a greater or lesser extent, are seen to be fulfilled. Many of the questions that pre-teens ask in the fan-mail that they write to stars, or to their fan clubs, reveal a desire to live through the star's life more fully, to identify with them in more detail. There are many requests for information to help this along, e.g.

What does —— eat for breakfast, please? Does he like toast, and does he allowed [*sic*] to leave the horrible crusts? . . . I bet he has a dog. What kind? I wish I had a big dog myself. (Boy aged twelve, to a fan-club secretary in London.)

There are lots of questions, too, about the relations between stars and their parents. Sometimes these are assumed (to judge by the tone) to be idyllic, but sometimes a revolt against parental authority is suspected as the background to stardom: this revolt, naturally, is felt to be successful.

It follows that those children with a more satisfactory home life, in terms of love, stability, and mutual regard, are less likely to need this kind of escapism to the same extent. These may join in, so as not to miss out, but remain on the sidelines, keeping their objectivity.

Sooner or later, however, the older group of children, who glance at them but quickly look away, seem to be living a more desirable life. This impression is strengthened by the disdain that those elder children express towards the younger ones. Being mistaken for a 'teeny-bopper' is perhaps the most hated fear that can alarm a teenager. The search for maturity, for being with the group that is just that much further advanced, will not admit any back-sliding.

It follows that a large number of young people are insecure about their status. They recognize, on the one hand, family ties and expectations, together with the values encouraged by teachers. (These may, sometimes, be not at all inconsistent with the formation of a gang and a cult: but more often at least the forms of expression chosen for the cult are rejected by parents and teachers.) On the other hand, there are all the blandishments of marketing and media to look for easy fun and thrills in a simplified world where criticism is suspended, and teenage mystique transcends any kind of social responsibility. It is not easy for children to decide what they want to be like, in these circumstances, or what to approve and what to reject. But further than that is the nagging doubt that their aspirations to be accepted at the higher level are doomed because of lack of maturity, talent, *savoir-faire*, attractiveness, connections, or for want of sufficient freedom from parental restraints. For a vast number of teenagers, acceptance at the right level looms so large in their mind's eye that any or all of these sources of insecurity are likely to plague them every so often. Teenagers within restricted circles—living in certain small towns or villages, or in boarding schools, for instance—are less subject to these pressures, since they very often have a sense of belonging to a unit which gives them a tightly controlled series of goals, e.g. the gradual accumulation of status and privileges in the miniature world of a public school. But this rarefied atmosphere is penetrated more and more often, nowadays, by news of what other teenagers are doing. Often, when attempts have been made to shut out modern influences at all costs, the reaction of teenagers who suddenly launch themselves into everything of which they feel they have been deprived is exceptionally strong.

Many of the more alarming traits that teenagers display become more intelligible if they are viewed as compensations for the insecurity that results from doubt about their ability to stand the scrutiny of their own age group, as well as that of the older age group to which they aspire. What, for example, have the following in common: smoking and drinking beyond the point of enjoyment; wearing clothes or shoes that are cold or uncomfortable, but which at least demonstrate a vivid difference from what others are wearing; experimenting with drugs; making sure that others hear all the music that they themselves are listening to; and aggression? Each is a way of emphasizing an insecure teenager's presence, while at the same time showing that he is rejecting part or all of the rules and conventions that he resents as restrictive. They can also be seen as ways of protesting at the double standard that society tries to impose on them—i.e. telling them with one voice that teenagers are wonderful, fun-loving creatures destined for greater freedom and pleasure than anyone in the past, and insisting on their following in the footsteps of their parents with the other. Yet another interpretation (and this is not inconsistent with those given so far), is that each act is a shrill demonstration of arrival within a group, and of one's worthiness to be in that group. Someone who does not smoke at fourteen, for example, may be suspected of being too immature to join such a group. Therefore he smokes. Eventually, if he can afford it, he may come to enjoy it. Most groups that have a code of aggression usually insist—with or without ritual—on some evidence that a newcomer is going to be suitably aggressive too. Typically, he may be instructed to 'mark' a conspicuous supporter of a rival football club, or to snatch a bag in a train or at a station.

Some years ago, when marijuana and other soft drugs started to become current among teenagers, and crazes developed around them, it was feared that a very large proportion of the teenage population might succumb to the habit, and gravitate towards harder drugs, while younger and younger children were encouraged to copy their elders and tag along. There is some evidence for the second of these fears being substantiated, but fortunately relatively few seemed to take the further step, towards heroin. Now, knowledge of soft drugs is fairly common among

8

many groups of teenagers, but it has lost, apart from some un-happy exceptions, a lot of its craze value. One possible reason for this is that although smoking 'pot' serves to show, for some child-ren, how sophisticated they are, it does nothing at all for group feelings. Smoking pot in fact tends to cut a person off, effectively, from any but the most repetitive actions with other people. There-fore it was failing at one of the purposes of teenage cult objects—to make the actual and the potential members of a group feel more at one with each other. Another pointer in this direction was given by an intelligent, precocious girl of fifteen:

We used to, once or twice, you know. . . . But we don't do it much now. It was fun at first—but now it seems so boring. . . . Some silly little kids you see trying it—I don't know where they get the money. . . .

In her case, introduction to soft drugs had apparently been by means of an enterprising pusher operating from an ice-cream van. But now, to her and to her friends, it had already become some-thing that 'younger kids' might do.

Drinking is, in all probability, a far more serious problem. Figures for alcoholism among teenagers are far worse than for drug addiction. Partly, this must be because it lends itself so per-fectly to group activities; and it is a field where teenagers can compete with each other, and issue challenges. This is by no means confined to boys: the challenges that girls issue to each other are usually more subtle, but no less real. People oppose the constraints that embarrass them socially, by drinking, which is particularly helpful to the more insecure. Further, it has enter-tainment value: at some stage, in group drinking, somebody is bound to do or say something that makes the others laugh. For all these reasons, drinking is very liable to enter into the teenage world. It will do no lasting harm to most, but alcohol is far more addictive than soft drugs, and because it provides an easy route to feeling secure socially, it is always going to be very dangerous to teenagers who need to be dependent on something.

Simplification is one way out, for teenagers, at any stage up to adulthood and independence, and beyond that too, Simplifying the choices to be made, the groups to be joined, and adopting a set of intransigent standards, gives a sense of position and pur-pose. That which has been called the 'noble idealism of youth' is partly a description of one kind of simplification. It refers to a young person's ability to judge a complex issue simply, straight-forwardly, and to want to act on that judgment immediately, with-out the caution, detachment, or cynicism that a more experienced person would bring to bear. It is also a self-protective measure, which makes it easier for someone to talk, think and act consis-tently, in a way that satisfies personal and social needs. There are many forms of simplification. One is dogged progression up the school ladder by doing the right sort of thing; one is dedication to an art or a hobby; one is to seize on a cause, which might be religious, political, or based on a desire to change a particular feature of local life, and pursue it wholeheartedly, so that it is reflected in one's entire behaviour; yet another is to follow the flag of aggression, joining a gang whose purpose could be to shock and extract whatever can be taken away from others, or to avenge an underprivileged group (racial or economic) by attacking whoever is identified with its attackers.

Since earlier puberty has meant that physical preparedness for pairing off outstrips emotional or social maturity for this, it is not surprising that *most* teenagers are very nervous of the other sex. Those who appear to be the most provocative and boastful in their boy–girl relations are often more nervous than those who seem quieter about them. A teenager who either brags about his or her conquests, or who goes out of his way to denigrate the opposite sex entirely, is the kind who is usually most concerned when an approach is suddenly made from the other side.

Teenage boys and girls are eager to impress each other because it helps cover insecurity, just as much as in order to win attention and affection. Different strategies are adopted: the typical male teenager will find a way of indicating that he is strong in sport, or academically, or has a cause that is burning him up, while the typical female teenager will be anxious to show that she is desir-able, and socially forward. *Both* sexes are liable to suggest that they have no enormous need for each other. That is part of the business of impressing somebody. Both are extremely anxious to avoid ridicule; and connected with this is the anxiety to be the one who is going to do the rejecting, if there is any rejecting to be done. They also become dependent on having elements of a common language, so they can bypass the problems of using for-mal English, and of lacking conventional formulae for addressing and answering each other, and for knowing when someone has over-stepped the mark: the rules of etiquette, both the middle-class variety, and the unwritten lower-class variants, were discarded some time ago. The elements of common language include catch phrases that are more suited to their age group; swearing, to indicate liberation, and also that here is an individual who expresses himself *hard*; badges, types of accessory; reference to battles of will between themselves and their parents. All of these serve to provide echoes of the way a teenager is expected to think, to another. Music, and adoption of musical styles, is perhaps the strongest and best-developed code that the teenagers have for this kind of communication with each other. E.g. 'She's reached Pink Floyd but couldn't graduate to Tangerine Dream', is a very clear description.

Teenagers today are *not* an entirely new kind of animal. Previous generations of teenagers have been deplored, and defended, just as much by their parents. But there are discernible trends among teenagers from one decade to another, which are worth noting. People can argue endlessly about where the trends come from, but as a general rule they can be described as responses to an intolerance of the values or demands that society is imposing. This fits neatly into the context of the trend in the early and mid-1960s towards the ideal of substituting war with love. In the background were the horrors of what could happen without an H-bomb treaty controlling tests, and the availability of nuclear weapons, and there was the situation in South-East Asia where seemingly endless destruction was threatened in the name of ideologies that many sought to question. It became a period of 'love-ins'; of wearing flowers in the hair; of pacifist anthems sung to Beatles rhythms. As a counter-balance to the forces who were bent on confrontation—given that this trend went far beyond national, or even Western boundaries—a historian might claim that the trend had been a timely one.

Clothing, hair and cosmetic styles, and accessories of all kinds, are usually tied in closely with the degree to which a teenager accepts that he is part of the prevailing trend. The mini skirt was an appropriate accompaniment to the more natural, deliberately unsophisticated ethos of 'make love not war'. So was the trend towards straight long hair, and a 'natural' look with a minimum of cosmetics except round the eyes. A swing back towards caftans and maxi-lengths can be seen as indicating a feeling that some mystique needs to be regained, for the body and for the personality. A reversion to Victorian styles can be read also as a reflection of a more passive state of mind, in which the confidence that one can change society by frontal attack has shifted towards a more fatalistic preference for a former era, thus indicating rejection of suspect principles of progress in life and in society through economic growth and modern invention. Precise explanations can be argued about, but the principle should be borne in mind that teenagers' fashions, especially those which they help to generate, or which they accept with particular enthusiasm, are there to be *interpreted*.

Often there is a period during which groups of teenagers do not know what they want to wear, and what they should represent. At such times they tend to opt for a kind of uniform—for sweater, jeans and training shoes. This makes them more comfortable, in that if they cannot identify with a cause, at least they can approximate closely to each other.

It is easy, at the present time, to tell the uncertain ones apart from those who are inclining towards the current trend of aggression. Following the Beatles came groups and individual performers who destroyed objects like guitars, or bourgeois symbols like prams, on stage; and violence has spread from areas where it was always endemic into cities, into transport, and places of entertainment where it is obviously recruiting parts of the teenage population who were supposedly immune. The 'martial arts' from the East have built up a huge cult following among the young. The clothes that signal this kind of move include shoes that look as if they were designed for use in street fights, and studded belts. It is now a sign of the times that the traditional Boy Scout knife, after decades of respectability, incurred the suspicion of the police and of other teenagers, and has had to be banned from being worn in public.

Not enough has been said about one most impressive trait that distinguishes the near-adult from an older person. This is the great energy that teenagers have for a project that really grips them. Once they regard something as worth doing, they cannot stop themselves from doing it, whether it means long hours of music practice or sports training after work, or waiting in long queues for promenade concerts, or humping sand-bags through villages cut off by floods—teenagers have the will to devote themselves utterly, if the cause seems worth while. Energy being used is wonderful. Providing causes—by indicating where they are, and by selling them if you believe in them—makes much more sense than ignoring teenagers, and leaving them to use up their energy in whatever way suits them. The price they pay for having great energy is to have a great capacity for boredom too. Some bored teenagers just look lethargic, but they usually find a way of kicking at a society that has been so misguided as to let them get bored, instead of feeding their imagination.

Chapter eighteen

Sport

There are many parents who imagine, in their mind's eye, a series of triumphal scenes in which their son or daughter carries all before them at one or more sporting events. Often they are re-living their own past in an idealized way: they like to see their children triumphing where they, themselves, would have liked to have excelled, but in fact only achieved partial success. While these parents may enjoy, or profess to enthuse more over their children's academic, artistic or social efforts, they feel a distinct glow whenever they see them running faster than others, or handling or kicking a ball more skilfully.

Other parents have a suspicion of athletics and sports, which comes out in feelings of impatience, boredom or antagonism when they have any talk of their children enjoying more than cursory acquaintance of games. But these tend to be a minority. They include some parents who were embarrassed or worsted at games when *they* were children, and suspect that this is liable to happen to their own children too; there are those who acquired a self-protection habit of disdain for 'the flannelled fools at the wickets, and the muddied oafs in the goals' and naturally want their children on their side; there are also parents who are anxious, or over-anxious, about possible side-effects of sport on health.

Parents' attitudes are very important, when looking at develop-ment in this area, because they influence to a large extent both the motivation and the opportunity to devote oneself to particular activities at the best time for the body to acquire agility and skill. If parents show themselves interested in, and impressed by, their children's performance on the sports field, they increase motiva-tion. If they attach a high enough importance to it, they will make sure that there are opportunities to get good coaching, and to practise. They will find out whether a school has a strong sports side, before committing their child to it.

In the same way that parents can supply motivation, they can also destroy it, by taking a negative or sarcastic attitude. They also achieve this same result unwittingly, sometimes, by pushing too far: they set standards of performance that their children can't reach, or find to need so much hard work and stamina, that they lose heart. No one enjoys a game if it means feeling you are on trial every time you play it.

There is a very close analogy here between sporting and musical achievement. In both cases, a child's interest is unlikely to get properly started without any prompting from parents. But push them too far, too quickly at either, so that they are improving technically at the cost of enjoyment, and dislike followed by apathy will gradually set in. Both are similar, too, for the fact that early experience, before the age of nine (when parents *have* to supply the opportunity if not the original idea), is extremely important if the child is going to become exceptionally good. That goes for swimming, as well as the violin.

Apart from parents' influence, there is the question of how competitive the child is. It is not always the most competitive child who wins races, or captains the hockey team: but this kind of distinction rarely occurs to a child who lacks a truly competitive spirit. The will to win is important in *most* sports. Even gymnastics thrive on a desire to perform better on the parallel bars than the others. Even the most team-orientated of team games, e.g. rowing, or tug-o'-war, demand a fierce sense of purpose. Which would *you* prefer to be pulling with—oarsmen who enjoyed a sense of togetherness and a certain nostalgia as they watch the mists rise over the Thames? Or a gang on whom you could rely to have one object exclusively in mind—to row the other crews into the ground and so lift the trophy at the end of the afternoon? This is not to decry fell-walking, or any of the sporting activities that give satisfaction and exercise to those who are definitely less competitive. It is to make the point that personality differences, and early experience of give and take in the nursery and kindergarten, are playing a big part in inclining somebody towards sport. This kind of personality is sometimes described as unnecessary to society, or even unpleasant and anti-social—depending on whether the speaker shares in it or not. But it is at the core of sport. And if it exists, it may well be better channelled into sport than into other aspects of life.

There are some children who are called 'natural athletes'. These will certainly have emerged victorious at some active game or other by the time they are nine. This is because they have a combination of good co-ordination—that is, they are agile and accurate in their movements, and can accurately calculate the movements of objects through space—and a strong competitive personality. Typically, they can run fast, they can throw and catch with ease, they have very good balance, and they are strong fighters too. These are the basic elements which characterize them, and although they may enthuse over one game in particular, they usually find the lure of something new irresistible. Sometimes they do several things very well, with the result that they never actually master any particular sport as well as they might. But if they are moving from one game to another on a seasonal basis, they can advance effectively on all fronts, as they grow older.

Schools very often have a number of 'sporting families': where there are brothers or sisters together at the same school, and one is outstanding at games, the other is outstanding at them as well. It is easy to see how, in the particular family at home, brothers and sisters are encouraged along similar paths when it comes to competing for parents' attention. This must be one reason, although there can be more simple, genetic reasons as well.

The other two powerful influences on sporting prowess are the opinions and regard of other children; and the encouragement given to this kind of activity by the school. Sports heroes are *popular*, it is the same in the playground as it is in the outside world, where thousands of adults will stop in the street to get a better view of a sporting giant, and will pay a great deal just to see the very best. Leaders of groups of children tend to be good at least at one kind of sport. If children cannot perform brilliantly at something themselves, they can at least gain some reflected glory from being part of a winning side, which may involve adulating the best of the games' players round about. Winning is important to most children, particularly if they are not mature enough (or too competitive) to accept minor defeats with equanimity. Opposing the best players is much more daunting to them than finding some means of identification with them. The phenomena of the boys who know every career detail of the head of the First XI;

8*

and of the girls who go to every gymkhana to cheer a particular older girl as she collects her cups and rosettes, and who wait hopefully in case she needs help with some item of her equipment, are both very well known. With this kind of reward available for the most successful, it is hardly surprising that doing well at sport is a goal for many who prize popularity and want more of it. Success feeds on success. Popularity is a reward for doing well, and in itself provides a spur to keeping on top, if not towards greater efforts.

Some schools set greater store by the *corpus sanum*, than by the *mens sana*. They will try to improve their sports facilities, their equipment, and their standards of coaching, and they will provide at least their better sportsmen with opportunities for fitting more practice time into the week. Other schools will restrict development in either of two ways: by putting a greater priority on the time to be spent at work, or refusing to allow much choice of sporting activity, so that those who are not at their best when playing, for example, football or hockey, are not given the opportunity of finding something at which they will really shine. Schools also differ in the extent to which they confer honours— becoming prefects, etc.—on those who are successful at sport as opposed to academically. In fact the idea that children should be good at one or the other, but not both, has no foundation in fact. It is a situation that is contrived at some schools, because it is an assumption underlying attitudes towards time-tables, and the encouragement given to concentrate on this or that. Research among gifted children (e.g. studies by Parkyn in New Zealand) shows clearly that if anything, early intellectual and athletic potential tend to go *together*, and not separately. Common sense must suggest that intelligent use of information is likely to be linked to good eye-and-hand co-ordination, and to a better grasp of strategy and tactics in a game. But popular myth, rehearsed and prompted by the school, puts scholarly children into a frame of mind that sports are a soft option for the dullards who cannot concentrate on 'work'. Similarly, those who show skill with their hands or feet are led to believe that 'being cooped up in a classroom' is strictly for the weeds. This contrast is usually stronger in boys' schools, or on the boys' side of mixed schools; this is only a matter of degree, but a possible reason is that skill at sports offers some boys a clearer temptation in the form of a career, rather than being complementary to other achievements.

As a result of all these influences, some children will naturally become intoxicated with sport; others will enjoy it, but lack the motivation to indulge in it with serious, long-term enthusiasm; and there will be a body of children who actively dislike it, and avoid it. One answer to help those in the last category to become more active, and to help some of those in the second category to want to obtain mastery of something, is to look for opportunities to introduce children to new games and sports. It is always possible that some totally unsuspected game will evoke a response, even among children whose dislike of team games or athletics has brought them to the conviction that 'it's all so *pointless*'.

In looking for something of this kind, it is worth making sure that a child can not only start to become enthused, but can also keep it up, at a suitable level. Thus it is rather inconsiderate to give a child a short series of preliminary fencing or riding lessons, and then admit that there is not the money or the opportunity to go on with them. It is also worth considering, from observation as well as from questions, where your child fits on the chart in Figure 11.

This chart looks complicated, but isn't. The two lines which cross at the centre represent dimensions of your child's personality. Near the top of the vertical line would come those children who have a great need to be with others, and to enjoy their company most of the time. They like doing things in a group, and feeling that they are part of a team. The further up they are on this dimension, the more they will appreciate belonging to a team of some kind—to play football, or lacrosse—or perhaps to a group or club, where they can learn judo or skating.

The second dimension (along the horizontal line) describes the difference between children in the kind of sporting acts they enjoy: the biggest difference is between those which demand all-out physical effort, above everything else, and those which are primarily a question of skill. Obviously, this is a matter of degree, since every sport requires a certain amount of skill, and I have purposely omitted games like bridge and chess which require very little expenditure of physical effort—at least until one is preparing for high-level competitions. Those sports and games which are closer to the left-hand side of the chart are more energy-orientated, those on the right need careful acquisition of skill plus a measured amount of energy.

A boy or girl who needs company but is best suited by a game

Figure 11 What kind of games will he or she enjoy?

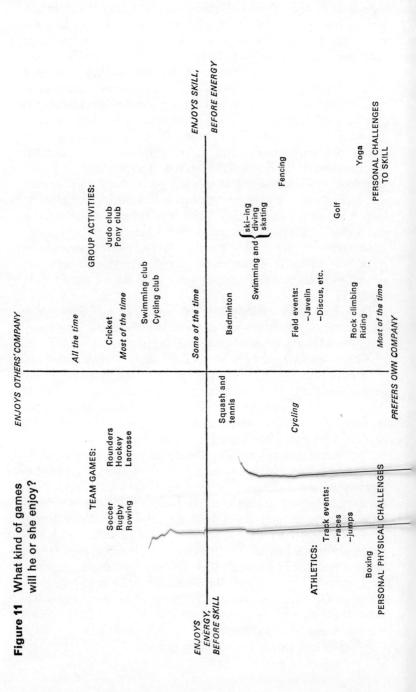

ENJOYS OTHERS' COMPANY

ENJOYS SKILL, BEFORE ENERGY

GROUP ACTIVITIES:

All the time

Cricket
Most of the time

Judo club
Pony club

Swimming club
Cycling club

Some of the time

Badminton

ski-ing
diving
skating

Fencing

Swimming and

Field events:
 —Javelin
 —Discus, etc.

Golf

Rock climbing
Riding
Most of the time

Yoga

PERSONAL CHALLENGES TO SKILL

PREFERS OWN COMPANY

TEAM GAMES:

Soccer   Rounders
Rugby   Hockey
Rowing   Lacrosse

Squash and tennis

Cycling

PERSONAL PHYSICAL CHALLENGES

ATHLETICS:

Track events:
 —races
 —jumps

Boxing
PERSONAL PHYSICAL CHALLENGES

ENJOYS ENERGY, BEFORE SKILL

where skill is more respected, may enjoy some kind of club devoted to one of the activities in the upper right quadrant of the chart. If he is more of a loner, he is better off with the activities in the lower part of the chart; and so on.

There are two other dimensions that will be considered as well: how competitive he is, and how anxious he is to distinguish himself, as opposed to the straightforward enjoyment of participating. Both these personality questions have a lot to do with how a child fits into a team. The choice of position in a football team, for example, often reflects a child's relative need to be conspicuous: if he cannot be a striker or a goalkeeper, he may be frustrated, to the point that a normally gregarious team-player may set up tensions that make him an outsider.

The chart can only be a rough guide, since personal curiosity on the part of the child towards a particular sport may dictate his choice. Even if he is not suited by it, the fact that his brother, or his father, goes out with the cycling club, or the fact that the PT teacher at school infectiously spreads enthusiasm for gymnastics or track events, can easily swing the issue.

Some, by the time they are twelve, will be thoroughly anti-sport, despite all the blandishments that can be offered from Figure 11. When they have taken a fixed attitude, it is often the result of a rebellion by an individualist against team games, and typically follows an event or a series of events where they have not only done worse than the rest, but have been laughed at as well. Such experiences cannot be erased. It is pointless trying to *make* somebody who is anti-sport into an enthusiast. Pressure is merely likely to convince him that he is the sort who disdains the trivia of the playing-field. 'I hated games at school' is a far more common complaint among those for whom games were compulsory. What can be done, is to suggest to the anti-sportsman that he might be interested in nature rambles, bird-watching, riding, fell-walking, fishing, train-spotting, plane-spotting . . . anything which has a *purpose*, or could be made to have a purpose that is less hearty, and more intellectual than 'sports' or 'games', yet which fulfils the function of providing exercise and fresh air. Many young yoga fans have been sold the idea as a mental discipline rather than as a form of physical culture. For best results, you must be prepared to do it yourself *too*.

It is worth making some efforts in this direction, since an exercised body is more likely to adopt better posture habits (avoiding considerable discomfort in later life), is more resistant after illness, and is probably, although there is no categorical proof of this, more resistant to illness itself. Exercise also goes some way towards correcting diet problems, but not the whole way. But diet is a bigger physical threat than most people believe. Between 1958 and 1974, research has indicated that the proportion of schoolchildren in the United Kingdom who are overweight has more than trebled. Being overweight does not simply mean being unattractive on a beach. There are serious long-term health risks. Some of the reasons for becoming overweight have been discussed earlier in this book, since research shows that the roots usually go back a long way into early childhood. But tendencies to get too fat can set in at any age. Eating is sometimes seen as a form of compensation, or self-comforting after a feeling that one has been missing out on something important. With an overweight child, it is always worth considering whether he is really unhappy; and in any event it is important to plan a better balanced diet for him. But exercise is important too, since it helps syphon off excess calorie intake, and it encourages muscle development, to contend with flab.

Man's nature demands that he is always trying to extend the limits of speed, and physical endurance. He also tends to try to achieve sporting records younger and younger, every decade. There are dangers in trying to do too much, too soon. There are two kinds: physical danger, and the danger of discouragement.

Peak ability at swimming is reached far earlier than at most other sports. In fact, if you are not edging up towards county championships at thirteen or fourteen, the chances of reaching the top rank are very slim indeed. Providing that a child gets really good warning, and that he is not propelled into endurance tests before he is ready for them, he will thrive on lots of practice, and will develop physically in a way that complements the techniques he is being taught. He can still become discouraged, however, if he is unwisely thrust forward into too many competitions where he is likely to finish well behind older, more experienced swimmers.

Diving, ski-ing and skating are also sports where a very high degree of mastery can be gained by the age of thirteen or fourteen, and sometimes earlier. But here there are aspects of style and technique which require a very experienced body, and a mature mind to put them into execution in the best way possible. It is important to *start* young, here, but with the expectation of a longer-term commitment to achieving the peak of one's ambitions.

All sports vary somewhat in this. Tables 5 and 6 attempt to give a comparative picture of what can be expected from youngsters of different ages, for different sports, given that they have no physical disabilities, ample opportunity to get coaching and practice, and a reasonable fund of interest and enjoyment. Girls are generally behind boys, but are very close indeed at swimming, and can be considered 'ahead' at riding.

Some sports cannot be analysed in this way. How do you measure, for example, ability to dribble, or positioning sense, at football or hockey?

It is interesting watching a succession of organized games in which children of different ages are playing. Every now and then it is clear that one or two of the players in each game are superior to the rest, but if they are discounted, it is possible to perceive differences in the *way* that each game is being played. The examples below are taken from boys playing football. The principles, however, apply generally.

Under nines

Only the goalkeeper's status is easy for the onlooker to recognize. Despite having, and knowing, their problems, much of the time there is a crowd of bodies near to, and following the ball. This 'beehive' moves from end to end. Many players shout 'foul', sometimes simulating that they have been fouled. When they fall, or are kicked, there are shouts and tears that seem to be more of rage than pain. They gloat over success; recriminate each other after failure. There is almost as much rivalry *within* each team as *between* the teams. Despite all this, they all seem to be enjoying the game; and they admire each other's successes, but not overtly. They go all-out, for as long as they can.

Nine- and ten-year-olds

There is more skill—particularly at stopping the ball, controlling it and passing it. The players are more conscious about where they are meant to be playing—although they argue about who should be marking whom, and about poaching inside each other's territory. There is some sense of positioning, but you have to *look*

Table 5 Sports attainments between eleven and sixteen—girls

Age	11	12	13	14	15	16
Running 100 m	15 secs (high) 18 secs (med.)	15·2 secs (high) 16·5 secs (med.)	14·5 secs (high) 15·5 secs (med.)	13·8 secs (high) 15 secs (med.)	13·4 secs (high) 14·8 secs (med.)	13 secs (high) 14·6 secs (med.)
400 m.			1 min. 20 secs (high)	1 min. 15 secs	1 min.	
800 m.						
Long jump	2·7 m (high) 2 m (med.)	3 m (high) 2·2 m (med.)	3·5 m (high) 2·5 m (med.)	3·9 m (high) 2·7 m (med.)	4·4 m (high) 3 m (med.)	4·8 m (high) 3·2 m (med.)
High jump	1 m (high) 0·7 m (med.)	1·1 m (high) 0·8 m (med.)	1·2 m (high) 0·9 m (med.)	1·3 m (high) 1 m (med.)	1·4 m (high) 1·1 m (med.)	1·5 m (high) 1·2 m (med.)
Swimming 100 m (free-style)	1 min. 55 secs (high) 3 mins (med.)	1 min. 50 secs (high) 2 mins 50 secs (med.)	1 min. 45 secs (high) 2 mins 40 secs (med.)	1 min. 35 secs (high) 2 mins 30 secs (med.)	1 min. 30 secs (high) 2 mins 15 secs (med.)	1 min. 25 secs (high) 2 mins (med.)
100 m (breast or back stroke)	2 mins 5 secs (high) 3 mins (med.)	2 mins (high) 2 mins 55 secs (med.)	1 min. 50 secs (high) 2 mins 50 secs (med.)	1 min. 45 secs (high) 2 mins 35 secs (med.)	1 min. 40 secs (high) 2 mins 20 secs (med.)	1 min. 35 secs (high) 2 mins 10 secs (med.)
400 m. (free-style)			9 mins (high)	8 mins (high)	7 mins 30 secs (high)	7 mins (high)

('medium' times uncertain)

Notes
'High' means top 10 per cent; 'medium' *here* means what could be attained by two girls in three who run/swim fairly frequently.

Age	11	12	13	14	15	16
Running 100 m	15 secs (high) 18 secs (med.)	14·5 secs (high) 16 secs (med.)	13·5 secs (high) 15 secs (med.)	12·5 secs (high) 14 secs (med.)	11·5 secs (high) 13 secs (med.)	10·8 secs (high) 12·8 secs (med.)
400 m			1 min. 15 secs (high) 1 min. 50 secs (med.)	1 min. 7 secs (high) 1 min. 40 secs (med.)	1 min. (high) 1 min. 25 secs (med.)	53 secs (high) 1 min. 20 secs (med.)
1,500 m					4 mins 35 secs (high) 6 mins (med.)	4 mins 10 secs (high) 5 mins 30 secs (med.)
Cross-country (target distance)			Up to 3 miles		Up to 4 miles	
Long jump	3 m (high) 2·2 m (med.)	3·5 m (high) 2·7 m (med.)	4·4 m (high) 3 m (med.)	4·8 m (high) 3·5 m (med.)	5·3 m (high) 3·7 m (med.)	6 m (high) 4 m (med.)
High jump	1 m (high) 0·8 m (med.)	1·1 m (high) 0·9 m (med.)	1·2 m (high) 1 m (med.)	1·3 m (high) 1 m (med.)	1·45 m (high) 1·1 m (med.)	1·8 m (high) 1·2 m (med.)
Swimming 100 m (free-style)	1 min. 50 secs (high) 3 mins (med.)	1 min. 45 secs (high) 2 mins 50 secs (med.)	1 min. 35 secs (high) 2 mins 40 secs (med.)	1 min. 25 secs (high) 2 mins 30 secs (med.)	1 min. 20 secs (high) 2 mins 15 secs (med.)	1 min. 15 secs (high) 2 mins (med.)
100 m (breast or back stroke)	2 mins 5 secs (high) 3 mins (med.)	2 mins. (high) 2 mins 55 secs (med.)	1 min. 50 secs (high) 2 mins 50 secs (med.)	1 min. 45 secs (high) 2 mins 35 secs (med.)	1 min. 50 secs (high) 2 mins 20 secs (med.)	1 min. 35 secs (high) 2 mins 10 secs (med.)
400 m (free-style)			8 mins (high)	7 mins (high)	6 mins 45 secs (high)	6 mins 20 secs (high)

Notes
'High' means top 10 per cent; 'medium' means what could be attained by two boys in three who run/swim fairly frequently.

for it, since passes are made direct, not for running on to. Tears are more under control, but not gloats. There is a tendency for some players to lose heart rapidly, once they believe they may be in a losing side.

Eleven- and twelve-year-olds

There is a big difference in the standard of the game now, for several reasons. Kicking and running with the ball is harder and faster. Some of the players, at least, have a sense of how the whole field might be used for building up attacks. Marking key men becomes a statutory, not a temporary obligation. At the same time, moving into spaces where they can be less under threat when collecting a pass becomes more important, and this changes much of the tactics within the game. Instead of running all-out, most manage to husband their resources for a fresh surge every so often. They have their preferred positions, but change around without much obligation. A few of the players are now obviously fish out of water: they have not developed their play as they have grown older, they are fatalistic, are at odds with their team-mates, and cannot wait to be allowed to drop football. A more sporting attitude is evident towards the other side's successes and failures.

Thirteen- and fourteen-year-olds

The game now has definite strategic elements in it, both in terms of attack and defence, as opposed to a series of tactical encounters. Players try to gear their game towards feeding a particular striker, or towards shutting out opposing attacks by contriving over-lapping cover. Frequently there are moments when some of the players seem to have a grand concept, which *could* work out well, if only some physical or technical deficiency weren't there to prevent the final achievement: now, strategic opportunities on an ambitious scale suggest themselves to the players, who suddenly find that they are simply not strong enough to execute them. Sometimes they perceive more ideas or dangers than they are able to communicate to each other, and there are recriminations over failure to understand plans. Captains assert their authority more severely now. There is a definite code observed by most players, governing reactions to accidents, etc., and although there are skilful attempts to mislead referees, there is a sense of how far it is reasonable to go. When they feel this code may be being broken, as opposed to bent, players are embarrassed by their *own* side. Those who disliked the game have now mostly left it, and the remainder are totally committed. This makes for a happier game.

Fifteen- and sixteen-year-olds

Some of the players in this age group have pretensions to playing at a very high level. They have devoted a lot of time and energy to achieving good ball control, to mastering tactics, and being very fit. They have watched high-level games, and find they can apply much of what they have learnt. Occasionally, this will include 'professional fouling', but since they are first and foremost enthusiasts, it is the positive points they tend to appropriate. Injuries seem to be more frequent in this period, since they play with total commitment, and try, for example, to jump a sliding tackle without loss of momentum, rather than being self-protective as well as goal-minded. They pace themselves through the game better, so that both sides can end with a grandstand finish, rather than staggering into the closing minutes. Some players have become very used to each others' ways and capabilities: true 'pairing' is sometimes seen, as between a link-man and a striker, or a 'stopper' centre half and a back who acts as 'sweeper'. Most have a fixed idea of their best playing position. There is less fatalism about the result, provided the teams are not too different in playing strength.

Since football is the passion of a large proportion of the male United Kingdom population, it is worth considering some of the steps that have to be taken by youths who want to play high-level football, and who actually make the grade. There is little doubt that, for most children, achievement of something like professional status depends primarily on these factors:

(a) An early intense interest (starting between nine and twelve) in a particular sport or game.
(b) Maintaining this interest without discouragement; by always keeping a new goal in view.
(c) Good co-ordination, and an instinctively quick and accurate response to each stimulus on the field; good eyesight, hearing, agility.
(d) Avoidance of injury, or serious illness.

(e) Good coaching (i.e. both technically 'good' and sensitively applied to the child as an individual) starting during the nine to twelve period.

(f) Opportunity to practise; and to pit one's skill against others.

The rest (which is itself very important) is a burning desire to succeed, despite opposition from the family and jealous outsiders. Clearly some of these requirements are expensive: few top skiers or riders, for instance, lack private means.

Some children are put on to 'agonistic' training schedules. What this involves is training and practising virtually every day, by a system whereby the personal best has always to be repeated, or bettered, within a few days. There is never any time for a mild, dilettante joy, or keeping it to a warming-up session when time is against one. This is real commitment. Attention is paid to muscles, and the slightest suspicion of a strain is examined carefully. A balanced diet, adequate but not over-filling, is insisted on. Altogether, it is an uncomfortable bed to lie on. Some young runners have lost their competitive fire, and (it is suspected) have become physically weakened by following such a regime. But the rewards are great for any who complete the course. For instance, there is the Californian swimmer Tim Shaw, who began winning significant races at the ripe age of ten. His agonistic training schedule did not start in earnest until he was about fourteen. The distance he covered *each day* in training went up from two miles by stages to around seven miles. Inexorably, world records fell to him, as he made himself inch towards them week after week. The first fell to his grasp when he was sixteen. At seventeen he held three world records.

But probably only a small minority can respond to such training with enjoyment, pride and even greater commitment. Strain on the heart is a danger which has to be checked. In fact, very close medical supervision is advisable if a child is to be treated like a thoroughbred racehorse.

This raises the whole question of how to keep a sense of proportion. Committed sportsmen *must* miss out on some other aspects of education and experience. Musicians do the same—but somehow society tends to consider them a special case, while querying the desirability of commitment to sport. One difference lies in the fact that a true musician improves with age, while a sportsman can go 'over the top' relatively early. (Some swimmers, for example, are considered to be superannuated at twenty.) This means that sportsmen need a broader preparation for life, and there is a case for preparing a second career very early on.

But the question still remains: should children be required to *work* so hard at something which is intended for pleasure and recreation? Effectively, they have little choice in the matter, because determined parents will often guide them into a sporting career come what may. A more comforting reflection is the point that children who resent their regime are either being badly coached, or are unsuitable for that kind of coaching, and this rapidly shows up in their performance.

Russian girl gymnasts took the world by storm in 1972. Here were young teenagers, proving themselves to be amazingly skilled, and at the same time to have individuality, a style and tastefulness in what they were doing. The USSR training methods have been revealed to be extremely sophisticated, and in their way to be just as demanding as those applied to Tim Shaw. For example, Olga Korbut, when training for the Olympic Games at fourteen, was allowed to read a book just before going to bed at night. Later, when she had won her medals, but was still destined for higher things, it was discovered by some research workers that the body continues to work out the efforts of pre-sleep activity during sleep; her schedule was immediately adjusted to include a training session last thing at night. At the same time, anyone observing her televised interviews must have been convinced that she derives a great deal of pride and pleasure from what she does, and shares this with her companions.

This is still not *normal* experience, however. Young sportsmen have to forgo a lot of companionship, particularly with the opposite sex, that others of their age must be getting. Certain types of social activity they may well miss altogether. And few of them get the satisfaction of making a particular study, whether academic, technological, or artistic, for which others may have the time. Knowing that, in training, the world centres around them, or around their team, must have a long-term effect on social behaviour, too. Sportsmen vary, but we have all met the ones whose sole conversation seems to be about their past or current achievements. These are areas that young sportsmen, and their parents, will neglect to their cost.

Most children need to get recreation out of sport—a break of routine, not the continuation of a hard grind. This is what it is, and should be, for most. As such, it is a wonderful medium for maintaining contact between parent and child. If they play something, or watch something from a grandstand, or discuss tactics and share enthusiasms together, they are keeping up an understanding and a bond that will endure a lot of family friction about education, drinking, smoking, staying out late, and so on. Leaving sport entirely to the younger generation makes no sense.

Arguably, it is this attitude which is partly responsible for the fact that nowadays some football matches have to be approached with caution, and each team's supporters may have to be segregated for their own safety. Crowd emotions are not like ordinary people's reactions in ordinary circumstances. A steadying influence, from older people, is needed to prevent excitement turning into thuggery. This is a debt to society, as much as to one's own family.

Chapter nineteen

Later years at secondary school

One of the aims of present-day educational methods is not to make children specialize too early in a small number of subjects. There are several good reasons for this. An undiluted course of maths and physics risks becoming tedious, even for very able and conscientious scholars. It is also limiting, in that the maths specialist might be left simply to imagine what a lot of literature, or history, might be like. He would not be encouraged to write more accurately, or more imaginatively, except within the somewhat rigid context of writing up his physics experiments. The scientist who cannot express himself, and the arts man who cannot mend a fuse or convert sterling into lire, have been, and are, real people. Part of this restriction of what might be called a 'general education' comes from not allowing sufficient time for its separate components. But the effects of specialization at an early age go deeper than that. As soon as children are given the idea that they are basically classicists, or historians, they will try to act this role. Subsidiary subjects which are not treated as seriously as 'real work' become regarded as a bit of a joke, and attention is withdrawn from them as soon as the pressure mounts to concentrate on main subjects. The habit of not treating something seriously dies very hard, once it is acquired. Further, there is the fact that academically successful children, even before they reach a sixth form, are likely to take some satisfaction from their superiority, and—with or without encouragement from teachers—draw comparisons between the kind of things that *they* are doing, as opposed to the soft options with which the others are left. Intellectual élitism is a matter of degree: it is not something that can be eradicated without losing a great deal of the pleasure that goes with knowing that you are doing well at your studies, in the company of others who are doing well.

But some children *want* to specialize. They decided long ago, for example, that they dislike languages, or that they dislike mathematics. 'When can I give it up?' is the question they often voice, to their teachers or to their parents. These children may be very good at their preferred subject: it often seems perverse to deprive them of extra time on something that they enjoy, while trying yet another ruse to kindle some interest in a subject they have rejected.

A simple expedient is to apply the principle, as many schools do, that children must be 'generalists' up to 'O' Levels, but may specialize for 'A' Levels. In many cases, this may well prove to be an appropriate balance. But there are two kinds of child who can suffer from having this principle applied insensitively, without allowing exceptions:

(a) Children of limited ability who might do well at one or two 'O' Levels, if allowed to specialize, but are far behind the others in the class and are making no headway at some of the basic subjects.

(b) Children of exceptional ability at one or two subjects, who have enthusiasm for them, but are building up a resentment of school, and possibly of education, as a result of being made to advance more slowly, across a broad front.

Schools vary considerably in how rigidly they make similar demands of all children at the 'middle school' level of fourteen and fifteen. It is worth finding out whether your own child might be feeling frustrated about non-specialization, to the point where such rigidity has to be broken down. Obviously, this has to be distinguished from cases where there is simply a temporary reaction against a particular subject. Younger brothers and sisters, when they see their elders going on to college or into a job, often tend to feel that it is time they, too, were allowed to concentrate on one discipline.

'Blind spots' at school have been discussed earlier in this book, since the best time to tackle the problem of helping a child to take to a subject he dislikes is when he is still at primary school. This is when a change of angle (e.g. an approach to arithmetic through nature study, dividing flowers or leaves into groups, and counting them), or a change of teacher can make a great deal of difference. By the time a child is fourteen, however, any blockage against a subject is likely to be much more difficult to shift. He has got used to saying 'I'm just no good at maths' until it has become part of his personality: repeat it often enough, and act out the role, and it becomes the truth. Some teachers who perceive active dislike of the subject they are teaching take what they feel is a pragmatic approach, to get the best out of the most unpromising examination material: 'Here's what you have to do to get through the exam with a decent mark . . .' I.e. never mind about this being interesting or useful, just swallow the pill in the right dosage, and pass. In the short term, this has the positive effect of helping someone to keep in a particular stream, or to scrape an 'O' Level, but the long-term effect is to *emphasize* the unpalatability of the subject.

Another influence that serves to establish these blind spots by the age of fourteen is the tendency for boys and girls to discriminate between 'male' and 'female' subjects. This is possibly greater where girls are concerned: considerably fewer girls take science subjects or mathematics at 'A' Level. But boys tend to show less interest in English studies, and in the use of English—as is implied in the facts about reading that are mentioned below. Talking to boys of fourteen, you get the impression that approval of a subject, in their terms, depends on its having some kind of practical value— either in itself, or as a stepping-stone towards further study, or a career. Looking below this superficial response, it is easy to see that many use it as a way of relegating schoolwork to a lower level of concern: it is to them a means to an end, not an activity in which they can take positive pride. For the more successful ones, it is different, but the majority are mainly concerned with establishing their own virility, and maturing to their own satisfaction, and schoolwork (with the arguable exception of science and technology) does not provide them with a suitable medium for this. Part of the difference in attainment levels between boys and girls across all subjects (girls are more successful, on average) may be explained by this.

Children get a certain amount of pressure to do better at school. Of course, this may vary from the mildest suggestion, 'Oh, do buck up!' once a term, to a situation where a child is almost constantly aware that he is being watched and assessed. The way that the pressure is applied also varies from the subtle '*That* was rather better, Ursula . . .' (as though waiting for more), to a declaration that only a shameless degenerate would continue to serve up the rubbishy work that has been disgorged of late. Some teachers have a knack of being insulting in a way that provokes a mixture of anguish and amusement that actually motivates a child to do better, while others simply contrive to depress a child, even if their remarks are mild. The nature of the pressure, therefore, is just as important as what is actually said. Parents who feel that there is a kind of rapport between the child and his main teachers, possibly based on respect despite dislike, are in a more hopeful situation than those who sense that their children are simply apathetic about what they might or might not derive from somebody's classes, or—worse still—are utterly disdainful of a teacher and what he is trying to do. When this happens, a frank talk with the head-teacher should be arranged, and it may be worth looking for another school, especially if you feel that a child's potential is being ignored or dissipated.

Occasional antagonism to a teacher, or his methods, is on the other hand *not* a good reason for considering a change of school. The principle described in Chapter 14, that it is in the nature of schoolchildren to find something or someone to grumble about, still applies at this age. The exception is where a child has got a very particular talent—in music, or art— or a determination to specialize in one subject in particular, and there is a feeling of a complete block to progress because the child cannot get on a productive wave-length with the one teacher in the school who is the key person for that subject.

Pressure from parents is also felt by many children. But there are many parents who cannot be bothered greatly with the details of their children's education. There is a happy medium, which is difficult to strike, between negligence and the kind of pressure that is nagging, incessant, and calculated to prevent a child from enjoying any free time because of the guilt they associate with not studying. Some degree of interest and concern in what is going on at school is important: it is, after all, a large proportion of his life as a child, and if it is of no concern to his parents it is a matter for anxiety, and for ticking off the days that remain before the prison sentence is complete. Several research studies show that the children of parents who *bother* enough to make contact with the school tend to succeed much more, academically. But some of these are at risk.

Possibly the worst comment a child can hear is, 'You're wasting *your* time and *our* money. Just think of the pounds your father and I have had to spend to send you to E—.' Why *should* he think about them? His parents almost certainly chose the school, and to pay the money. Nor is he really interested in what his parents have had to forgo to send him there. Martyrs are usually self-made.

But *some* pressure undoubtedly helps. There are three main categories of positive pressure, which some might prefer to call 'help'. In the first place, a child wants to know that you care about how he is doing, and whether he is *enjoying* school, which is more important to him than getting distinctions. Second, there is selective praise: this means taking the trouble to notice what he has been doing, and make an appropriate comment when he has obviously moved a stage further, or when in the school's eyes, or in his own eyes, he has made some kind of breakthrough. The third category is to provide an atmosphere which helps a child to work. One basic step, for a day-school child, is to make sure that he can actually do homework in the evening—without having to sit in the cold while the rest of the family watches television. But many children need more than this. It is really only a minority who seem able to plan the time they are going to spend doing homework: others are likely to start the evening, or the week-end, feeling that they have plenty of time, but end up in a panic five minutes before bedtime, anxious about what is going to be said about their blank exercise books. When there are several homework items, and some out-of-school activities to fit in as well, the problem of planning is very considerable. This is where parents can be helpful, reminding without nagging, and arranging evenings so that some basic elements of routine can be followed. This is important. The feeling that homework is always a losing battle can destroy enjoyment, and eventually success, in a subject. For this reason (as well as because the alternative is unnatural) parents should be prepared to discuss homework too.

Children who board are less easy to help in these ways. Many parents only discover there have been problems when an end-of-term report is offered by a trembling hand. Nobody wants to spend precious hours of half-term holidays going over the minutiae of struggles with algebra, so how are parents to help? There are two things they can do, apart from encouraging their children to talk as freely as they like about school during holiday time. One is to make it clear that either the post or the telephone can be used for discussing seemingly insoluble problems, especially when a child cannot understand his teacher's 'explanation' of a knotty point. The very *fact* that this facility exists is more important than being able to talk convincingly about surds or past participles on the telephone. It gives confidence.

One of the key differences between children that has a lot to say about their interest in formal education, and what they are getting out of it, is the amount they read. This is not just a question of taking the class history book or the reader home, and obediently ploughing through it by way of homework. Whether a child is a *self-starter* at reading is much more indicative.

Only recently the first advance report of the Schools Council Research Project into Children's Reading Habits, 10–15, has been produced by Whitehead, Capey and Baddren (*Children's Reading Interests*, Evans/Methuen Educational, 1975). This is perhaps the only really authoritative investigation into children's reading habits using a large sample. While it is representative of children in state schools and direct grant schools, it does not cover those in independent schools: but although the proportion of voluntary readers may be higher in these latter schools, there is no reason why similar sub-groups of children (in terms of reading) should not be found there also.

The most dramatic findings are perhaps the large proportions of children who do not do any reading on their own at all; the rate of decline of voluntary reading between the ages of ten and fourteen; and the big differences between boys and girls, both in the amount they read, and in the nature of their reading. Thus, at ten, 87 per cent of all children read at least an occasional book on their own. As time goes on, many drop books for comics. By the age of fourteen, reading books becomes *less* frequent, particularly for boys. At this stage, more boys who *do* read are reading non-fiction: they are pursuing their own interests through print, whether these be football, cars, or the martial arts. Girls are much more likely to be reading fiction.

This kind of picture deserves some comment. Several researchers have remarked on the fact that use of words improves with the amount of attention you pay to them, and the amount of enjoyment you derive from them. Several factors could be holding children back from reading, and they are worth considering.

(a) He is a poor reader; finds it involves too much hard work, relative to satisfaction.
(b) There are no positive incentives: few books at home; poor school library; no class library; no encouragement from parents or teachers.
(c) There are *dis*incentives: parents, friends despise books; parents, teachers have pushed books *too hard*.

(d) There are too many activities competing for his attention: e.g. games, television, homework, etc.

The writers of the report referred to above draw attention to those instances where an unlikely class in an unlikely school yielded a good library, a teacher who was keen and imaginative about reading, and successfully encouraged a healthy crop of readers. Usually, grammar schools, or any school which has 'creamed' the local intellectual talent, has a higher academic standard, and a higher proportion who read voluntarily. But this need not be the case exclusively—nor is it.

Parents have a role to play, as well as teachers. If they cannot provide space which is adequately heated, and away from the television set, they cannot reasonably expect either homework or private reading from their children. Similarly, if they are not themselves in the habit of enjoying a book in the evening, at least sometimes, they cannot be surprised if their children never pick up the idea for themselves. The stage at which parents could communicate the magic of books (and the fact that they are to be enjoyed by young *and* old), by reading stories with their children, and talking about them, is just before bedtime. But they can still be seen to use books themselves, and to treat them as worth discussing with each other.

Reading is sometimes regarded by psychologists as an escape; or as a means of extending one's personal life into areas which one cannot reach in reality. 'Identification', or imagining oneself in the role of one of the characters, and going through all his joys, fears and disappointments, can be looked at either as a way of getting out of a humdrum routine; or of breaking new ground, of trying oneself out in experiences about which curiosity is extremely strong. The degree to which children 'lose themselves' in a book is often vividly emphasized in their bad temper when they are forced to emerge from it, or even when they have finished it, and are so moody, that they are unable to enter into anything else. Everyone experiences identification at some stage, either in day-dreaming or when immersed in a book. Criticism is sometimes levelled at those who lose themselves in books for days on end (and are therefore 'bookworms') that they must be lacking something in everyday life, to make them want to spend so much time in fantasy. There is *some* truth in this: if *every* girl had a pony, for example, would so many pony books need to be read? But there are other satisfactions derived from reading: it arouses the imagination about places, needs, reactions, processes, just as much as about how nice it would be to turn into someone else. It is always exciting to share thoughts about stories, too, with others who have been through them. Finding that another person has 'read' a book in an entirely different way, is always a surprise.

One role that books are also said to serve is as a sounding-board of how people behave towards each other, in different circumstances: this is an extension of social experience, in which a child can come to terms with vicarious rebuffs unscathed.

Those who find that books are not so much accessible as there to provide pleasure have a great advantage of *confidence* when it comes to serious study, quite apart from the pleasure itself. But no one can be forced to enjoy a book. Strong pressure can have the reverse effect. A boring book does the same, too.

Television and films are often blamed for destroying interest in books, as well as killing conversation. However, the facts show that the healthiest sales of classic books often follow successful television or film series. A television-bound anti-book child can often be lured back towards prose by seeing his parents enthusing over a paperback that is capitalizing on one. It is also a mistake to be too hard on comics, and on books that fall far below the standard of reading that you feel is desirable as an educational pastime for the child's age group. These are not *always* substitutes for 'the real thing': slow readers often need something like them to gain confidence and speed, while very bright children occasionally enjoy a small amount of 'regressive reading', as if to underline the point that they are being stretched, academically, a lot of the time.

When children do not read, it is because they do not get much out of it. When they do not study hard, and concentrate at passing examinations, it is by and large for the same reason. It is easy to talk about stimulating interest, and presenting schoolwork in a more interesting way, but when children have become accustomed to treating it all as boring, this becomes increasingly difficult in practice.

A popular statistic in the mid-1970s, especially among those who consider that the raising of the school leaving age to sixteen has been premature, and against the interests of the majority, is the 80 per cent of over-thirteens to whom it is believed that 'academic studies are basically irrelevant'. This is a massive proportion. It is probably an exaggeration, in that even some of the more outwardly cynical rebels may in fact be deriving *something* from their last years at school, despite failure at exams, and self-avowed boredom, in those lessons where imagination was used. However, the figure underlines the bleakness behind the desks where little or no success is expected, but the grind is unremitting.

It does not *have* to be so bleak for the non-academic. There are very broadly two kinds of children who leave school without any formal qualifications. The first are greatly relieved to be free from a work-pattern that had little meaning, and are determined not to let themselves into a situation where they are expected to be intellectual again. Typically, they come out strongly against learning, and anything like books or art which smacks of it. Eventually, they may discourage any excursions into these areas among their children. The second category come away with some regret, but less resentment. They compensate for academic failure by acquiring expertise in particular areas, and some time may attend evening classes, or become mature students. Both kinds may throw themselves energetically into a career, sometimes in order to prove that they are the equals of anybody in, say, a particular line of business. But the first has closed the door firmly on education as such; while the second has kept it open. This door re-opens suddenly, sometimes, when learning all at once acquires a practical value. When a young adult realizes the value of learning a language, or how an engine works, he may take to it in a way that suggests it never had any practical meaning before.

Children themselves are far more likely to have a viewpoint on academic qualifications now than they were in the past. This catches many parents unawares. A viewpoint is not a word to give to the passive, bland acceptance that exams are in the nature of things, and that since most of the people around put a high value on passing them, one had better do the same oneself. This characterized many schoolchildren in the past, whether they were successful or not. If they rebelled, it was often rebellion that was more important to them than the issue of exams. Now they are more aware of arguments about the principle of asserting understanding and skill in these terms, the diverseness they encourage, the barrenness of intellectual élitism, the point or value of going to a university, the practical help that qualifications might afford in a job interview. Are there not better ways of spending time at school than in swotting for exams? All this is grist for current debate, and there are no simple answers to the questions they raise. Children in many schools nowadays realize this at a remarkably early age. Teachers in many schools are divided on these issues, too: it would be strange if they did not transmit some of their feelings.

As society changes, as the rewards obtainable for different types of work draw closer together, it may be inevitable that the advantages that qualifications used to provide as a 'way in' to better-paid and more respected jobs must decline, even if they would never disappear. Regarding education as a passport to better things should decline, too, except probably where the closed-shop professions are concerned (e.g. medicine, and law) and when the public need for help is continuous, rather than periodic (e.g. architecture). An educational purist would say that this is all to the good: a child subsidized by the state to gain educational opportunities, should develop his skill and knowledge for the good of society, rather than for personal material gain. But it is a more difficult question, because lack of incentive reduces the number of those who are prepared to go in for further education. This in its turn means that society stagnates intellectually and technologically.

What this means is that our children, being more questioning, will increasingly decide for themselves what value they are to put on further education. The biggest influence, bigger than most, though not all their teachers would agree, will be the economy. Whereas in the past parents could direct their children's footsteps towards this kind of goal without too much trouble, they are now increasingly powerless to do so. It has to be a *considered dialogue*, if today's adolescents are to take much notice of the points parents want to make. Pushing, nagging and fateful warnings have little effect: but objective discussion may.

Chapter twenty

The new adult: must there be a generation gap?

For many families, the question in the chapter heading scarcely seems to apply. Everyone retains a sense of harmony, liking, and mutual respect, as the children proceed from early to late teens, and operate more and more as self-sufficient individuals. This is how it should be. But it often isn't. And even in happily united families, there are still times when it seems as if the changes in interests and demands of the children are a serious threat to understanding.

There are many ways in which a 'generation gap' can be described. But explaining it is far more complicated and uncertain. There are too many kinds of generation gap, for one to draw up a neat picture outlining what to encourage, what to avoid, and what corrective action to take that will be adequate or appropriate in a particular given circumstance.

One kind of gap is the result of a very long-term process. It may have its roots in one or other of a child's parents never really feeling any deep love for him; or perhaps getting into that state of mind where it is believed that the child 'simply doesn't respond', which is usually a reflection of a parent's lack of patience or sympathy for an individual personality. When parents and child have never been close, it is hardly surprising that a gap should manifest itself when the child is growing up and expressing his own views on what he should do in life, and what he should reflect.

Another kind of gap is caused by a failure, on the part of parents, to allow the irrelationship to progress much further than that of adult-to-child. This means not allowing for any kind of progress to be made between, say, showing a child how a job is done, and adopting an adult-to-adult line which allows either party to advise the other on how best to do the job. Nobody becomes an adult overnight: but nobody is content, either, to remain on the receiving end of an advisory service once he is entering his teens. There has to be some adjustment. Parents often enjoy, without realizing it, the sense of affording protection and support to their children, in a way that denies that their child is making any real gains in understanding or experience. Why parents do this is a complex matter. Partly they are expressing their genuine love, and a desire to keep their children from harm. Partly they enjoy perpetuating a role which they enjoy. Denying one's children's age is a music-hall joke as a means of pretending to be as young as ever. But joke or not, it seems a threat to one's status as a young parent to sense that a son or a daughter is advancing rapidly towards independence. Some find it easier to come to terms with a child's increasing physical age than to credit the increases in knowledge and judgment that are also taking place.

There are several different ways in which this problem is reflected in parents' behaviour. The most obvious is to meet each demand for greater independence with suspicion: 'Why *should* he?' is the automatic reaction to a request to choose one's own clothes, throw up one spare time activity in pursuit of another, or make one's own way home instead of returning from some event with the family. A more logical reaction, and a more realistic one, is to ask yourself, 'Why *shouldn't* he?' There still might be a very good reason why not to allow a particular request, but the emphasis in outlook is quite different. It is accepting the fact that here is a young individual who wants to try his strength, at the cost of a few mistakes.

Another example is to speak for him, when he is perfectly capable of expressing his own feelings. This is often encouraged by visitors who may nod in the direction of a twelve-year-old, and ask, 'How is Sandra getting on? How's her swimming?' Few Sandras appreciate their mother or father trying to answer this directly—even if they remain silent. 'I'm not sure: Sandra, how's it going?' is far less presumptuous, and a far more polite way of turning the question. Depending on her level of social sophistication (which at twelve may be anything between highly polished and rudimentary), she may giggle, she may say vaguely, 'Oh, it's all right I suppose', or she may launch into a running commentary on her latest 100-metre freestyle triumph. It may be embarrassing, momentarily. But denying her the opportunity of entering into adult conversation is to perpetuate embarrassment, to destroy maturity, to provoke resentment, and to open up the generation gap.

Parents who are very good at talking with eight-year-olds may be very indifferent when it comes to talking with a twelve-year-old. If they continue to presume a lower level of understanding than is really there, it is not surprising if the dialogue becomes stilted, or if the twelve-year-old ducks out of future meetings. It is the same principle in businesses, or any kind of working environment: if you treat some people as if they are stuck at a particular point of development (e.g. clerical work, or fitting simple components together), and do not allow them more scope or responsibility, some of them will come to believe they are like that, while others will resent the gap between what they and others are doing. These last will look for a way out, and a way to make trouble. But even parents who understand this, find it hard to talk naturally, as one person to another, with their child. Instead, they try to ingratiate themselves. A patronizing tone is very quickly rumbled by any child with average intelligence.

There are, however, more subtle barriers that make communication more difficult. One is, very simply, that parents often find that even with the best will in the world their children's interests seem boring, inane, or calculated to irritate parental nerves or to be downright threatening. When this feeling is uppermost, it is impossible not to let it tinge the words you use to your children. Nobody can expect to share all their children's enthusiasms: but there is no reason for not enjoying *something* together. Parents lose out on this when they expect their children to become interested in a hobby that they themselves have long enjoyed. This might be anything—from collecting antiques to water ski-ing. Many children would in fact enjoy it, except in a situation where

(a) Mother or father is the undisputed source of all knowledge about it, and
(b) It has long been associated with the household's spare time.

Children are intrigued by what is *new*. A novelty drive is a kind of instinct, typical of the young of any race, which has survival value for that race. At five, a child may be fascinated by the sight of his grandfather's stamp collection. It is new to him. At eight, when he is allowed to help do some sorting of the stamps, he is thrilled. Participation in it is new for him. At ten, when it is clear that there is little that he can contribute (since grandpa knows exactly how he wants his collection to develop), he is dead bored at the very idea of seeing it again.

Chris and Margaret have two teenage children, aged fifteen and fourteen. Other parents are often struck by the easy-going relationship that this pair enjoys with their children. This does not mean that they avoid confrontations, when some basic family rules are queried and discussed. But the confrontations are straightforward, with each side stating what they believe, and then working out a compromise. There are outbreaks of temper sometimes, but these are short-lived, and without bitterness. Both sides *know each other* very well. They *care about* what each other is doing. Sometimes they make fun of each other's doings and prejudices, but there is a sense of imminent co-operation, even when they are enjoying a quiet laugh. Some parents would feel, instinctively, that there is not enough *respect* or deference about the way Chris and Margaret are addressed by Dick and Jill. They do not realize that this easy-going backchat is founded on love, on mutual interest, on greater understanding of each other's reactions (of where they are thick-skinned, and where they are sensitive), and on a desire to keep each other's respect.

This overheard conversation is typical of what can be heard in their household, most Saturday mornings:

Dick, 'Is there anything that needs doing in our horrible garden this weekend?'
Chris, 'You could try making it less horrible by cutting the grass.'
Dick groans, then, 'Oh, the machine's broken down! I forgot.
That's all right then.' (Fans himself in pretended relief.)
Margaret, 'No it isn't. Webb's brought it back the other day. Works a treat. It's only waiting for a good driver.'
(This is a reference to Dick's protestation that he is perfectly capable, at fifteen, of driving the family car round a disused airport. Chris is still steeling himself to face this.)
Dick groans again.
Chris, 'You do the grass, I'll dig over where the beans have got to go, and we'll be on the golf course before 12.'
Margaret and Jill together, 'Are you two skyving off again?'
Chris, 'Well, we must get some practice in before our match next week.'
Margaret and Jill exchange glances. Margaret offers to help Jill with a dress she has started. This relieves Jill, who says, 'Thanks, Mum. I'll even come on your dreary tour of the antique shops this afternoon if you like.'

Margaret explained to me later that Jill would need the dress for a party that evening. She would have had qualms a year ago, at the thought of her daughter, at fourteen, going to a mixed party to be held in somebody's basement, when there would be a juke box on loan, dark corners, and many of the features associated with a night club. 'But I know the family in whose house it is. They seem sensible about alcohol, and they're keeping it to young teens. They believe as I do, that you've got to be prepared to meet them half-way.' Nevertheless, she seemed nervous about the event, and twice repeated the statement that she would be setting off at eleven o'clock to bring Jill home, and to ferry back her 'escort', Jim, as well. Jim and his family are friends of the family. 'I feel better,' Margaret says, 'when I remember that Jim is really much more worried that something will go wrong than I am.'

In the past year, Margaret has threaded an intricate path through her daughter's wishes, and the group impulses of her daughter's friends. She has refused permission to join in events over which she could have no control: a pop festival, and a late-night barbecue after a moto-cross rally, had both to be ruled against. 'So had a coach party to an airport to see a pop group arrive,' Margaret added. 'There was no way of telling whether she would be one of a couple of hundred, or one of ten thousand. I may have been wrong about that one, and certainly Jill thinks so, but you can only follow your instinct.' On the other side, Margaret has attended one open-air pop concert, at a distance from Jill (who implored her to keep well out of sight). 'Terribly noisy, but I found what it was all about, and the next time, I felt happy about her going off with her group of friends, because I knew what went on.'

When Margaret talks to Jill about an event of this kind, she normally says what she means in simple terms. There is no 'Because *I* say so, dear,' although there is occasionally a 'No, I'm sorry but you can't: I've decided'. The first time that she actually told Jill '. . . you see, I'm afraid that in the dark you'll get too excited, you may be given a drink that makes you drunk, and somebody may take advantage of this and hurt you', it had been difficult to say. When Jill wanted to know more—'Mummy, are you afraid that somebody will make me be sexy with him and then I'll be pregnant?'—Margaret squirmed, and simply nodded. 'Well, I won't let him!' Jill had insisted; and then there was a discussion of how difficult this might be to control, if some of the unknowns at the event in question were used to drink, drugs, or capitalizing on young girls' inexperience. But she was pleased that she had a daughter with whom she *could* discuss these things.

They have always done a number of things together. Margaret consults her daughter about her own projects for dress-making or clothes buying (although she sometimes has to overrule the advice), as well as encouraging Jill to express her preferences rather than simply having things provided for her. They do some dress-making together, and they go swimming together. At the former, Margaret is the leader. At swimming, Margaret has more recently had to submit to instruction from Jill as well as from Jill's teacher, to get a faster crawl. 'It's better now that she's more patient with me,' is Margaret's comment on this.

Chris found that although *he* enjoyed watching football, it bored his son; although Dick was interested in going to see drag racing, this left Chris cold. Amateur dramatics turned Dick off as soon as he perceived that a five-line part was all he would expect in his first production. Chris went to a 'martial arts' evening class for senior beginners at his son's school, in the belief that he might be able to share some or the excitement that Dick felt when he talked about Karate or Kung Fu: but he felt a bit ridiculous being the oldest and clumsiest of the trainees, and he strained a hip muscle while aiming a kick at an imaginary opponent. Golf, at least, was something that both found they could enjoy learning. Chris had played a little before, but they are both now evenly matched. They are very competitive with each other, and they enter handicap pairs tournaments together, with a determination to sweep all before them. Chris has tried to get some of Dick's friends to try the game, with some success.

Chris has had fewer occasions to intervene and stop his son from doing something he wanted badly than has been the case with Margaret and Jill. The main difficulty has been over driving the car. They have not got a long drive, and unlike some other fathers Chris is unwilling to break the law by teaching his son to drive on the open road. But he has taught Dick what to do with the controls, and has arranged some lessons for him on a simulator, so that as soon as he can get a provisional licence he will have a flying start.

Occasionally, Chris admits, he gets left behind by what his son is doing. Dick earns some money helping out at a local garage, and comes back with enthusiasms for parts of a car of which Chris is sometimes completely unaware. Kindling any spark of interest in the garden has been notably unsuccessful. 'I tried too hard, I think,' says Chris. 'I proposed one day that it would be fun to choose two rows each in the vegetable patch, and see which of us could produce the best beans and carrots during the summer. He saw straight through that one. He told me he had better things to do with his summer than watching carrots grow.' The obvious subterfuge did not work. Saying in a straightforward way, 'Look here, I need some help if we're going to grow any decent vegetables this year,' got a reasonable response.

It seemed worth dwelling at some length over Chris's family, partly because they seem to be people who suffer less than most from any generation gap, and because they still come up against problems that beset most parents of teenagers. They are not always successful in the way they cope with these, as I have tried to show. But they always have a kind of basic understanding on which they can fall back when there is a row.

Part of this basic understanding seems to be that they like each other as people—quite apart from any family feeling. They respect each other's territory and possessions, and do not exert pressure or blackmail to get their own way. At their present ages, most of the contact is between the child and the parent of the same sex. This has not always been the case. At nine and ten, Dick's first port of call when he was experiencing trouble at school was Margaret. At the same period, and for rather longer, Jill expressed her great admiration for Chris by trying to monopolize his time, most weekends, and many evenings.

Avoidance of pressure may well be a key element in their family relationships. The parents do not expect or force their children to have the same interests or cultural values as they have; and as far as they can they are encouraging towards the varied assortment of friends that their children make. Even more important, they do not urge their children to strain after academic honours; nor have they any fixed ideas about what kinds of career Dick or Jill might follow. This does not mean they do not care. On the contrary, they talk about school, about subjects, and about exams, and on a few occasions they have been moved to question the school's methods with the head-teacher. But they try to avoid making their children feel that they must do this or that out of duty to them or to 'the family'.

With some children, pressure of that kind might not make a great deal of difference to family solidarity. These are children who succeed academically without too much trouble. But nowadays children are increasingly impatient of academic and career goals that are either boring for them, or very hard for them. They are quicker now to reject such goals, and when they do this it often means rejecting their parents' expectations. Any guilt they feel is often worked out in aggressive demolition of *all* their parents' values. Paradoxically, if in some cases parents put up a barrier against entering a particular business or profession by suggesting that it was not really suitable, they might find their son or daughter more curious about it and asking how they might get in.

By and large, resistance to pressure is a common finding among teenagers who either 'drop out' of what they call the academic and business rat-races, or who adopt some other dramatic life style that is chosen for its distance from parents' ideals. There are exceptions, of course. The children who also are simply less intelligent, or who are more easily led, are also likely to gravitate to what seems both an easier and more adventurous way of living—pressure or no pressure.

Some work done by sociologists in the USA points towards increasing loss of contact between father and son, in terms *of what the father does and why he does it*, as a prime cause of anti-social behaviour among teenagers, and of the generation gap itself. Similarly, the economic importance to a household of having a second wage-earner decreases the extent to which a mother can be around to present a meaningful pattern of purpose in life to her teenage daughter. The economic need for working overtime can intensify both these effects.

In former times, many more jobs were self-explanatory; and many more jobs were easy for mothers and children to visit, and either watch, or at least to understand better since people tended to live closer to their work. Some fathers can still show their children some tools of their trade, and point out to them the results of the work to which they have contributed. Builders and architects, grocers, and those who are engaged in developing new biscuits in a pilot production plant . . . it is a *long* list. But many of them do not bother to extend their business concerns into their homes. Better to forget them, and relax. Others, like systems analysts, public relations officers, and men who work with microcircuits, have a hard job explaining what they do, why they do it, and how exactly anybody benefits. But for a child to want to plan his career in a way that is at all similar to that of his parents, he must presumably develop a feeling for that to which his parents have devoted their working lives. One starting point for alienation, then, is not understanding what your parents have been doing, and not seeing anything there to emulate or transcend.

Naturally, some parents are defensive about their work. They may not do it very well, or at a high enough level to satisfy them; or they may find their daily grind supremely boring. These parents are unfortunate; but it is all too easy for them to communicate to their children a sense of futility about joining a machine-like organization, and saving to pair off in flats or houses and have children just like most of the previous generation. By refusing to discuss what they do, parents increase the likelihood of children opting for a radically different kind of life.

Another form of generation gap is intellectual. On one hand there are children who have received better education than their parents, and show a snobbish horror for those interests and enter-tainments that they feel they should leave behind. Many of the new interests they acquire they cannot talk about with their parents because it demands too much preliminary explanation, which the parents find patronizing. On the other hand, there are children who have formed a broader base of friends and interests than their middle-class parents. These children may reject the intellectual pressure on them, and dismiss the attitudes of their parents as precious, bourgeois, or fossilized.

Neither of these reactions is entirely avoidable. It is natural for each generation to be slightly different from the preceding one in intelligence, if not in interests, education, and in the influences surrounding it. The first generation to go to college invariably finds it hard to adjust conversations in its parents' home. But complete alienation is another matter. This can and should be avoided.

Obviously, this is not *only* a question of what parents are like and do. Children vary in the need they feel to be part of the group of friends, and how far this dominates their behaviour, and their attitudes towards their parents. Their personality may make them naturally more curious about new experiences and other ways of living; they may react particularly strongly to being warned away from these things. It is perfectly possible, in other words, to have a child who is especially likely to be on the other side of the gap. Some will derive a feeling of compensation for bad school work, or a sense of failure in other respects, by opening the gap up, and taking their bemused parents by surprise.

But the burden of maintaining contact lies primarily on the

9*

parents. Before their children are nine, this will have been a matter of building a solid structure of love and security that establishes a positive relationship. After nine it means taking an interest; helping; asking advice instead of always giving it; looking for things to do that will make the family home seem less predictable and less boring; keeping an ear open for any badly expressed appeals for a talk or consultation about something that is a fear or a problem; noticing and respecting ways in which teenagers are more sensitive; making it clear when there is a serious worry—but refusing to transmit a series of 'fussy' warnings; and showing interest in, and hospitality towards, one's children's friends. Finally when they really do go wrong, it means being charitable and helpful, rather than recriminating and anxious about the family name.

Here are two brief case histories (each very different from Chris and Margaret's family above) which illustrate failure and limitation, respectively, on several of these points. It is always possible to argue that the children's personality, and the influence on them, would have made it very difficult for any parents to maintain communication. But as in many other cases, social workers drew my attention to what parents *could have done* to help.

Angela

Angela is now sixteen. She is tall, but rather thin, and her looks suggest an older person. Her complexion is pasty, and her hair and clothes usually give the impression of needing attention. She has a rather vacant look when she meets you, as if to imply that you are merely one of a number who have made it their business to talk to her since she became a 'problem'.

She has always had most of the things in life that she has wanted. At fourteen, for example, she was the possessor of a pony, and a pair of skis, a sizeable wardrobe, and a jewellery box that overflowed. She was a moderate performer at her expensive private school, but fairly popular. It was a surprise to many (her parents included) when she was first warned and then expelled from school for having a small hoard of cannabis.

Although there had been a few rows at home about the time she was to be expected back from parties, and although Angela had had to be forbidden to smoke cigarettes at home, her parents had had vague inklings that she was meeting various experiences more rapidly than they felt was for the best. There was the Pony Club, for example. If you were a member and you were fourteen, it seemed vital that you should go to their dances. Her parents knew who she would be going with, and their families. They were somewhat alarmed when she was driven home from her first dance at midnight, helpless with laughter. They attributed this more to high spirits than to the vodka that had been in the cider cup. And they had no idea that smoking pot was an exciting part of the Pony Club ritual.

When Angela's parents decided their daughter's personal habits needed their attention, she was already committed to bridging the gap between her age and the older, swinging sophisticates of the Club. By the time they decided that they should forbid this and forbid that, she had passed well out of range of any feeling of closeness with them. They simply became nuisances that somehow she had to get round.

She was put into a state school by her parents, partly out of pique. There she quickly joined up with the older girls who had no intention of contributing more than sarcasm to lessons or school activities. She was rejected by some for her 'classy ways' but accepted by others as an interesting window on what went on at the Vodka Martini level. One teacher who made some efforts to get in contact with her claims that Angela considered her stay at the new school to be 'a kind of prison sentence': she believes that Angela's interpretation of her being put there as a punishment must have added to her sense of distance from her parents, and her determination to back away from their influence, if not from the money they provided. It certainly put her in the wrong state of mind for gaining anything from school. At any rate, she opted out and went to live with some older friends in a flat in West London, while still fifteen.

Angela's parents objected, but felt they could do little, even when they had established where she was living. She refused to have anything to do with them, and seemed to be accepted as part of the group in her flat. They were told she intended to become a model. When they visited her, they were swiftly insulted for their pains. They talked to their lawyer, who told them what would be involved in asserting their legal rights, and in getting Angela to be declared a ward of court. It would have been an acrimonious, long-drawn-out business, expensive and very much under the public gaze. They were in two minds about it, and were still arguing when the police got in touch with them. Angela had been stopped for shop-lifting. Drugs had been found at her flat when the police followed through with a visit. They were preparing a report for the juvenile court, so that publicity was inevitable anyway.

There are various possibilities open to the magistrates at the juvenile court in these situations. The main aim in their minds nowadays (rather than punishment for its own sake) is to make some kind of arrangement, and give practical help so that the child becomes and feels part of society, rather than remaining at odds with it. Part of this, where his family exists and is suitable, is to get him integrated into his family. Sometimes attendance at a special school has to be prescribed; usually a social worker is appointed the task of watching how the child gets on, with his family, at school, and with his plans for the future. The social worker usually knows about job opportunities, and also training schemes, youth clubs and sports and other organizations in which a young person can make new friends and find new interests. Psychiatric help is sometimes needed, and is provided.

Angela was told to return home, and social workers tried to help her and her parents strike up some kind of way of living with each other, and to find a common purpose. Instead, however, there were rows: Angela left home again, and was seen three months later, once more under the auspices of the police. She was said to be an accessory in a case of robbery with assault in a seaside town. In the interval she had been introduced to Chinese heroin. She had a septic arm from a dirty needle, but she was still at a point where, luckily, a cure would be less agonizing than it is for many. Her future is entirely uncertain.

Angela's parents are critical of Angela; of her friends; of the insidious effects 'of all these bad ideas coming at young people through the mass media'; of Angela's school; of the 'wetness' of a certain social worker. They are less critical of themselves, although they are prepared to point out 'how difficult it is to bring up young people today', and that 'we've not been much good at it'.

It's doubtful whether there ever was an *easy* time to bring up young people. Human nature finds difficulties with strict regimes, as well as with *laissez-faire* families. Angela's parents gave up, at some stage—when, exactly, is hard to say, but it was probably when they suddenly realized that they needed to establish principles and impose them, rather than assuming that all would be for the best. Suddenly having to change from a comfortable middle-class confidence in the idea that all would be well because they could afford to give her a happy interesting childhood, proved to be too much for them.

Being close with a son or daughter who is rapidly growing up does not come automatically. It has to be worked for, preferably on a basis of mutual trust and understanding that was prepared a long time beforehand. But there are plenty of cases where children have rebelled against their homes, their schools, and most of the people and institutions around them, but the parents have kept on trying to make some contact with them, with the result that there are good times, as well as bad. Children need a link with another generation if they are to have any time for its feelings or its ideals. Giving up contact—e.g. 'We never could understand him', 'It's no use in trying to reason with *her*', or 'They're living in a world of their own, these days, these kids'—is to sever that link.

'There are lots of parents that I meet,' a psychiatric social worker with a long case-book maintains, 'who seem to have got used to treating their children like sophisticated pets. They do bridge, golf, fishing, charity work even, and spend many hours decorating the house or gardening . . . but they never have much time with their children. They buy them clothes, feed them, educate them, and give them money. But they don't talk or play with them much. When they are surprised that their children get into trouble, you have to wrestle with a long-established attitude of mind that they should somehow just develop by themselves.'

Not all children, when they stop being children, are liable to be rebels. More serious, sometimes, are the problems of those who are *too* good; *too* timid to stand up for themselves; nervous of responsibility; and ill-equipped for making their way through life. 'Dependency-seeking' parents have been described earlier. They want to have somebody permanently dependent on them. In Victorian times, it was fairly common for one member of a large family to be deputed to 'stay behind and look after mother (or father)'. This satisfied certain practical needs as well as whatever dependency-seeking motivation was still present after bringing up such a family. It also created some unpleasant tensions, personal misery, and a sense of a wasted life. Nowadays there is less social approval for this practice, but some parents still have a strong desire to prolong their children's dependency.

Fathers' resentment of their daughters' boy friends is a classic by-product of the wish to continue a relationship beyond its allotted span. It is very difficult for a father who has strong feelings against a particular admirer to be sure whether he is *really* being objective, or simply expressing a fear that this one might be too successful.

Of course, mistakes will be made: but by parents as well as children, over boy friends and girl friends. Often children of both sexes will go through some phase of romantic idealism that seems utterly naïve to their parents. Equally often, parents will express misgivings that are over-cynical about the relationship in question, or over-stress a materialist viewpoint. Communication is certainly difficult when these two forces are in opposition. But it is better to try to maintain it, on a quiet level, than *either* trying to bottle up one's feelings altogether, *or* to insist categorically that one is right. It is enough to say that the biggest and most permanent rifts between the generations usually have something to do with disapproval of choice of a sexual (if not a life) partner.

Studies of divorce trends show that, in the United Kingdom at least, marriages which take place a year or more before the partners are of average marrying age (twenty-one for women, twenty-three for men) are particularly vulnerable. A fair proportion of these are 'shot-gun weddings', where the bride is pregnant, and since these can involve considerable resentment, open or concealed, they constitute a special category. But even *allowing* for this category, divorce statistics do not favour early marriage. As for experimental marriages, although there are no statistics there are no obvious grounds for supposing these are more successful among the young.

However, when relationships break down, the one person who does *not* resume instant popularity is the parent who delivered solemn warnings. The merest hint of 'I told you so' is enough to suggest, far-fetched as it may seem, that this was the unpleasant influence in the background that turned everything sour.

Anthea

There are many situations that older children are liable to present their parents with nowadays that catch them by surprise. This feeling of astonishment is easily reflected in their response, and by itself this threatens to promote a sense of generation gap. Bob and Lorraine had this one, 'out of the blue'.

Their daughter Anthea, sixteen, asked if her current boy friend could come round that evening. ('How nice that we are communicating!' thought Lorraine.) Nigel, a twenty-six-year-old, had met them briefly, just once before.

'Well,' said Nigel, after five minutes of inconsequential small-talk, 'I think it's time we came to the point.' Anthea nodded enthusiastically. 'Anthea and I—well, we're rather keen on each other—' 'So we thought we ought to tell you that we want to live together.' 'Yes, well—there we are, you see. . . .'

Bob threw his whisky right back down his throat. 'Good of you to tell us,' he murmured huskily.

Lorraine smiled, and suggested that there was little to be gained by starting a family straight away. The young couple agreed with this sentiment. 'It's not as if we were getting *married*,' said Anthea.

'Thank God they're not getting married,' said Bob, after Anthea had shoved her suitcase in Nigel's car, and departed to a new life style.

'Yes—but I thought he was quite nice, really.'

'Could have been much worse, I agree.'

The parents were in a state of shock, but were beginning to come to terms with their experience. Anthea was not 'of age'—but then, she was legally entitled to be married, she was a wage-earner, she was a strong personality, and she could run a kitchen, possibly a home. Had they tried to insist that Anthea stayed, they realized they would not have achieved anything. They were not sure of their ground, anyway: 'If we said we were outraged, or anything like that, it would simply be hypocritical,' Lorraine explained. Both wanted their daughter's friendship, and to be able to help her. Neither of these would be easy to achieve if they outlawed her and her friend. As it was, they had Nigel's and Anthea's address and telephone number, and an invitation to come over for dinner the following evening. Lorraine had made sure that Anthea knew pretty well all she needed to know about sex a good while before this event. No questions had been evaded. A few months before, Lorraine had been quizzed about contraceptive pills. It all seemed to fit into place.

Anthea and Nigel have now been living together for some time.

They appear to be happy. Moreover, there is little generation gap between Anthea and her parents.

Obviously it might *not* have worked in this way. Every sixteen-year-old is at a different emotional level, and has found different expectations of the kind of relationship he or she might have with the opposite sex. It is probably true to say that girls are more socially mature at this age than boys, but this is only an average, and the margin cannot be as great as all that. All parents have to decide for themselves, how they would react to this situation. It is by no means as uncommon as Bob and Lorraine first imagined.

Some will feel hypocritical about seeming to approve or to give way. They might disagree with Bob and Lorraine, that denying to their daughter what they felt they might have done themselves (since they believe this behaviour has practical and possibly social advantages) would constitute the real hypocrisy. If parents feel shocked, it is usually right for them to say so. This is different from opposing all individuality in their children. Nor does it mean, necessarily, laying down the law. If they really want to influence their children for what they feel is the better, they will tell them precisely why they believe their children are doing wrong, and be prepared for discussion.

One way out which parents sometimes adopt is to use a form of emotional blackmail. This is to build up a sense of guilt in their son or daughter, powerful enough to restrain them from doing anything contrary to family morality. When this happens the foundations have really been laid very deep, a long way back in childhood. Only a reminder is now necessary to rouse this guilt at appropriate moments, e.g. 'How *could* you think of doing such a thing—after all we've done together', or 'You can tell *me* about it, John, but it would break your mother's heart.'

This kind of appeal serves a short-term purpose, in getting a child to conform. But this way of making somebody conform to what his parents want should not be confused with the idea of getting him to accept his parents' ideals as being relevant to himself. The stronger the emotional pressure, if divorced from personal conviction, the stronger is the resentment underlying a superficial conformity. This creates a 'pseudo-morality', where the child perceives no real need for the taboos he observes, and may well break them dramatically whenever he feels that the cost need no longer deter him.

There are certain methods that parents use to preserve grown-up children's dependence or attention which are well recognized by psychologists as typical of less successful parent–child relationships. A good example is the 'double-bind' which mothers typically employ over sons to secure deference and regular visits: 'Of course you mustn't notice what *I* say, you've got your *own* life to lead.' This is the classic 'menopausal' remark, so called because it exemplifies the neurotic self-pity that sometimes accompanies the 'change of life'. (Of course men can be *just* as 'menopausal' as women.) The subtlety of this remark lies in the implication that even if the hearer is not feeling guilty, then he certainly ought to be. At the same time, how reasonable and self-denying the speaker's words are, on the surface! Those who prove to be inadequate, in later life, at establishing satisfactory relations with others, are frequently found to have suffered from 'double-binding' in their teens, which effectively prevented them from ever feeling really comfortable about the rights and wrongs of claiming personal rights.

There are several questions, similar to that posed by Nigel and Anthea, which are liable to take present-day parents by surprise. It is worth while being prepared for them—even if you believe they are rather unlikely. *What* you reply must be your decision: there are no really 'correct' answers, because so much depends on the individual son or daughter, and everyone has to make up their own minds as to what kind of adult behaviour is sensible and acceptable. Here is a selection of the questions that are all perfectly possible, and which should be thought about *before* they are actually put:

(a) 'I want to go on holiday with John/Jane/a friend. . . .'
(b) 'Can John/Jane/etc. stay the night? . . . With me, I mean?'
(c) 'I want to go and live on my own with John, Jane, etc. . . .'
(d) 'Can we have some whisky/vodka, etc., at my party? Will you stay away please?'
(e) 'I don't feel like starting/finishing university. Do you mind if I go straight out and get a job?'
(f) 'Christmas at home is a dead bore. Can I go camping/ski-ing, etc., with some friends?'
(g) 'I want some advice on contraception. Will you help me? . . . Will you help me find a good gynaecologist?'
(h) 'Can I take driving/gliding/parachute lessons/have a motorbike, etc.?'
(i) 'Some friends are driving to Singapore. Can I go with them?'
(j) 'I'm going on a demo for a few days. OK?'

Table 7 Reasons for reconciliation failing

Parents	Children
Recrimination: 'I still think you're behaving irresponsibly.'	Anxiety to prove a point: 'So you're coming round to my way of thinking, now.'
Regret: 'We don't seem to hit it off any more.' 'If only you'd continued your studies.'	Impatience: 'All right, let's talk then.' 'What do we say to each other?'
Meanness: 'I suppose you need more money, now.'	Imputed meanness: 'You always have been so tight over money.'
Appeals to nostalgia, pathos: 'Your own little room is always waiting for you, you know.'	Pride: 'I don't *want* your help, and I certainly don't want your money.'

Both parties	
Lack of sense of humour:	'He/she doesn't seem capable of taking it seriously.'
Lack of ability to laugh at yourself.	
Conviction that you are right:	'He/she doesn't seem prepared to give an inch.'
Attacks on a third party *as a means* of attacking each other:	'You don't still see that idiot John/ Jane, etc., do you?'

Not all these questions will be asked. Some will make their own decisions, without asking. Parents who discover by chance that one of their taboos has been contravened, or that asking permission to make a serious change has been deliberately avoided, have a more difficult choice to make, in some ways. They can ignore, or deplore the situation: in the first case, they may lose respect, in the second, depending on how forcibly they go about it, they may prejudice future contact.

Somehow or other, a large part of what a grown-up child becomes has been contributed by the parents. Disowning the results is an act of self-condemnation.

But most teenagers, despite wanting to be different, to surprise, and to shock at least *part* of the time, do not want contact broken. They regret scenes which go beyond retrieval, which end up with each side taking up positions from which retreat is impossible without loss of dignity. In short, they are more accessible than many parents feel. It is always worth trying again.

Many attempts at reconciliation between parents and children founder because of the difficulties that each party has in looking objectively at what they are saying and doing. Asking a relative or friend who gets on with both sides to act as an intermediary can help a lot.

A friend of mine found himself, aged seventeen, telling his father about some of Bach's music that he had particularly enjoyed during his first year at college. 'But, you know,' said his father, 'Beethoven was much greater.'

'Well—I prefer Bach.' There was a bitter argument, and he left home. That was over thirty years ago. *He has never seen his father again.* What a waste! So much for the assumption that the absurdities of the 'generation gap' are a new phenomenon. It must be worth making more effort.

Table 7 gives some of the more common reasons why reconciliation between parents and children breaks down. It is worth a look in case it can give a more objective view of a delicate situation.

Chapter twenty-one

What kind of adult?

There are no obvious moments when a child becomes an adult. This goes for most Western societies, where there is a succession of approximations towards adult status and adult behaviour that sometimes merge into each other: being allowed to marry, or to vote, or to live apart from one's parents, and be self-sufficient as to means, are all parts of this progression. The Registrar General in the United Kingdom classifies everybody who is sixteen and over as 'adult', but in practice the demarcation is not nearly so simple.

In more primitive civilizations, this transition was, and is, more formally organized. There are certain conventional 'rites of passage' that mark the occasion, and supply proof that the child-candidate is worthy of becoming a man. Some societies have 'rites of passage' for girls, too. But for them, it is more often a case of becoming married, whereupon they acquire the status (sometimes this is deferred) to look after their own household, or their own part of a household. The classic test applied by many tribes has been to dismiss a promising young male from the tribal village for a certain period, and see whether he was capable of surviving in the wilds: this would justify his re-admittance on his return.

'Getting the key of the door' at twenty-one no doubt had considerable significance originally, but it has long since become a kind of folk-lore joke. However immature an eighteen- or nineteen-year-old might be in certain respects, it has long been impossible not to regard at least some of them as adults—particularly if their occupation is to protect or serve society in the police, the armed forces, and the fire and ambulance services. The argument is that if we are asking them, as individuals, to risk their lives for the good of society, they cannot reasonably be refused the basic rights of any member of that society. When they are married, and starting a family—or, at any rate, establishing separate households in their own right—their household is downgraded if they are denied basic rights, and a society that respects individuals cannot have downgrading of any of its households.

The truth is that in the United Kingdom independence is there for the grasping at sixteen. There is virtually nothing that parents can do about it, except perhaps to delay it briefly. Technically, they can have recourse to the law, and make arrangements for their children to be found and brought home, if they have left it; they can apply to have their child declared a ward of court, if they feel that under somebody else's influence he or she is destined to suffer. They can do this until their children reach the age of eighteen, although an extension might be possible if it can be shown that the young person is mentally incapable of exercising judgment and looking after his own affairs. But this power of parents is more apparent than real. Time is on the *children's* side, and if they are thwarted over a serious matter, the pattern is usually for them to look on their parents' act as a blow to their personal freedom, and their right to do as they please with their own life. They do not forgive this very easily, and they are likely to remember it a long time afterwards. Even where parents exercise moral or financial pressure, it comes down to the same thing. There are plenty of cases, involving both sexes, of somebody opting out of college, or of marrying as soon as they reasonably can, simply to cut the ties more quickly. Both these courses of action can be extremely unfortunate, in different ways. It is scarcely worth a parent's while to be a contributory cause of them.

Since the child–adult boundary is so ill-defined, it is hardly surprising that there should be conflicts on the way. Parent and child will argue over what stage has actually been reached, and over what is appropriate for that stage in the modern age. There has to be compromise, if parent and child are going to enjoy each other's company in the future. It works best when both sides:

(a) recognize when the particular issue at stake is felt by one party to be especially important, dangerous;
(b) avoid getting into situations where one is holding out for trivial rules, or concessions, as if they were major ones.

Once again, this really comes back to the question of how well parent and child are managing to communicate with each other.

It is worth remarking that adulthood, in Western society, has become very much a psychological matter. Anyone of sixteen (or earlier even in some circumstances) who is sufficiently strong-willed can say, 'I am an adult', and play out the role, if they wish. Many take off in the summer, sleeping rough or squatting, and (sometimes) they come back in the autumn. Against this, there are plenty of people in their twenties or thirties who are outwardly normal in many respects, but have remained, psychologically, children. Their emotional dependence, their inability to take decisions, is pathetic, and they are a threat to anyone—except the most domineering—who views them as a potential life partner. When you meet them, you feel like shouting at them to grow up, because their refusal to be self-sufficient is infuriating. But of course they cannot grow up just like that, because they have not been given enough incentive to make their own decisions, or stick to them. These people often achieve a measure of independence, over time, by learning to live in a sheltered community, such as a university, or certain schools, or even some branch of the forces—'sheltered' in this context refers to the fact that the surroundings are very well organized, which means that the individual simply has to fit in with rules and conventions, rather than endure the agony of free choice.

Many parents will have had clear clues well before this of the kind of adult their child is likely to be. But such is the instinct to protect that they normally prefer not to contemplate them in this light until they have actually left the nest. Parents of a sixteen-year-old are more likely to underestimate his viability on his own than to exaggerate it.

There is also a rosy glow of fantasy surrounding many parents' ideas of what their children will be like, grown up. Children are often visualized avoiding the mistakes of their parents; they are seen getting to college where the parents couldn't manage it, or enjoying a society, as opposed to a suburban, wedding, or running just that bit faster than father ever could, and scoring a winning try. This is harmless enough when it is kept under control, as a pipe dream and nothing more. But parents are often driven, de-spite their better judgment, to press their children into a mould that fits the fantasy, instead of encouraging them at what *they* happen to be good at, and enjoy. Many of the children who run away and settle down on the beach at Brighton prove, after dis-cussion, to have been refugees from being pressed into a mould they did not fit.

Table 8 Influences on young adults' characteristics

Influences encouraging the characteristic	Characteristic	Influences discouraging the characteristic
Warmth and affection Stable home background Belief, trust placed in the child	Fits easily into social groups Is accepted by new social groups	Awareness of conflicts between parents and the child's school, friends, etc. Insisting on rigid code Over-protection
Warmth and affection Satisfaction of demands —to experiment —for (some) independence Treating as intelligent individual	Speed and reliability of becoming —a mature adult —independent, self-reliant	Withdrawal of affection Reserve, neglect, rejection Treating as childish; derision
Parents' attitudes, behaviour towards others More rewarding than punishment Strong personal attachment	Responsibility to society Conscience in interpersonal relationships	Parents' cynicism, behaviour towards others More punishment than reasoning Rejection by own age group
Withdrawal of love as punishment Changes in attitudes by parents Loss of close relative/friend Strong criticism	Anxious Diffident	Praise, encouragement for achievements Consistent attitude from parents

The chart in Table 8 shows a number of influences on the way children develop into adults. It includes references to many of the better-attested findings from psychological and social research. Some of the more basic personality characteristics are not reflected here, because *their* roots go back a very long way into childhood, and probably into genetic history—e.g. generosity, obstinacy, competitive spirit, etc. For the purposes of Table 8, these omissions do not matter, since we are dealing here with the results of ways of dealing with children that last a long way through their childhood, rather than the influence of very early experiences.

It is remarkable how often, once one gets away from theories and looks only at facts established by research, the very simple question of whether a person had a warm relationship with his parents or not, as a child, seems to be predictive of positive character traits. Other work also shows that the reverse is also true: that when a child has been deprived of any such warm relationship, the chances of developing negative character traits are that much greater. When Table 8, in fact, is stripped down to its barest minimum, this is what is left. Possibly the other major principle is that of consistency. When somebody has, as a child, enjoyed a feeling that his parents always love him, at a deep level, irrespective of the many upsets and crises that interrupt any normal childhood, then he is much more likely to take his place in the world with assurance, and not to suffer from some social handicap. It should be noted that a number of very great men had a very unpleasant childhood, leaving them with a nagging need to compensate for something by striving continuously for greater and greater success: but this is not the same as leading a happy life, or making friends, or helping society.

These findings must be encouraging to many parents who cannot, for one reason or another, give their children all the advantages they believe would be helpful to them, e.g. an expensive education, foreign trips, visits to the theatre, and the like. If they can give security in a happy home, it is worth far, far more.

This extends further, into adulthood as well. As a rule, young adults baulk at the idea of their parents 'interfering', by giving advice on jobs, marriage, or where to live. But if they are aware of their parents in the background, and that they are interested enough to ask how things are going, they feel that much more confident. The sense of continuity across generations may be something that they pretend to deplore, but it is a source of strength that is usually regretted when it is lost. The amount of speculation, time and money that many people without roots spend looking for more details about their families, or their distant relatives, is evidence of this. The other key element that reappears in most of the research findings is that of positive rewards proving stronger than blame, criticism, or punishment. An individual who has had insufficient experience of being praised for having a good idea, for trying hard, for making it work, for being imaginative, or even just for helping others, and behaving nicely, is not well placed to make much progress in the future—for himself or for society. It is no good for parents to say, about a young adult who lacks drive, confidence or pertinacity, 'Well, he never did much that was good enough to be praised': this is merely a criticism of their own standards, their powers of observation, and perhaps their interest. Intelligence, and talent, come into the picture only in a relative way. A young adult with, for example, severe learning problems, may have been given the right encouragement for making what might seem tiny steps forward, and turn out to be a much better adjusted, a more helpful, and a happier human being than a potentially brilliant scholar who puts his teachers' backs up, and feels frustrated because he gets no encouragement. Here again, it is not the very rich, or the very intelligent parents who necessarily help their children the most. It is the parents who really love them, and want them to succeed, and believe that they can, within realistic limits.

Here are some books which are worth looking at, for anyone who wants to dig deeper into certain aspects of children's development. An asterisk beside the name of a book indicates that it is considerably more demanding for the average reader.

Jolly, Hugh, *The Book of Child Care,* Allen & Unwin, 1975. This is put first, because it offers a wide-ranging compendium in which virtually any query or problem about looking after children is thoroughly analysed.

Davie, R. *et al., From Birth to Seven,* Longman, 1972.

Doman, G., *Teach Your Baby to Read,* Cape, 1965.

Foss, B. M. (ed.), **Determinants of Infant Behaviour,* 4 vols, Methuen, 1969.

Piaget, J., **The Language and Thought of the Child,* Harcourt Brace Jovanovich, New York, 1926, Routledge & Kegan Paul, London, 1971.

Piaget, J., **Play, Dreams, and Imitation in Childhood,* Norton, New York, 1951, Routledge & Kegan Paul, London, 1967.

Robertson, James, *Young Children in Hospital,* Tavistock, 1970.

Rowlands, Peter, *Children Apart: Problems of Early Separation from Parents,* Dent, 1973.

Rowlands, Peter, *Gifted Children and Their Problems,* Dent, 1974.

Vernon, M. D., *Reading and its Difficulties,* Cambridge University Press, 1971.

Whiting, J. W. M., and **Child, I. L.,** *Child Training and Personality,* Yale University Press, New Haven, 1953.

Wood, Margaret E., **Children: The Development of Personality and Behaviour,* Harrap, 1973.

INDEX